Post-everything

MANCHESTER
1824

Manchester University Press

Post-everything:
An intellectual history
of post-concepts

Edited by

Herman Paul and
Adriaan van Veldhuizen

MANCHESTER UNIVERSITY PRESS

Published by Manchester University Press
Altrincham Street, Manchester M1 7JA

www.manchesteruniversitypress.co.uk

British Library Cataloguing-in-Publication Data
A catalogue record for this book is available from the British Library

ISBN 978 1526 1 4819 3 hardback

First published 2021

The publisher has no responsibility for the persistence or accuracy of URLs for any external or third-party internet websites referred to in this book, and does not guarantee that any content on such websites is, or will remain, accurate or appropriate.

Typeset by
Servis Filmsetting Ltd, Stockport, Cheshire

Contents

Figures

Notes on contributors

Roger E. Backhouse is Professor of the History and Philosophy of Economics at the University of Birmingham and Erasmus University Rotterdam. He is author of *Founder of Modern Economics: Paul A. Samuelson*, Volume 1: *Becoming Samuelson, 1915–1948* (2017), and he is currently working on the second volume.

Edward Baring is Associate Professor of History and the University Center for Human Values at Princeton University. He is the author of *The Young Derrida* (2011), and *Converts to the Real: Catholicism and the Making of Continental Philosophy* (2019).

Hans Bertens is Emeritus Distinguished Professor of the Humanities at Utrecht University, the Netherlands. He publishes in Dutch and in English, mainly on American literature and postmodernism. His English-language books include *The Idea of the Postmodern: A History* (1995), *Literary Theory: The Basics* (2013), *Contemporary American Crime Fiction* (2001; with Theo D'haen), and *American Literature: A History* (2012; also with Theo D'haen).

Howard Brick is Louis Evans Professor of History at University of Michigan. He is author of *Transcending Capitalism: Visions of a New Society in Modern American Thought* (2006), and co-author (with Casey N. Blake and Daniel H. Borus) of *At the Center: American Thought and Culture in the Mid-Twentieth Century* (2020).

K. Healan Gaston is Lecturer on American Religious History and Ethics at Harvard Divinity School. She received her BA in Religious Studies from Brown University and her PhD in US History from the University of California at Berkeley. Gaston is the author of *Imagining Judeo-Christian America: Religion, Secularism, and the Redefinition of Democracy* (2019). Her work to date has focused on the logics of religio-political discourses, the co-constitution of the religious and the secular, and the relationship between history and ethics.

Stéphanie Genz is Senior Lecturer in Media Studies at Nottingham Trent University. She specializes in contemporary gender and cultural theory. Her book publications include *Postfemininities in Popular Culture* (2009) and, with Benjamin A. Brabon, *Postfeminism: Cultural Texts and Theories* (2nd edn, 2018). Her current work centres on sexist liberalism/liberal sexism in post-recessionary culture that belies assumptions of gender equality and sexual freedom.

Yolande Jansen is Socrates Professor of Humanism in Relation to Religion and Secularity at the Free University Amsterdam and Associate Professor of Social and Political Philosophy at the University of Amsterdam. She is the author of *Secularism, Assimilation and the Crisis of Multiculturalism: French Modernist Legacies* (2014) and the editor of *Detention, Deportation, Drowning: The Irregularization of Migration in Europe* (2016). In 2020, she co-edited with Nasar Meer a double special issue of the journal *Patterns of Prejudice* titled 'Genealogies of "Jews" and "Muslims"; social imaginaries in the race–religion nexus' (volume 54, numbers 1–2, February–May 2020).

Jasmijn Leeuwenkamp is a PhD candidate at the Amsterdam School of Cultural Analysis (ASCA). In her research project, preliminary title 'Human Rights Beyond the Nature/Culture Divide', she analyses the possibility to reconceptualize human rights from a non-anthropocentric perspective.

Herman Paul is Professor of the History of the Humanities at Leiden University, where he directs a research project on 'Scholarly Vices: A Longue Durée History'. He is the author of *Key Issues in Historical Theory* (2015) and *Hayden White: The Historical Imagination* (2011).

Andrew Sartori is Professor of History at New York University. He is the author of *Bengal in Global Concept History* (2008) and *Liberalism in Empire* (2014), and co-editor of the journal *Critical Historical Studies*.

Stephen Turner is currently Distinguished University Professor at the Department of Philosophy, University of South Florida. His recent books include *Cognitive Science and the Social: A Primer* (2018) and, edited with Christopher Adair-Toteff, *The Calling of Social Thought: Rediscovering the Work of Edward Shils* (2019).

Leire Urricelqui is a university assistant at the Political Philosophy Department at the University of Graz, and a PhD student at the University of Lucerne as part of the research group '"Meddlesome and Curious". On the Realization of Democratic Freedom in Forms of the Non-Identical'. She has been a visiting scholar at Centre Léon Robin – CNRS Paris (2018–19) and at the University of Amsterdam (2019–20).

Adriaan van Veldhuizen is a scientific researcher for the Dutch government, and is on the editorial board of literary journal *De Gids*. Until 2020 he was also an assistant professor in Philosophy of History at Leiden University. He has written and edited books, articles and essays on history, philosophy and literature.

Acknowledgements

This volume emerges out of a workshop held on 31 August and 1 September 2017 in the Trip House in Amsterdam, a seventeenth-century neoclassical city palace that is nowadays the seat of the Royal Netherlands Academy of Arts and Sciences (KNAW). The irony of discussing post-concepts in a historic building full of antique art and furniture was hard to miss. While we examined rhetorical strategies for 'getting rid of the past', the decorated ceiling above our heads tried to keep classic architectonic forms alive. From the walls, solemn oil portraits of white male luminaries eavesdropped on our conversations on postfeminist identity. In one of the coffee breaks, we found ourselves exploring how images of weaponry inside and outside of the building – the Trip brothers made their fortune in the arms trade – related to the post-colonial sensibilities discussed just a few minutes before. Clearly, the past can be present in unexpected ways, challenging simple, secessionist accounts of historical change.

Nonetheless, what a privilege it was to spend two days in this historic location, thanks to yet another historical figure: the nineteenth-century Dutch prime minister Johan Rudolph Thorbecke (1798–1872). It was the Thorbecke Fund, established by Willem Thorbecke (1920–2014) in honour of his great-grandfather, that provided generous funding for our workshop as well as for the open access publication of this volume. Although the link between Thorbecke's liberal constitutionalism and the rise of post-concepts in post-war sociology and theology is not immediately evident, it so happened that the *auctor intellectualis* of the Dutch constitution of 1848 started his career as a historian and philosopher. Thorbecke's 1824 book *Ueber das Wesen und den organischen Character der Geschichte* (On the Nature and the Organic Character of History) shows his deep fascination for historicist notions of development. If this volume points to the persistence of such 'developmental historicism' in the post-Christian and post-ideological imagination, it testifies to the long-term influence of a mode of thinking that was dear to the young Thorbecke.

Turning now to the living, we would like to thank the commentators who greatly contributed to the liveliness of our discussions: Sascha Bru, Peter van Dam, Meike de Goede, Liesbeth van de Grift, Rajesh Heynickx, Yolande Jansen, Merel Leeman, Matthijs Lok, Bram Mellink, Marion Pluskota, Henriette Steiner, and Peter-Wim Zuidhof. One of them, Yolande Jansen, helped us improve the balance between 'older' and 'newer' post-concepts by turning her improvised remarks on post-humanism into a fully fledged chapter, co-authored with Leire Urricelqui and Jasmijn Leeuwenkamp. We are indebted to K. Healan Gaston, whose detailed comments on our book proposal and draft introduction were particularly helpful. Also, we are grateful to Martine Koot (KNAW) for her practical help in organizing the workshop, to Manon van den Brekel for carefully editing a whole pile of draft chapters and to Caroline Schep for preparing the index. At Manchester University Press, Emma Brennan cheerfully shepherded the manuscript through to publication. Finally, we thank our copy-editor, Anita Joseph, for correcting a lot of small mistakes.

Introduction:
Post-concepts in historical perspective

Herman Paul

Post-concepts

When the *Oxford English Dictionary* named 'post-truth' its Word of the Year 2016, this was broadly interpreted as evidence of a disturbing change in political mores. The sudden popularity of post-truth – within a single year, use of the term had increased by around 2,000 per cent – was understood as indicative of a new type of political discourse, embraced most unscrupulously by Donald Trump, in which 'objective facts are less influential than appeals to emotion'.[1] At the same time, the term revealed uncertainty about the implications of this emotional regime. Unlike, say, 'political emotivism', post-truth did not attempt to identify key characteristics of the Trump era. What the term expressed instead was that a twittering president challenged conventional understandings of political communication, White House strategy planning, and American foreign diplomacy. The post-concept, in other words, conveyed that a familiar world was disappearing in the rear-view mirror and that it remained to be seen into what new reality President Trump was propelling his country.[2]

This does not merely apply to the Word of the Year 2016. Post-truth is one of many post-concepts that commentators use in their attempts to make sense of a changing world. Western societies are routinely described as post-industrial, post-traditional, and post-Christian. Our world order is labelled as post-Cold War, post-American, post-neoliberal, and post-hegemonic. Post-racial and post-ethnic are among the most emotionally charged and politically loaded concepts in the current public debate.[3] In addition, every culturally literate person is familiar with postmodernism (perhaps even with post-postmodernism as popularized by architects and urban planners like Tom Turner).[4] William Brittelle and other composers who prefer to draw eclectically on pop, jazz and classical music advertise their music as post-genre.[5] Old-style feminists have been overhauled by postfeminists and post-postfeminists (not to mention post-post-postfeminists, who astonish feminists with fewer posts by preferring full-time parenting over a professional career).[6] Also, in the humanities and social sciences, it hardly seems possible to read a state-of-the-art survey article without stumbling upon at least a handful of post-concepts. While poststructuralist and post-colonial belong to every student's basic vocabulary, current debates in literary studies, for example, revolve around post-theory and postcriticism.[7] Meanwhile, philosophers and cultural theorists try to develop posthumanist frameworks for understanding the challenges that intelligent robots, uploaded minds, and other posthuman beings pose to us, humans without post-prefixes.[8]

Surveying this plethora of post-concepts, two social scientists recently sighed that 'one would think only a new titan from the end of the world would come up with another "post" term'.[9] However, one does not have to be a Jürgen Habermas or a Slavoj Žižek to found a Post Carbon Institute, launch a Post-Post-Race album or establish a Post-Imperial menswear brand. Posts are literally everywhere. They continue to pop up in the most unlikely places, from political think tanks and designer studios to news-rooms and graduate students' offices. Given this fact, it seems far safer to predict that the last post has not yet been sounded.

Post-everything

How new is this habit of adding post-prefixes to proper nouns? Writing in 2007, an influential Peruvian author characterized the twenty-first century as a departure from all that came before it. 'We are at a new beginning,' he declared, 'in an era that is "post-" everything we have ever known: a postmodern, postindustrial, postcapitalist, postcolonial, and post-socialist society.'[10] Interestingly, however, similar observations had already been made in the 1970s. In 1974, for example, sociologist Dennis H. Wrong wrote with thinly veiled disapproval about 'the post boys' in his field – figures like Daniel Bell who defined the Western world as 'post-industrial, or post-bourgeois, or post-capitalist, or post-modern, or post-economic, or post-Christian, or post-Marxist, or post-traditional, or even post-civilized.' In Wrong's perception, 'enough posts abound in contemporary social thought to build a picket fence!'[11] (As we shall see in a moment, this was not an unapt metaphor, given that post-concepts indeed tend to 'draw a fence around a part of reality [and] call that the past'.)[12]

Wrong's survey of post-concepts was indebted to Bell's *The Coming of Post-Industrial Society* (1973) – a book that combined advocacy of one specific post-concept with somewhat amused commentary on the sudden popularity of such concepts in the social sciences. Noting that the post-war United States had been characterized as post-bourgeois and post-collectivist, among other things, Bell concluded: 'It used to be that the great literary modifier was the word *beyond*: beyond tragedy, beyond culture, beyond society. But we seem to have exhausted the beyond, and today the sociological modifier is *post*.'[13] This was confirmed by others who observed that 'Post-Civilization, Post-Modern, Post-Industrial, Post-Historical, Post-Ideological, Post-Electronic, Post-Technological, Post-Christian, Post-Freudian, Post-Affluent' were gaining popularity as labels for the present age.[14] Indeed, already by 1968, sociologist John Porter signalled that post-industrial, post-capitalist and post-bourgeois had 'been in currency for some time' – although Porter's apologies for adding yet another neologism (postmodern) to the list shows that post-concepts had not yet become common parlance.[15]

On the one hand, these observations show that concepts like post-capitalism and post-ideological have histories that stretch at least half a century back. Although post-ideology became a popular term in the 1990s, after the fall of the Berlin Wall and the end of the Cold War, the adjective can be traced back, ironically, to the start of the Cold War, in the 1950s, when sociologists like Edward Shils embraced the term mainly to discredit Marxist modes of social analysis.[16] Likewise, although post-capitalism has enjoyed high visibility since the publication of Paul Mason's book of that title in 2015, the term was actually introduced by Anthony Crosland and Ralf Dahrendorf in the 1950s.[17] While postmodernism entered common parlance in the 1980s and 1990s, American poet-critics such as Randall Jarrell and John Berryman already used the term in the 1940s.[18] Post-industrial, though most popular in the 1960s and 1970s, even reaches back to 1914, when Ananda Coomaraswamy and Arthur J. Penty published an edited collection of *Essays in Post-Industrialism*.[19] And so one could go on: all of these post-concepts have histories – often intertwining histories – that can be traced in rich detail.

On the other hand, the 1970s commentators quoted above did more than notice the emergence of certain new post-concepts. What intrigued them most of all was the popularity of post-prefixes *as such*. Writing in 1964, the journalist Karl E. Meyer still associated this language with a cohort that he called 'the post-generation – post-ideological, post-New Deal, post-Freud, post-Joyce, post-coital and now even post-New York Post'.[20] Ten years later, Wrong's remarks on 'the post boys' in American sociology suggested something similar. As post-concepts had a ring of being novel and provocative, they were not instantly picked up by everyone.[21] However, from the mid 1980s onwards, when the English-language translation of Jean-François Lyotard's *La Condition postmoderne* (1979) popularized the term postmodernism,[22] post-concepts became increasingly more common. This only accelerated when, around 1990, the adjectives postcolonial and poststructuralist established themselves in academic jargon.[23] Judging by a series of critical interventions varying on the title of Kwame Anthony Appiah's 1991 article, 'Is the Post- in Postmodernism the Post- in Postcolonial?', post-language turned out to be infectious.[24] Post-concepts were coined or defined in analogy to each other, thereby creating a network of post-terms, which in turn became an indispensable resource for scholars advocating 'turns' or 'paradigm shifts' in their respective fields of study (think of the post-positivist turn in philosophy, the post-secular turn in religious studies, and the post-racial turn in cultural theory).[25] All this suggests that while individual post-concepts may have histories of their own, the phenomenon of interpreting the world through post-lenses also emerged out of a particular historical background.

The age of the post

For this reason, this volume presents itself as an intellectual history of 'the age of the post', that is, as a history of how people began to conceive of themselves, their societies or their understanding of the world as moving beyond something that no longer met the demands of the time. Just as the nineteenth century was, among other things, an 'age of questions' – a period when commentators spent much energy debating the 'Eastern question', the 'woman question', the 'tuberculosis question', and the 'social question'[26] – so the second half of the twentieth century was, among other things, a time when post-industrial, post-bourgeois, post-Christian, and postmodern were broadly experienced as capturing the 'spirit of the age'. This volume raises the question: What made these post-prefixes so attractive?

Posing this question does not imply commitment to the thesis that mid-twentieth-century Western societies 'entered a new phase of [their] history, marked by a varied and widespread use of the prefix "post"'.[27] Instead of proposing a periodization scheme ourselves, we would like to inquire why twentieth-century intellectuals felt urged to engage in periodization by distinguishing between stages in the evolution of Western societies or by relegating certain ideas or practices to the past. So instead of treating the emergence of post-terms as indicative of a major shift in Western societies, we are curious to find out what these terms reveal about people's 'relations to the past' or 'regimes of historicity' – their experience of change as well as their sense of continuity and their negotiation of distance and proximity.[28]

Against this background, the volume's leading questions are: When did the 'post-age' start?[29] To what extent did early post-concepts, like post-industrial and post-Christian, define the conceptual parameters within which later ones could operate? Why did post-terms stick? Did they testify to what Frank Kermode, writing in 1967, called 'the sense of an ending' or, in a more activist key, reveal a desire to move beyond the inheritance of a pre-war world?[30] Where did diagnosis end and advocacy or criticism begin? To what extent did post-concepts draw on 'epochal' modes of historical thinking? If post-prefixes mark distance or dissociation, then what kind of distances (temporal, ideological, aesthetic) did they allow for? What were the political contexts in which post-ideological and postcolonial could flourish? How did 'post' relate to other prefixes, such as 'anti' and 'neo'?[31] And who were 'the post boys' behind all this? To what extent are we, current users of post-terms, indebted to figures like Will Herberg, Daniel Bell, Robert Bellah and Ihab Hassan, whose names repeatedly turn up in this volume because they helped popularize multiple post-terms?[32]

Existing literature

Whoever consults existing scholarship in the hope of finding answers to these questions is likely to make three discoveries. First, there is not exactly a lack of articles on the defining features of individual post-terms. Second, despite this wealth of literature, historical studies on the emergence, spread and uses of post-concepts are virtually non-existent. Third, most existing studies are interventions in theoretical debates instead of retrospectives – which may help explain both why there are so many of them and why historical questions are not most prominent among their concerns.

This does not imply, of course, that studies like Appiah's aforementioned article have nothing to say about, for instance, the modes of distancing at work in terms like postmodern and postcolonial. Appiah helpfully argues that, in these cases at least, the prefix does not denote a historical transition, but serves as a 'space-clearing gesture' that calls into question an 'exclusivity of insight' claimed by modernism and colonialism alike.[33] Consequently, the 'post' in postcolonial does something different than the 'post' in post-industrial. Whereas, for Bell, post-industrial referred to an epochal 'change in the social structure' of American society,[34] the 'post' in postmodern and postcolonial corresponds to a change in perspective more than to a perceived change in reality. So a first insight that can be drawn from existing literature is that post-prefixes can refer to two kinds of history: the *historia res gestae* (the historical process as interpreted by twentieth-century commentators) and the *historia rerum gestarum* (the stories through which people make sense of their pasts, each with their own limitations and underlying assumptions).

Having said this, the question on which of these two levels post-concepts operate is not always easy to answer, given that discontinuities of the kind

captured in the term post-industrial are, of course, created in the historical imagination and therefore always a matter of interpretation. As such,
the 'post' in post-industrial can be a 'space-clearing gesture', or a form of
critical dissociation from previously held positions, just as much as shorthand for a transition in historical reality. As Ella Shohat has argued, this
ambiguity is characteristic even of postcolonialism. In her reading, this
post-concept 'implies both going beyond anti-colonial nationalist theory
as well as a movement beyond a specific point in history' – that is, beyond
colonial regimes in the so-called Third World and struggles for independence that helped bring about decolonization in the course of the twentieth
century. Unlike Appiah, therefore, Shohat maintains that the adjective postcolonial not only marks a distancing from colonial types of discourse, but
also signals 'a passage into a new period and a closure of a certain historical
event or age, officially stamped with dates'.[35] Apparently, the first thing that
understanding a post-concept requires is elucidating what the root term (the
noun following the prefix) denotes. What exactly is it that the post-prefix
seeks to challenge, criticize or reject?

A second relevant distinction is made by Arif Dirlik, who distinguishes
between two kinds of relations between prefix and noun. Apart from post
'as transcending the immediate past', there is post 'as being conditioned in
a historical sense by what came earlier'.[36] This is to say that post-prefixes
can be markers of change-in-continuity, but also signs of continuity-in-
discontinuity. Arnold Toynbee's musings on the post-Christian condition
of 1950s Europe are a case in point. On the one hand, Toynbee observed
with regret that Christian faith seemed increasingly less relevant, not only to
individual citizens, but also to public institutions in Europe. On the other,
he warned that democracy, freedom and human rights cannot flourish if
severed from the soil that nourished them. For Toynbee, then, the 'post' in
post-Christian was simultaneously a marker of discontinuity (rapid secularization) and a marker of continuity (Europeans remaining heirs to their
Christian past, whether they liked it or not).[37]

Helpful as these conceptual distinctions may be, historical questions of
the sort raised above hardly figure in the existing literature. Indeed, examples like Toynbee's, from the immediate post-war period, are strikingly
absent, not only from specialized articles, but also from broadly conceived
volumes like *Past the Last Post: Theorizing Post-Colonialism and Post-
Modernism* (1991) and *The Post-Marked World: Theory and Practice
in the 21st Century* (2013).[38] Judging by these studies, most authors
examine post-constructions in order to stimulate conceptual theorizing.
They examine older post-terms, such as postmodernism or poststructuralism, with an eye to defining or challenging new ones. Much of the relevant
literature, in other words, engages with post-constructions from theoretical

or conceptual points of view, without paying more than cursory attention to historical backgrounds. Existing scholarship has little to say about where post-concepts came from, who brought them into circulation, how they spread, and what they meant.[39]

Aims and methods

This volume, by contrast, seeks to put these historical questions centre stage. It does so by offering intellectual histories of some of the most influential post-terms from the past hundred years: post-capitalist, post-Keynesian, post-Christian, post-ideological, postmodern, post-secular, poststructuralist, postcolonial, postfeminist, and post-traditional. The chapters collected in this volume ground these concepts in varied and shifting historical contexts. They explore their articulation, proliferation, reception and redefinition, pay attention to tensions around alternative meanings, even within single texts, and highlight the range of interpreters, in and outside of Western academia, that mobilized these post-concepts. Although the result is, of course, far from comprehensive, it does show how fruitful it is to complement conceptual reflection with intellectual historical study. As highlighted in the epilogue, historical analysis as offered in this volume can add much-needed depth and nuance to contemporary debates about what it means to 'live in world of "posts"'.[40]

In order to ensure maximum cohesion and allow for comparison between chapters, the volume has been organized around five interpretive principles.[41]

The first of these is *positioning*: All post-concepts are 'positioning concepts' with relational meanings. While they assert a genealogical connection to their root concepts, they also facilitate what Appiah calls a 'distancing of the ancestors'.[42] Following Mark Salber Phillips, this volume assumes that such positioning is best understood as a multidimensional activity with epistemic, aesthetic, moral and political dimensions.[43] These modes of positioning, moreover, can combine in complex ways: aesthetic distance, for example, can accompany political proximity. Distance and proximity are also relative rather than absolute terms: they mark the ends of a continuum. This implies that the positioning work done by post-terms forces us to consider two questions in every instance: What continuities and discontinuities with the root concept does this particular post-construction imply? What new definitional possibilities emerge with the use of a post-prefix in this context?

Performativity: Post-concepts do not simply mark, reflect or interpret a pre-existing demarcation between two periods of time. Rather, they establish and enact that demarcation. They define a visible fault line – the 'fence' alluded to above – between past and present and propose a specific understanding of the difference between them. Indeed, as Barbara Adam notes, post-terms often produce sharp boundaries where none exist by turning 'ongoing and embedded processes into disembedded, static states'.[44] Accordingly, distances between past and present are not simply there, they are always created, for specific purposes, in different manners at different times.[45] So the question is: What prompts such historical 'otherings' and what agendas lie behind them?[46] And to what extent do such efforts draw on historicist notions of development, especially in distinguishing 'eras' or 'epochs'?[47]

Transfer: Temporal borders are not the only boundaries involved in the use of post-constructions. As virtually every chapter in this volume illustrates, post-terms travelled across disciplinary, linguistic and geographical boundaries. Indeed, many such concepts – think of postcolonialism and postmodernism – became inherently interdisciplinary by resonating throughout the twentieth-century humanities and social sciences. These concepts also traversed geographical and linguistic borders. Yet these travels often involved key shifts in meaning. The authors in this volume therefore raise questions like: Why was 'French post-structuralism' largely made in the US and how did it travel (back) to Europe? What were the mechanisms of transfer in such cases?

Interconnectedness: Although the volume is organized around individual post-concepts, it reveals unexpected patterns of interaction between post-concepts at two levels. First, there often were significant overlaps in meaning, as in the shared historicist assumptions that shaped both post-Christian and post-ideological discourses. Second, the terms often intersected in the biographies of individuals. In circles around the World Council of Churches, for instance, Hans Hoekendijk helped spread multiple post-concepts, from post-Christian and post-ecclesiastical to post-bourgeois and post-personal. One wonders, did these constructions reinforce one another? Did they draw on shared assumptions?

Conceptual webs: The chapters in this volume proceed from the assumption that every concept rests on a wider conceptual web of ideas and associated terms that anchor and deepen its meanings. As Jason Josephson argues, concepts are 'nodes in a conceptual network and gain their function according to their links to other nodes'.[48] These links, says Josephson, take on different forms, from simple relations of difference or similarity to more complex forms of interaction. Thus, in addition to tracing the genealogy of particular post-concepts, the chapters in this volume also attend to wider webs of concepts that sustain them. They ask not only, 'How has this post-construction been used over time and across space?' but also, 'What wider web of concepts and terms sustains each of its various meanings?'

It is worth highlighting that precisely this contextualizing approach allows the volume to trace post-constructions through a broad range of genres and fields. By comparing how sociologists, economists, historians and religious scholars diagnosed their time or positioned themselves vis-à-vis existing approaches in their fields, it tries to excavate a discipline-transcending history replete with unexpected connections, transfers and parallels between fields that are too often studied in isolation from one other. In doing so, the volume encourages historians of sociology, historians of theology and historians of political thought to transcend their disciplinary boundaries and work together towards a rapprochement between the social sciences and the humanities (including philosophy and theology).[49] Some chapters even show affinity with history of knowledge approaches as advocated by Lorraine Daston and others.[50] They seek to transcend yet another boundary: between academic and non-academic circuits of knowledge production and knowledge circulation. Post-terms lend themselves well to such treatment, as professors never had a monopoly on post-terms. On the contrary, part of what makes 'the age of the post' so interesting is that pastors, poets, journalists and politicians sometimes used post-terms just as eagerly as social scientists and humanities scholars.[51]

Structure of the volume

The essays collected in this volume are clustered in three broadly chronologically organized parts. Tracing the emergence of post-language among mid-twentieth-century intellectuals, Part I shows how prominent religious thinkers were in introducing terms like post-Christian, post-Protestant and post-secular. Also, the chapters on post-Christian and post-ideological show how deeply 'post boys' such as Christopher Dawson, Raymond Aron, Edward Shils and Daniel Bell were indebted to historicist modes of thinking. In suggesting that an 'era' or 'age' had come to an end, these intellectuals all drew on stadial philosophies of history. By contrast, the 'postcapitalist vision' as articulated in Europe and the United States alike eschewed such bold demarcations between past and present. In Howard Brick's analysis, it was 'characterized by a great deal of ambivalence and uncertainty' – even though it also favoured developmental modes of thinking.

In the second part of the volume, devoted to the heydays of 'the age of the post', such explicit philosophies of history recede into the background. Even if postcolonial started as a periodizer, most of the post-terms that rose to prominence in the 1970s, 1980s and 1990s expressed intellectual distance – from New Criticism, in the case of poststructuralist, or from mainstream economics, in the case of post-Keynesian – more than historical change. At the same time, while some of this distance was clearly intended, post-terms were not only labels of self-identification, they often also served as derogatory terms. As Brian McHale observed in 1982: 'Most writing about postmodern writing to date has been polemical or apologetic.'[52] By examining these polemic exchanges from a historical point of view – attentive to key players, cultural contexts and mechanisms of transfer – the chapters in Part II relate abstract concepts, sometimes associated with 'high theory', to the concrete realities of conference organizers that invited Jacques Derrida to the United States and groundbreaking volumes like Bill Ashcroft, Gareth Griffith and Helen Tiffin's *The Empire Writes Back* (1989). At the same time, such contextualizing treatments do not imply that the theoretical issues at stake are placed between brackets: Stephen Turner's chapter deftly shows the difficulties inherent to how Alasdair MacIntyre, Robert Bellah and Anthony Giddens define the post-traditional.

Part III, finally, subjects some more recent post-constructions to critical scrutiny. Chapters on postfeminism and posthumanism illustrate how deeply the post-prefix has become ingrained in the language of cultural theory and cultural criticism. As Adriaan van Veldhuizen argues in his epilogue to the volume, this suggests that what he calls the 'post-family' is unlikely not to bring forth more children, nephews and nieces. With post-truth now routinely being invoked as a label for our time, there are few signs that the age of the post is approaching its end.

Notes

1 Alison Flood, '"Post-Truth" Named Word of the Year by Oxford Dictionaries', *The Guardian* (15 November 2016).
2 For more recent connotations of the term, see the epilogue to this volume.
3 Helpful titles include David Theo Goldberg, *Are We All Post-Racial Yet?* (Cambridge: Polity Press, 2015) and David A. Hollinger, 'The Concept of Post-Racial: How Its Easy Dismissal Obscures Important Questions', *Daedalus*, 140 (2011), 174–82.
4 Tom Turner, *City as Landscape: A Post Post-Modern View of Design and Planning* (London: E. & F. N. Spon, 1996).
5 David Hajdu, 'The Genre of Post-Genre', *The Nation* (13 March 2018).
6 Ruth Godden, 'Joys and Pains of Full-Time Parenting', *The Times* (3 January 2004).
7 Elizabeth S. Anker and Rita Felski (eds), *Critique and Postcritique* (Durham, NC: Duke University Press, 2017).
8 See Chapter 11 on posthumanism by Yolande Jansen, Jasmijn Leeuwenkamp and Leire Urricelqui.

9 Arpad Szakolczai and Bjørn Thomassen, 'Introduction: Rethinking Social Theory with Anthropology', in Arpad Szakolczai and Bjørn Thomassen (eds), *From Anthropology to Social Theory: Rethinking the Social Sciences* (Cambridge: Cambridge University Press, 2019), pp. 1–19, p. 5.

10 Gustavo Gutiérrez, 'Memory and Prophecy', in Daniel G. Groody (ed.), *The Option for the Poor in Christian Theology* (Notre Dame, IN: University of Notre Dame Press, 2007), pp. 17–38, p. 32.

11 Dennis H. Wrong, 'On Thinking About the Future', *The American Sociologist*, 9 (1974), 26–31, 27. Closely related to the 'post boys', in Wrong's assessment, were the 'thanatologists': authors who caught public attention by boldly proclaiming 'the Death of God, or of Man, or of the Family, or the End of Liberalism, or of Ideology, or of Culture, or of Literature, or, more bathetically, of the Novel'.

12 Constantin Fasolt, *The Limits of History* (Chicago, IL: University of Chicago Press, 2004), p. 12.

13 Daniel Bell, *The Coming of Post-Industrial Society: A Venture in Social Forecasting* (New York: Basic Books, 1973), p. 53. These sentences were almost literally taken from 'Starting from the Post', *Public Interest*, 24 (1971), 108–9 – a short article that listed no less than nineteen post-concepts proposed by theologians and, especially, social scientists. See also 'The Nation: A Parcel of Posts', *Time* (25 October 1971).

14 Eleanore Price Mather, *Edward Hicks, Primitive Quaker: His Religion in Relation to His Art* (Wallingford, PA: Pendle Hill Publications, 1970), p. 33.

15 John Porter, 'The Future of Upward Mobility', *American Sociological Review*, 33 (1968), 5–19, 5 n. 1.

16 See Adriaan van Veldhuizen's chapter in this volume.

17 See Howard Brick's contribution to this volume.

18 See Hans Bertens' chapter in this volume.

19 Ananda K. Coomaraswamy and Arthur J. Penty (eds), *Essays in Post-Industrialism: A Symposium of Prophecy Concerning the Future of Society* (London: T. N. Foulis, 1914). Cf. Howard Brick, 'Optimism of the Mind: Imagining Post-Industrial Society in the 1960s and 1970s', *American Quarterly*, 44 (1992), 348–80, 351, 375 n. 12.

20 Karl E. Meyer, 'Ironist and Iconoclast', *The New Leader*, 47 (1964), 27–8, 28.

21 Post-concepts have not seldom elicited ironic commentary along the lines of Umberto Eco's famous quip: 'God is dead, Marxism is undergoing crisis, and I don't feel so hot myself.' Umberto Eco, *Travels in Hyperreality: Essays*, trans. William Weaver (San Diego, CA: Harcourt Brace Jovanovich, 1986), p. 126.

22 Niels Brügger, 'What about the Postmodern? The Concept of the Postmodern in the Work of Lyotard', *Yale French Studies*, 99 (2001), 77–92.

23 See Edward Baring's and Andrew Sartori's contributions to this volume.

24 Kwame Anthony Appiah, 'Is the Post- in Postmodernism the Post- in Postcolonial?', *Critical Inquiry*, 17 (1991), 336–57. In 'Varieties of Nationalism: Post-Revisionist Irish Studies', *Irish Studies Review*, 4 (1996), 34–7, Willy Maley asked: 'Is the "post" in post-colonialism the same as the "post" in post-nationalism?' (34).

Five years later, David Chioni Moore added: 'Is the Post- in Postcolonial the Post-in Post-Soviet? Toward a Global Postcolonial Critique', *PMLA*, 116 (2001), 111–28. More recent variations on Appiah's title include Graham Huggan, 'Is the "Post" in "Postsecular" the "Post" in "Postcolonial"?', *Modern Fiction Studies*, 56 (2010), 751–68 and Shu-mei Shih, 'Is the *Post-* in Postsocialism the *Post-* in Posthumanism?', *Social Text*, 30 (2012), 27–50.

25 For the rhetoric of 'turns' in the humanities, see the forum section, 'Historiographic "Turns" in Critical Perspective', *The American Historical Review*, 117:3 (2012).

26 Holly Case, *The Age of Questions: Or, a First Attempt at an Aggregate History of the Eastern, Social, Woman, American, Jewish, Polish, Bullion, Tuberculosis, and Many Other Questions over the Nineteenth Century, and Beyond* (Princeton, NJ: Princeton University Press, 2018).

27 Francesco Coniglione, 'Introduction: From the Age of "Posts" to the Knowledge Society', in Coniglione (ed.), *Through the Mirrors of Science: New Challenges for Knowledge-Based Societies* (Heusenstamm: Ontos, 2010), 13–32, 13.

28 Herman Paul, 'Relations to the Past: A Research Agenda for Historical Theorists', *Rethinking History*, 19 (2015), 450–8; François Hartog, *Regimes of Historicity: Presentism and the Experience of Time*, trans. Saskia Brown (New York: Columbia University Press, 2015).

29 I borrow this term from Gregory L. Ulmer, 'The Post-Age', *Diacritics*, 11 (1981), 39–56.

30 Frank Kermode, *The Sense of an Ending: Studies in the Theory of Fiction* (New York: Oxford University Press, 1967).

31 Jeffrey C. Alexander, 'Modern, Anti, Post, and Neo: How Social Theories Have Tried to Understand the "New World" of "Our Time"', *Zeitschrift für Soziologie*, 23 (1994), 165–97.

32 Although there has been some debate on the relevance or irrelevance of hyphens between prefix and noun, the variety of spelling conventions in our source material is too large to allow for any generalizations on this issue.

33 Appiah, 'Post- in Postmodernism', 348, 341–2.

34 Bell, *Coming of Post-Industrial Society*, p. x.

35 Ella Shohat, 'Notes on the "Post-Colonial"', *Social Text*, 31/32 (1992), 99–113, 101. For a critical response see Stuart Hall, 'When Was "the Post-Colonial"? Thinking at the Limit', in Ian Chambers and Lidia Curti (eds), *The Post-Colonial Question: Common Skies, Divided Horizons* (London: Routledge, 1996), pp. 242–60.

36 Arif Dirlik, '[Interview]', in Shaobo Xie and Fengzhen Wang (eds), *Dialogues on Cultural Studies: Interviews with Contemporary Critics* (Calgary: University of Calgary Press, 2002), pp. 9–46, p. 20.

37 See my own chapter in this volume.

38 Ian Adam and Helen Tiffin (eds), *Past the Last Post: Theorizing Post-Colonialism and Post-Modernism* (New York: Harvester Wheatsheaf, 1991); Krystyna Kujawińska Courtney, Izabella Penier and Sumit Chakrabarti (eds), *The Post-Marked World: Theory and Practice in the 21st Century* (Newcastle upon Tyne: Cambridge Scholars Publishing, 2013).

39 Notable exceptions include Tanya Ann Kennedy, *Historicizing Post-Discourses: Postfeminism and Postracialism in United States Culture* (Albany, NY: State University of New York Press, 2017); Howard Brick, *Transcending Capitalism: Visions of a New Society in Modern American Thought* (Ithaca, NY: Cornell University Press, 2006) and Hans Bertens, *The Idea of the Postmodern: A History* (London: Routledge, 1995).

40 Joyce Appleby, 'Introduction: Jefferson and His Complex Legacy', in Peter S. Onuf (ed.), *Jeffersonian Legacies* (Charlottesville, VA: University Press of Virginia, 1993), pp. 1–16, p. 14.

41 I would like to thank K. Healan Gaston and Adriaan van Veldhuizen for their help in formulating these interpretive principles.

42 Appiah, 'Post- in Postmodernism', 342.

43 Mark Salber Phillips, *On Historical Distance* (New Haven, CT: Yale University Press, 2013).

44 Barbara Adam, 'The Temporal Landscape of Global/izing Culture and the Paradox of Postmodern Futures', in Barbara Adam and Stuart Allan (eds), *Theorizing Culture: An Interdisciplinary Critique after Postmodernism* (New York: New York University Press, 1995), pp. 249–62, p. 258.

45 Chris Lorenz and Berber Bevernage (eds), *Breaking Up Time: Negotiating the Borders Between Present, Past, and Future* (Göttingen: Vandenhoeck & Ruprecht, 2013).

46 Johannes Fabian, *Time and the Other: How Anthropology Makes Its Object* (New York: Columbia University Press, 1983).

47 I take 'developmental historicism' in Mark Bevir's sense of the word, as short-hand for a mode of historical thinking that highlights 'development' over time while distinguishing sharply between distinct 'periods' or 'epochs', each with their own typical zeitgeist: Mark Bevir, 'Historicism and the Human Sciences in Victorian Britain', in Bevir (ed.), *Historicism and the Human Sciences in Victorian Britain* (Cambridge: Cambridge University Press, 2017), pp. 1–20.

48 Jason Ānanda Josephson, *The Invention of Religion in Japan* (Chicago, IL: University of Chicago Press, 2012), p. 77.

49 As advocated by Wolf Feuerhahn, 'Les sciences humaines et sociales: des disci-plines du contexte?', *Revue d'histoire des sciences humaines*, 30 (2017), 7–29. See also Rens Bod et al., 'A New Field: History of Humanities', *History of Humanities*, 1 (2016), 1–8.

50 Lorraine Daston, 'The History of Science and the History of Knowledge', *KNOW*, 1 (2017), 131–54. See also 'History of Science or History of Knowledge?', special issue of *Berichte zur Wissenschaftsgeschichte*, 42 (2019), 109–270; Johan Östling et al. (eds), *Circulation of Knowledge: Explorations in the History of Knowledge* (Lund: Nordic Academic Press, 2018).

51 Well before 'history of knowledge' became a common phrase, Lutz Raphael described the often entangled relations between societal practices and social sci-entific knowledge in terms of a 'scientification of the social'. See Lutz Raphael, 'Die Verwissenschaftlichung des Sozialen als methodologische und konzeptuelle Herausforderung für eine Sozialgeschichte des 20. Jahrhunderts', *Geschichte*

und Gesellschaft, 22 (1996), 165–93 and Kerstin Brückweh et al. (eds), *Engineering Society: The Role of the Human and Social Sciences in Modern Societies, 1880–1980* (New York: Palgrave Macmillan, 2012).

52 Brian McHale, 'Writing about Postmodern Writing', *Poetics Today*, 3 (1982), 211–27, 212.

Part I

The emergence of a prefix (1930s–1960s)

1

'Our post-Christian age': Historicist-inspired diagnoses of modernity, 1935–70

Herman Paul

Introduction

'"Post-Christian Era"? Nonsense!' declared one of Europe's foremost theologians, Karl Barth, in August 1948, at the first assembly of the World Council of Churches in Amsterdam.

> How do we come to adopt as self-evident the phrase first used by a German National Socialist, that we are today living in an 'un-Christian' or even 'post-Christian' era? ... How indeed do we come to the fantastic opinion that secularism and godlessness are inventions of *our* time; that there was once a glorious Christian Middle Age with a generally accepted Christian faith, and it is now our task to set up this wonderful state of affairs again in new form?[1]

The World Council assembly was an appropriate venue for raising these questions, as several high-profile attendees used the very phrase, 'post-Christian era', in their diagnosis of the times. Even Martin Niemöller, a collaborator of Barth in the German Confessing Church, stated at the Amsterdam conference that 'we already talk about a "post-Christian age", in which we live and see the Christian church nearing its decline'.[2] Apparently, by 1948, 'post-Christian era' had become a familiar turn of phrase, at least in circles of the World Council of Churches. But where did it come from and what did it mean?

Barth's emphatic statement notwithstanding, 'post-Christian age' was not a phrase of National Socialist origin. Admittedly, it resonated among secularists of right-wing political leaning, especially in the 1930s and early 1940s. By 1948, however, it had been adopted on a fairly wide scale by Christian theologians and church leaders who worried about the advance of anti-Christian forces in European societies. 'Post-Christian age' had come to resemble 'secularization' in that it invoked narratives of dramatic change, rich with emotional resonance, that different religious and political parties could use to their own purposes.[3] What Barth could not foresee was that soon after World War II, secularist intellectuals would abandon their habit of diagnosing the times as 'post-Christian'. In the 1950s and early 1960s, 'post-Christian age' would come to serve primarily as a *Kampfbegriff* between two specific groups of Christian intellectuals: reform-inclined church leaders in and around the World Council of Churches who advocated a thorough rethinking of theological beliefs and church practices in the light of new societal circumstances, and more conservative Christians who interpreted such reformism as capitulation to a secular zeitgeist or as evidence that secularization did not halt before the doors of the church.

These underlying narratives of progress or decline touch upon one of the key questions in the (sparse) historical literature on post-prefixes: What did the 'post' in 'post-industrial', 'postmodern' or 'postcolonial' intend to convey? Did 'post' serve as a marker of critical dissociation, indicating that the root concept was no longer seen as representing a desirable condition? Or was 'post' an equivalent to 'beyond' in a chronological sense of the word, announcing the dawn of a new age in which the industrial, modern or colonial experience had become a thing of the past?[4] Drawing on examples from Germany, France, Great Britain and the Netherlands (with a brief excursion to the United States),[5] I will argue that the 'post-Christian age' was interpreted almost without exception in terms of historical stages. Seen through the prism of stadial philosophies of history, the 'post-Christian age' was believed to open up a new chapter in the history of Europe.

Indeed, despite the fact that the image of an imminent post-Christian era could be adapted to serve the religious-political agendas of conservative Catholics as easily as those of aggressive atheists, a striking similarity between the mid-twentieth-century authors who took the lead in exploring the post-Christian is their indebtedness to what Mark Bevir calls 'developmental historicism', characteristic of which are (1) the belief that history amounts to a progressive unfolding of ideas or principles and (2) the habit of dividing this historical process in distinct eras, ages or periods.[6] Whether the post-Christian age was welcomed, as by Otto Petras, or perceived as a threat to everything holy, as in the case of Christopher Dawson, the philosophies of history underlying their diagnoses of modernity all varied on historicist themes. So, although the authors discussed in this chapter *positioned* themselves quite differently vis-à-vis the post-Christian age (or what they understood this to be), the *conceptual schemes* on which they relied in this defining and positioning were more similar to each other than one might expect in the light of their different political, religious and philosophical backgrounds.

This finding is important for two reasons. First, it allows us to situate 'post-Christian' among other twentieth-century post-concepts. As I will return to in the conclusion, 'post-Christian' resembled 'post-capitalist' and 'post-industrial' more than 'postliberal' or 'post-secular'. Whereas the latter group of concepts referred to *intellectual positions* held by individuals (with the prefix denoting a critical stance vis-à-vis the root concepts), the former group described the features of a *historical epoch* (the 'modern age'). Second, this shows, *pace* Mark Bevir, that developmental historicism did not disappear in the early twentieth-century 'crises of historicism'.[7] Mid-century assessments of the post-Christian predicament illustrate just how powerful the legacies of nineteenth-century historicism still were at that time.[8] The historicist connotations of 'post' in 'post-Christian' demonstrate, in other words, that the authors discussed in this chapter were not yet 'post-historicist'.

Otto Petras

Who was the 'German National Socialist' whom Karl Barth held responsible for coining the phrase 'post-Christian age'?[9] Barth may have thought of Alfred Rosenberg, the Nazi ideologue, or Janko Janeff, a Berlin-based Bulgarian Nazi propagandist who in 1939 had greeted the dawn of a 'post-Christian time' and a 'post-Christian culture'.[10] However, taking into account that Barth was notoriously sloppy in his references,[11] it is more likely that he referred to Otto Petras, who in the mid 1930s had gained attention with a treatise on the emergence of a 'fundamentally post-Christian world'.[12] Though not a National Socialist, Petras was a right-wing intellectual and admirer of Erich Ludendorff – hence politically situated at great distance from the staunch critic of nationalism that was Barth. A former Lutheran village pastor, Petras had abandoned his faith and found employment in a pedagogical institute.[13] From the late 1920s onwards, he was a frequent contributor to *Widerstand*, a National Bolshevik periodical edited by Ernst Niekisch that also served as a platform for conservative thinkers like Ernst Jünger.[14] Petras's 1935 book, *Post Christum* (After Christ), brought these threads together, arguing that Christianity was not dying, but already long dead. The book caused some stir: even Thomas Mann read it 'with interest and aversion'.[15]

What, then, made *Post Christum* such a remarkable study? To Barth's surprise, no doubt, Petras's pronouncement of death was partly inspired by the most vehement critique of liberal Protestantism that the Weimar Republic had seen emerge: Barth's *Der Römerbrief* (The Epistle to the Romans) in the edition of 1922. In uncompromising prose, this work had accused the German 'cultural-protestant' tradition for forgetting that God is the 'wholly Other', whose revelation in Christ is not the basic axiom of a religious worldview, but a thunder strike destroying all man-made religion.[16] Interpreting Barth's insistence on the infinite distance between God and human beings as the original essence of Christianity, Petras argued that, historically speaking, exclusive faith in the 'heavenly world above' had soon diminished to the point of disappearing altogether in the nineteenth-century theologies that had redefined Christianity into a programme for human self-actualization in a religious key.[17] Literally quoting Barth, Petras therefore concluded that 'Christendom as we have known it has come to an end'.[18]

Yet there was a crucial difference between Barth and Petras. When Barth argued that 'the *Christian*-bourgeois or *bourgeois*-Christian age has come to a close', he referred to a period in which the church had perverted its witness by making the gospel subservient to social order and bourgeois morality.[19] For Barth, the liquidation of this unholy alliance created opportunities for a new appreciation of the gospel. His iconoclasm, in other words, served a reformation. Petras, by contrast, equated the end of the 'Christian age' with the dawn of an age in which Christian faith no longer had any legitimate place. It had become anachronistic in the sense of representing a superseded stage in the development of the 'spirit'. Unlike Barth, who rejected all idealist philosophy of history, Petras saw history as a process driven by 'powers from the deep' (*Kräften der Tiefe*). Independent of human agency and consciousness, these 'powers of history' brought forth that what was 'historically necessary' (*geschichtlich Notwendig*). Historical phenomena like Christianity were thus no products of human hands, let alone created by divine purpose, but 'necessary emanations of the deep'.[20]

Unmistakably, this argument betrayed the influence of post-Kantian idealism or, more specifically, Hegelian philosophy of history as further developed by Young Hegelians like Bruno Bauer – a staunch critic of religion who as early as 1855 had announced the end of the 'Christian-Germanic age'.[21] Although Petras also closely aligned himself with Franz Overbeck, who had denounced the 'Christian age' as a figment of the imagination,[22] Petras felt especially inspired by Bauer's argument that Christianity had once been a creative manifestation of the spirit, but ceased to be so when the spirit had further developed itself.[23] The secularization template on which Petras drew was thus a narrative developed by Left Hegelians in the years around 1848.[24] Consequently, when Petras argued that Christianity had 'exhausted its creative power', thereby suggesting 'that we live *post Christum* in a deeper sense than indicated by the calendar', this implies that the 'post' referred to a next stage in the development of the spirit.[25] The 'post' reveals, in other words, how deeply Petras had drunk from the well of post-Kantian philosophy of history.[26]

Hans Ehrenberg

Petras's *Post Christum* reached an audience well beyond self-defined secularists. In particular, it was read widely among Christian theologians who worried about the advance of secular ideologies like 'godless Bolshevism'.[27] 'The end of the Christian age' (*das Ende des christlichen Zeitalters*) became a recurring phrase especially in defensive responses to the perceived dangers of Communism. For many German commentators, the end of that epoch was a looming threat that ought to be averted, first of all by diagnosing the powers intent on relegating Europe's Christian identity to the past. To that end, various terminological proposals were made. Some theologians perceived Communism as a key example of what the Jerusalem meeting of the International Missionary Council in 1928 had labelled 'secularism'.[28] Others perceived Communism and, after 1933, National Socialism as 'political religions', thereby emphasizing their incommensurability with Christianity.[29] Still others discerned in the Communist and National Socialist worldviews a resurgence of mythological thinking or a return to 'pagan' sources that justified the label 'neo-paganism'.[30]

It was in this context that Hans Ehrenberg introduced the phrase 'post-Christian', in a meaning different from Petras's. Ehrenberg was a philosophy professor of Jewish descent who at age forty-one had given up his chair in Heidelberg for a Lutheran pulpit in Bochum.[31] If his philosophy background made Ehrenberg an atypical pastor, so did the stream of publications that he unleashed. As early as 1932, he interpreted Communism as an offspring of European Idealism that had turned itself against the Occidental tradition, its Christian elements in particular. In Ehrenberg's view, this provoked a 'war of religion' between European Christianity and the 'antitheism' that was Communism.[32] The 'anti' in 'antitheism' conveyed that Ehrenberg not simply conceived of Communism as a return to pre-Christian paganism. Although he believed Communism to be 'the most pagan paganism that has ever existed', he emphasized that it was pagan in a modern key, unimaginable without the 'Occidental spirit' on which it drew and against which it reacted.[33]

In the 1940s, Ehrenberg expanded this analysis by arguing that the superiority of German National Socialism over, for instance, State Shinto in Meiji Japan was primarily due to its Christian background.[34] Whereas Shintoism was a 'primitive religion', 'post-Christian' Nazism simultaneously struggled against and relied on a religion that had 'formed man and world, order and life, politics and culture'. Therefore, when Ehrenberg placed Nazism on the top rung of a Fascist ladder, he did so because he believed that Christianity – the religion on which Nazism drew in its rebellion against it – represented the highest stage of religious development. 'The line ascends steeply from Japan via Turkey and Italy to the giddy heights of Nazism.'[35] Ehrenberg's 'post' thus conveyed an almost opposite message than Petras's. For Ehrenberg, 'post-Christian' referred to the Christian arsenals from which Nazism borrowed its weapons. 'The material is almost equally pre-Christian and post-Christian, but the main substance is post-Christian ... and the dynamic power is exclusively so.'[36]

Unlike Petras, then, Ehrenberg did not hail the emergence of a post-Christian era. He rather used the phrase to warn his readers against a political religion that was successful partly through ingeniously exploiting resources borrowed from the world's most advanced religion: Christianity. Underlying this argument, however, was a philosophy of history not unlike Petras's developmental historicism. Ehrenberg, too, assumed that reality is best interpreted through the prism of 'ideas', 'systems' or 'worldviews'; that these ideas develop over time, meanwhile translating themselves into social, political and cultural patterns; that some ideas have greater potential than others, as illustrated by the various stages of progression realized by the 'world's religions'; and that distinct phases can be distinguished within this development. For someone who had studied with Wilhelm Windelband, published on Immanuel Kant and G. W. F. Hegel, lectured on 'the philosophy of history and civilization', and worked in close proximity to Ernst Troeltsch and Alfred Weber, these commitments were perhaps not altogether surprising.[37] Ehrenberg's entire cultural milieu was shaped by the legacies of Idealist historicism.[38]

Arnold Toynbee

To what extent can similar historicist influences be detected in Great Britain, a country that, at much smaller scale, had had its own tradition of philosophical Idealism?[39] Interestingly, when 'post-Christian' entered the vocabulary of British intellectuals, the meanings attached to this diagnostic concept resembled Ehrenberg's. This was due in the first place to the historian and international relations expert, Arnold J. Toynbee. The first volumes of *A Study of History* (twelve volumes, 1934–61) had earned Toynbee a reputation for cultural-political diagnosis from a long-term historical perspective. As early as 1940, Toynbee told an Oxford audience that such a long-term perspective made the modern Western world appear as distinctively 'post-Christian'. Like Ehrenberg, Toynbee applied this label in the first instance to secular ideologies with quasi-religious features: 'Communism, which is another of our latter-day religions, is, I think, a leaf taken from the book of Christianity – a leaf torn out and misread.'[40] Toynbee considerably widened the scope of the phrase, however, by including Communism's democratic other into the post-Christian realm:

> Democracy is another leaf from the book of Christianity, which has also, I fear, been torn out and, while perhaps not misread, has certainly been half emptied of meaning by being divorced from its Christian context and secularized; and we have obviously, for a number of generations past, been living on spiritual capital, I mean clinging to Christian practice without possessing the Christian belief.[41]

This implied that not only totalitarian 'neo-paganism' was post-Christian, but that Western society at large had become a 'post-Christian secular civilization'.[42] Not 'they', but 'we' had secularized to the point of becoming 'ex-' or 'post-Christian'.[43] In the early 1940s, when the rise of 'secular society' as a catchphrase in British media was still two decades away,[44] this was a controversial thing to say. As late as 1952, in his Reith Lecture for the BBC – by then still a Christian broadcast company[45] – Toynbee assumed his listeners to be 'surprised – and even a little indignant – to hear me speak of our western community' as being as thoroughly post-Christian as Communist Russia.[46] Critics like Douglas Francis Jerrold charged Toynbee for precisely this reason: they felt he was exaggerating the 'post-Christian' element.[47]

For Toynbee, however, 'post-Christian' was a term of hope, not of despair. In his 1940 Oxford lecture, delivered just weeks after the German invasion of France and written under the influence of a befriended Benedictine monk,[48] he made the argument that even if Western civilization would come to an end, 'Christianity may be expected not only to endure but to grow in wisdom and stature as the result of a fresh experience of secular catastrophe'.[49] These were remarkable words for a historian who had always analysed world history through the prism of civilizations, without paying much attention to religion. The 1940 lecture marked a watershed in Toynbee's thinking in so far as it prioritized religion over civilization, to the extent of making the future of Western civilization depend on a rediscovery of its Christian roots.[50] Interestingly, 'post-Christian' served this call for spiritual renewal to the extent that it suggested that Europe's Christian heritage was implicitly still very much present. Recognizing that democratic values such as individual liberty could only flourish on Christian soil was a first step towards a recovery of Christian faith as Europe had known it. In Toynbee's own words:

> We are uncertain about Christian beliefs and yet are very certain about something which is a consequence of our Christian beliefs, a political or social consequence – this belief in individual freedom and in the value of the individual soul. But perhaps the situation can't remain like this; perhaps we shall

have either to recover a theological basis for our belief in individual liberty or else to abandon our belief in individual liberty.[51]

'Post-Christian', then, acquired apologetic meaning in so far as it encouraged rediscovery and rearticulation of Christian assumptions underlying democratic values such as individual liberty. Even if Toynbee occasionally allowed himself to slip into nostalgia, thereby turning the post-Christian into a site of estrangement ('I feel more at home in either the Christian World or the pagan Greek World than in our present post-Christian world'),[52] he confidently believed that some of the ambiguities of secularization could be resolved if Christian views of God and human nature could be rearticulated in language accessible to modern human beings. Interestingly, as the 1950s progressed, Toynbee increasingly rephrased this in more ecumenical terms, highlighting the self-sacrificing love that he saw as central to all 'higher religions'.[53]

Although Toynbee did not share Petras's and Ehrenberg's German Idealist historicism – he had studied in Oxford, not in Berlin[54] – he, too, consistently inscribed the present in narratives of *longue durée* development. Also, like Ehrenberg, he emphasized the incomplete secularization of modern political ideologies: they continued to draw on Christian resources. Unlike his German colleague, however, Toynbee highlighted the potential this offered instead of the threat it posed. A democracy 'living on spiritual capital' is not yet fully secularized: it is still capable of justifying itself on religious grounds. For Toynbee, this was an opportunity that Western democrats engaged in a Cold War could only ignore at their peril.[55]

Christopher Dawson

While Toynbee highlighted the similarities between Christianity and other faith traditions, a more specific apologetic programme was carried out by his friend and colleague, Christopher Dawson. A Roman Catholic convert, Dawson approached the 'post-Christian' from a different angle to Toynbee. With T. S. Eliot, V. A. Demant, and Maurice Reckitt, among others, he belonged to a group of mostly Anglo-Catholic intellectuals known as the Christendom group.[56] Already by the early 1940s, this group perceived the modern Western world as fundamentally post-Christian. In words that could have been written by Toynbee, they understood this to mean that modern Westerners had retained 'a real devotion to some of the ethical and social results of the Christian outlook', but largely forgotten 'the doctrine and feeling upon which these results [had] been reared'.[57] Yet the key question for these Christendom thinkers was not how religious love could heal a world increasingly plagued by technologically induced suffering, but how 'the formation of a new Christian culture', as Eliot put it, could prevent the Western world from plunging into neo-paganism.[58] In Dawson's robust prose, Western culture had to choose between 'total secularization or a return to Christian culture'.[59]

Characteristically, Dawson placed much historical weight on this choice by arguing that nothing less than the course of European history was at stake. When Europe, after its 'pre-Christian' stage, had been Christianized in the Middle Ages, it had become 'a society of peoples with common moral values and common spiritual aims'.[60] This unity had been broken, however, in the age of revolutions, which had inaugurated a 'post-Christian' phase in European history. Characteristic of this last stage, in which Europe found itself internally divided over religious as well as political issues, was its lack of prospect: post-Christian Europe was falling prey to destructive forces unleashed by secularizing powers. 'There is no going forward on this path. If the peoples of Europe desire to survive, they must seek a new way.'[61] For Dawson, this renewal required a retrieval of Europe's 'spiritual inheritance', that is, a rediscovery of the religious roots of Western civilization. 'Civilization can only be creative and life-giving in the proportion that it is spiritualized.'[62] In Dawson's developmental scheme, the way forward thus required a step backward – a returning to the Christian stage, not by artificially restoring medieval Christendom, as some of Dawson's critics feared, but 'by relating the instruments of culture to their true spiritual ends', just as Thomas Aquinas and Albert Magnus had done in the heydays of medieval Christendom.[63]

Unlike Toynbee, Dawson mainly held his fellow Catholics responsible for this renewal of Western culture. Instead of summoning church-leavers back into the fold of the church or expecting them to undo the 'secularization of culture', he emphasized Catholic agency. This was partly because Dawson perceived the post-Christian condition as having been made possible by Christian failure ('Our civilization has become secularized largely because the Christian element has adopted a passive attitude'), partly also because Christians alone still enjoyed direct access 'to the sacred tradition of the Christian past which flows underneath the streets and cinemas and skyscrapers of the new Babylon'.[64] Following this argument, Dawson spent much of his life, mostly notably as a Harvard professor of Roman Catholic Studies (1958–62), advocating educational practices aimed at fostering Catholic *ressourcement* in a post-Christian age.[65]

Dawson's grand historical vision had more than a few affinities with historicist thinking, especially in so far as it paired a developmental view of history with stadial modes of periodization ('the seven stages of Western culture', 'the six ages of the church').[66] Most characteristic, however, was

Dawson's explicit call for the retrieval of Europe's Catholic heritage, born out of the conviction that the Western world had become too secular. Ironically, for this reason, the 'post' in Dawson, the devout Catholic, resembled that of Petras, the staunch critic of religion. Despite their different evaluative stances, both took the prefix to denote a radical dissociation from true Christianity.

Hans Hoekendijk

Secularization stories of this kind not only circulated among atheists or among Christians who saw it as their task to counter the decline of Christian culture. Such stories were also told by progressive Christians who urged the church to stay in touch with the development of Western society at large. If society had become 'post-Christian' in Petras's sense of the word, then the church could no longer assume, as it had done in the heyday of Christendom, that people would intuitively know who God is or have a latent desire for their sins to be forgiven. Therefore the church would need to reinvent itself – its theology, its rituals, its organization – if it were to remain 'relevant' to a generation for whom Christianity was a thing of the past, or so the Dutch theologian Hans Hoekendijk, among others, maintained.[67]

Although Hoekendijk had attended Barth's 1948 lecture in Amsterdam,[68] the former missionary and recently appointed professor of missiology at Utrecht University chose to ignore Barth's warnings when he argued in 1952 that Europe had entered a 'post-Christian, post-ecclesiastical, post-bourgeois, [and] post-personal' stage of history. While acknowledging that the shadow of the cross still loomed large over Europe, Hoekendijk maintained that especially younger generations had moved beyond the cultural milieu with which the church was most familiar. Whereas the church was almost exclusively populated by representatives of what Hoekendijk called 'the third man', Europe was witnessing the emergence of a new type of human being, called the 'fourth man', who neither felt a need to attend church nor saw any good in rebelling against it: 'As the fourth man sees it, the church has so completely identified herself with the culture of the third man that for that reason alone he will consider all that church business as something not addressed to him. You do not respond to it anymore with a yes or no; you are no longer anti-clerical; you just do not have a thing to do with it.'[69]

Hoekendijk's writing was marked by strong contrasts indeed. The Utrecht missiologist distinguished the 'Sisyphean existence' of the fourth man from the 'bourgeois' mentality epitomized by its predecessor as sharply as he rejected church practices that he perceived as out of joint with the times. Concretely, Hoekendijk argued that 'solidarity' with the fourth man required the church to invest in lay apostolate – a more radical alternative for full-time clergy than the 'worker-priest' known in the French Roman Catholic Church – and in para-church organizations such as house churches and cell groups.[70] 'All silly stateliness and all hocus-pocus, which so often spoil our church life, can be forgotten, yes, *must* be left behind in such groups.'[71] Likewise, in Hoekendijk's missionary vision, ancient cathedrals should be abandoned in favour of fellowship houses, silence centres in apartment blocks or portable chapels spread across the city like telephone boxes.[72] The advance of the fourth man, in short, required drastic missionary measures.

Where, then, did this post-Christian figure come from? As a character profile of 'modern man' not unlike William H. Whyte's 'organization man' and Herbert Marcuse's 'one-dimensional man', the fourth man originated with the German sociologist Alfred Weber (Max's younger brother).[73] In Weber's historical imagination, European history could be divided into four phases, which he saw embodied by the hunter-gatherer, the agrarian settler, the bourgeois citizen and the mass man, respectively.[74] The fourth man image thus presupposed a long-term historical narrative with clearly delineated phases. This, moreover, was a developmental narrative in so far as Weber, to his regret, saw no way back: historical change could not be undone.[75] Although Hoekendijk was too eclectic in his intellectual tastes to accept all of this historical baggage, some of his critics, including especially the Dutch theologian Hendrik Berkhof, perceptively noticed that his insistence on irreversible societal change with which the church should quickly catch up was premised on a philosophy of history that schematized social and religious variety into rather rigid historical stadia.[76] In so far as Hoekendijk borrowed with Weber's fourth man some of the historicist sensibilities out of which this image had originally emerged, he assigned more weight to 'individuality' than to 'development'.

Hoekendijk's argument that the church should 'radically' renew itself in order to be 'relevant' to post-Christian citizens struck a chord among liberal Protestants across the world. While British authors in the 1950s often cited Dawson, Toynbee or C. S. Lewis as theorists of the 'post-Christian',[77] Hoekendijk served as an important source for American theologians. Figures as diverse as Samuel H. Miller, Loren E. Halvorson, Howard Moody and Harvey Cox, the influential author of *The Secular City* (1965), all attributed the phrase 'post-Christian' to the Dutch missiologist.[78] Interestingly, this happened at a time, around 1960, when quite a few American Protestants believed they were witnessing the fulfilment of Paul Tillich's 1936 prophecy that the 'Protestant era' would soon be over.[79] This caused the 'post-Christian age' to interfere rather closely with the 'post-Protestant era' that historians of religion Martin E. Marty and Winthrop S. Hudson believed the United States to have entered into becoming a pluralist country – 'post-Christian' though not yet 'post-religious', as sociologist of religion Will Herberg put it.[80]

In all these cases, 'post' implied discontinuity rather than continuity. Although theologian Sidney E. Mead exaggerated when he argued that 'post-Christian' and 'post-Protestant' were phrases reflecting 'the somber mood of those identity-conscious people who are sure there was a past but who can find little basis for assurance that there will be a future',[81] it is true that past–present divides were often drawn sharply, with little eye for the continuous presence of the past that Toynbee and Dawson preferred to highlight. Among liberal Protestants in particular, the perceived breach with the Christian past was such that religious scholar Bruce Morgan was able to claim that only an 'un-linear and thus essentially non-Christian philosophy of history' could blind Christians to the 'uniqueness' of the post-Christian moment.[82] So, here, too, the 'post' began to denote an 'over and done with', without much nostalgic feeling for the world that was lost.

Jacques Ellul

Few responded with more irritation to this discourse of radical change than Jacques Ellul, a French sociologist of technology and Reformed lay theologian affiliated with the University of Bordeaux.[83] Although Ellul did not eschew bold generalizations – he had a reputation for being markedly pessimistic about the moral prospects of 'technological society'[84] – he called into question the 'uncriticized presuppositions' that made theologians such as Hoekendijk perceive their age as dramatically different from earlier periods in history. 'Thus it is assumed that society is evolving, that it has little in common with the past, and that we are involved in situations which are entirely new. One seldom takes the trouble to specify what is new, but is content instead with featureless generalities about science and technology.'[85] With an indignation reminiscent of Barth, Ellul wondered whether liturgical and theological reforms aimed at reaching out to 'post-Christian man' had any empirical basis. 'What if the analysis is wrong?'[86]

These were typical questions for a man who seven years earlier had written a book-length critique of commonplaces such as 'modern man has come of age' and 'make way for the youth' – stereotypical phrases that emphasized in one way or another that 'the times they are a-changin''.[87] Although Ellul acknowledged cataclysmic transformations in Western technological culture, he was less convinced that human nature changes in tandem with technology or that God reveals himself differently to human beings with a car in their garage than to people travelling by horse or track boat. Consequently, he found himself criticizing 'an entire segment of Protestant writing today', especially in so far as it followed 'Hegelian-Marxist' templates in attributing normative significance to historical change.[88]

How did this stance affect Ellul's understanding of 'post-Christian civilization'?[89] In his most elaborate musings, from 1973, Ellul distinguished two senses in which he was prepared to call the Western world post-Christian. Echoing Ehrenberg, Toynbee, Dawson, as well as the French economist Georges Lasserre,[90] Ellul emphasized that Western society still showed the marks of Christianity: 'We have not ceased to be products of the Christian era, but we have managed to reject what is specifically Christian in this product and retain only its psychic aspect. Thus, post-Christian society is a society of men who are at the point to which Christianity brought them but who no longer believe in the specific truth of the Christian revelation.'[91] Secondly, Ellul understood 'post-Christian' to signify that the Christian tradition no longer supplied shared values or a common frame of reference. Christians had become a countercultural minority, as Ellul could tell from personal experience as a Protestant in a country divided by Catholic–secular conflict.[92] Yet instead of framing this in terms of transition from one historical period into another, Ellul understood it as a long overdue correction to the 'monumental error' that had been Christendom. Just as Barth had welcomed the end of the 'bourgeois-Christian era', Ellul believed that Christians could 'thank God' for the liquidation of a settlement that had obscured the extent to which Christian hope is eschatological and hence independent from earthly powers. 'Christendom is dead. Long live post-Christendom!'[93]

On the one hand, then, Ellul disagreed with Barth's critique of the post-Christian. Yet on the other, he shared his deep suspicion of historical categories taking precedence over theological arguments.[94] Just as Barth had identified 'historicism' as one of the two arch-enemies of Christian theology ('psychologism' being the other one),[95] so Ellul believed that Christians should reject 'conformity to history', because their standard of judgement is not historical development, but 'the coming break with this present world' that is the eschaton.[96] In contrast to Hoekendijk and his American admirers, Ellul thus minimized the importance of historical change as a theologically relevant category. 'History has no privileged significance. It is nothing but a sort of appendage to man. Man is the important thing, not history. The latter exists because man lives, and history adds no value whatsoever to man.'[97]

Conclusion

According to religious historian Sydney Ahlstrom, it was in the 1960s that the idea of a 'post-Christian world' took root in the popular imagination.[98] There is some truth to this: 'post-Christian' was never a more popular phrase than in the early 1960s. Yet as Hugh McLeod has argued, many of the ideas that became fashionable in the 1960s were not new: '[M]any of them went back to the early twentieth century, the nineteenth century, or even earlier.'[99] This was also the case for 'post-Christian age'. As this chapter has shown, the phrase emerged in 1930s Germany in the context of what Ehrenberg called a 'war of religion' between Christianity and various forms of 'antitheism', including Communism and National Socialism. Whereas Petras and other self-designated secularists welcomed the 'post-Christian era' as an age of emancipation, Ehrenberg instead warned against the 'neo-paganism' of post-Christian powers intent on relegating Christianity to the past. Similar ambiguities continued to mark the phrase during the 1950s and 1960s. Toynbee and Dawson experienced 'post-Christian civilization' as a context of estrangement. Hoekendijk, by contrast, encouraged his fellow-believers to adapt their churches to a 'post-Christian age'. Clearly, then, 'post-Christian' not only *meant* different things to different authors; the term could also be mobilized in the service of different *positions* vis-à-vis Europe's Christian heritage.

Nonetheless, what all versions of the phrase had in common was an underlying commitment to a mode of thinking about history that inscribed the post-Christian 'age' in a narrative of *longue durée* development in which several distinct 'eras' or 'epochs' could be distinguished. Known as developmental historicism, this mode of thinking distinguished 'post-Christian' in its mid-twentieth-century incarnations from more recent post-concepts, such as 'postliberal' as defined by George A. Lindbeck and other Yale theologians in the 1980s and 'post-secular' in Jürgen Habermas's definition of 2008. None of these authors claimed that a postliberal or post-secular era was about to succeed a liberal or secular age. Lindbeck, rather, proposed a theory of religion intent on overcoming classic dichotomies between 'tradition' and 'innovation' in American theology,[100] just as Habermas's post-prefix marked a stance of dissociation from a secularist position denying the legitimacy of religious voices in the public domain.[101] 'Post-Christian' resembled 'post-capitalist' and 'post-industrial' – two early twentieth-century adjectives that also reached their greatest popularity in the 1960s – in so far as it announced the dawn of a new era. Like 'post-capitalist' and 'post-industrial', 'post-Christian' presupposed a historicist philosophy of history that made 'ages' and 'eras' appear as plausible categories in the first place.[102]

The larger implication of this is that, by the 1960s, developmental historicism had not yet ceased to make its impact felt on social and religious thought. Despite the 'crisis of historicism' proclaimed by the German theologian Ernst Troeltsch in the interwar period,[103] and notwithstanding the rise of 'modernist' categories of thought, especially after World War I,[104] developmental historicism as late as the 1960s offered categories for interpreting experiences of profound societal change. Although historicist assumptions were challenged by a broad range of early and mid-twentieth-century thinkers, theologians included,[105] these critiques did not cause developmental historicism to recede into marginality immediately. The 'post' in post-Christian demonstrates that Petras, Ehrenberg, Toynbee, Dawson, Hoekendijk and Ellul did not yet live in a 'post-historicist' world.

Notes

1 Karl Barth, *Die Unordnung der Welt und Gottes Heilsplan: Vortrag gehalten an der Weltkirchenkonferenz in Amsterdam, 23. August 1948* (Zollikon-Zürich: Evangelischer Verlag, 1948), pp. 16–17, quoted in English translation from 'No Christian Marshall Plan', *The Christian Century*, 65 (1948), 1330–3, 1332.

2 Martin Niemöller, 'Das christliche Zeugnis inmitten der Welt', *Evangelische Theologie*, 8 (1948), 123–9, 124. Unless otherwise noted, all translations are mine.

3 J. C. D. Clark, 'Secularization and Modernization: The Failure of a 'Grand Narrative', *The Historical Journal*, 55 (2012), 161–94; Jeremy Morris, 'Secularization and Religious Experience: Arguments in the Historiography of Modern British Religion', *The Historical Journal*, 55 (2012), 195–219; Hermann Lübbe, *Säkularisierung: Geschichte eines ideenpolitischen Begriffs* (Freiburg: Alber, 1965).

4 Ella Shohat, 'Notes on the 'Postcolonial', *Social Text*, 31/32 (1992), 99–113; Stuart Hall, 'When Was 'the Post-Colonial'? Thinking at the Limit', in Iain Chambers and Lidia Curti (eds), *The Post-Colonial Question: Common Skies, Divided Horizons* (London: Routledge, 1996), pp. 242–60; Kwame Anthony Appiah, 'Is the Post- in Postmodernism the Post- in Postcolonial?', *Critical Inquiry*, 17 (1991), 336–57; Graham Huggan, 'Is the "Post" in "Postsecular" the "Post" in "Postcolonial"?', *Modern Fiction Studies*, 56 (2010), 751–68.

5 Although the six authors discussed in this chapter were, of course, not alone in exploring the post-Christian condition, I have selected them as case studies because of their high visibility in their respective countries, their impact on how 'post-Christian' was understood, as well as the variety of theological backgrounds from which they engaged with the term.

6 Mark Bevir, 'Historicism and the Human Sciences in Victorian Britain', in Bevir (ed.), *Historicism and the Human Sciences in Victorian Britain* (Cambridge:

Cambridge University Press, 2017), pp. 1–20, p. 2. These two features correspond to what Friedrich Meinecke classically identified as defining characteristics of *Historismus*: an 'evolutionary' mode of thinking that emphasizes 'development' (the present can only be understood genealogically, as a product of long-term historical changes) combined with an 'individualizing' approach that stresses the distinctiveness of individual stages or phases within this process of change. Friedrich Meinecke, *Die Entstehung des Historismus*, vol. 1 (Munich: R. Oldenbourg, 1936), pp. 2–5.

7 Speaking about Great Britain, Bevir argues 'that the decline of developmental historicism can be traced to the rise of modernist ideas in the late nineteenth century and the way in which the First World War undermined the Victorian faith in reason and progress'. Bevir, 'Historicism and the Human Sciences', p. 3.

8 This ties in with Gary Dorrien's thesis that the German Idealist tradition cast a longer shadow over twentieth-century theology than is usually acknowledged. Gary Dorrien, *Kantian Reason and Hegelian Spirit: The Idealistic Logic of Modern Theology* (Chichester: Wiley Blackwell, 2012).

9 Following Barth, Martin Niemöller also postulated Nazist backgrounds in 'Warum wollt ihr sterben ...' (1949), in Niemöller, *Was würde Jesus dazu sagen? Reden, Predigten, Aufsätze 1937 bis 1980*, ed. Walter Feurich (Berlin: Union, 1980), pp. 62–73, p. 67.

10 Janko Janeff, *Dämonie des Jahrhunderts* (Leipzig: Helingsche Verlagsanstalt, 1939), pp. 185, 191. Although Alfred Rosenberg's *Der Mythus des 20. Jahrhunderts: Eine Wertung der seelisch-geistigen Gestaltenkämpfe unserer Zeit* (Munich: Hoheneichen-Verlag, 1930) was one long plea for abandoning Germany's Christian heritage in favour of a National Socialist worldview, the book did not yet refer to a 'post-Christian age'.

11 Cornelis van der Kooi and Katja Tolstaja, 'Vorwort', in Karl Barth, *Der Römerbrief (Zweite Fassung)* (1922), ed. Cornelis van der Kooi and Katja Tolstaja (Zürich: Theologischer Verlag, 2010), pp. viii–xxxviii, pp. xxiv–xxvi.

12 Otto Petras, *Post Christum: Streifzüge durch die geistige Wirklichkeit* (Berlin: Widerstands-Verlag, 1935), p. 15. Another indication that this was the book Barth had in mind is its occurrence in Karl Barth, *Die Kirchliche Dogmatik*, vol. 1, pt. 2 (Zollikon-Zürich: Evangelischer Verlag, 1945), pp. 69, 353. See also Karl Barth and Eduard Thurneysen, *Briefwechsel*, vol. 3, ed. Caren Algner (Zürich: Theologischer Verlag, 2000), pp. 617–18 n. 22.

13 Armin Mohler, *Die konservative Revolution in Deutschland 1918–1932: Ein Handbuch*, 3rd edn (Darmstadt: Wissenschaftliche Buchgesellschaft, 1989), pp. 466–7.

14 Paul Noack, *Ernst Jünger: Eine Biographie* (Berlin: Alexander Fest, 1998), pp. 84, 86–7.

15 Thomas Mann, *Tagebücher 1935–1936*, ed. Peter de Mendelssohn (Frankfurt am Main: S. Fischer, 1978), p. 225. Equally critical was Mann's acquaintance, Ricarda Huch, in her 'Post Christum', in Kurt Ihlenfeld (ed.), *Die Stunde des Christentums: Eine deutsche Besinnung* (Berlin: Eckart-Verlag, 1937), pp. 191–7.

16 Karl Barth, *Der Römerbrief*, 2nd edn (Munich: Chr. Kaiser, 1922). For background and context, see Peter E. Gordon, 'Weimar Theology: From Historicism to Crisis', in Peter E. Gordon and John P. McCormick (eds), *Weimar Thought: A Contested Legacy* (Princeton: Princeton University Press, 2013), pp. 150–78.

17 Petras, *Post Christum*, p. 15.

18 Ibid., p. 54, quoting Karl Barth, *Das Evangelium in der Gegenwart* (Munich: Chr. Kaiser Verlag, 1935), p. 33.

19 Barth, *Evangelium*, p. 33 (emphasis in original).

20 Petras, *Post Christum*, pp. 7, 11, 13–14.

21 B. Bauer, *Die russische Kirche: Schlussheft* (Charlottenburg: Egbert Bauer, 1855), p. 12; Douglas Moggach, *The Philosophy and Politics of Bruno Bauer* (Cambridge: Cambridge University Press, 2003), pp. 180–7.

22 Franz Overbeck, *Christentum und Kultur: Gedanken und Anmerkungen zur modernen Theologie*, ed. Carl Albrecht Bernoulli (Basel: Benno Schwabe, 1919), p. 72.

23 Petras, *Post Christum*, pp. 34–7, referring to Bruno Bauer, *Christus und die Caesaren: Der Ursprung des Christenthums aus dem römischen Griechenthum* (Berlin: Eugen Grosser, 1877).

24 As Ian Hunter has argued, secularization narratives of the sort that would come to dominate twentieth-century thinking about religion emerged in archetypical form in relation to the European revolutions of 1848, most notably among German philosophers, the Young Hegelians included. Ian Hunter, 'Secularization: The Birth of a Modern Combat Concept', *Modern Intellectual History*, 12 (2015), 1–32 and 'Secularisation: Process, Program, and Historiography', *Intellectual History Review*, 27 (2017), 7–29.

25 Petras, *Post Christum*, p. 11.

26 On the idealist roots of the *Widerstand* movement to which Petras belonged, see Michael Pittwald, *Ernst Niekisch: Völkischer Sozialismus, nationale Revolution, deutsches Endimperium* (Cologne: PapyRossa Verlag, 2002), pp. 212–37. Back in 1913, Petras's PhD thesis on Kant's understanding of evil had included a chapter on Kant's philosophy of history: Otto Petras, *Der Begriff des Bösen in Kants Kritizismus und seine Bedeutung für die Theologie* (Leipzig: J. C. Hinrichs, 1913), pp. 47–57.

27 Joachim Müller, *Das Ende des christlichen Zeitalters* (Wernigerode: Licht im Osten, 1938), p. 3.

28 David M. Gill, 'The Secularization Debate Foreshadowed: Jerusalem 1928', *International Review of Mission*, 57 (1968), 344–57.

29 Günter Jacob, 'Christliche Verkündigung und politische Existenz', *Junge Kirche*, 2 (1934), 309–21. See also Christian Johannes Neddens, '"Politische Religion": Zur Herkunft eines Interpretationsmodells totalitärer Ideologien', *Zeitschrift für Theologie und Kirche*, 109 (2012), 307–36 and Werner Ustorf, 'The Missiological Roots of the Concept of "Political Religion"', in Roger Griffin, Robert Mallett and John Tortorice (eds), *The Sacred in Twentieth-Century Politics: Essays in Honor of Professor Stanley G. Paine* (Basingstoke: Palgrave Macmillan, 2008), pp. 36–50.

30 Müller, *Ende des christlichen Zeitalters*, pp. 37–8; Erich Göttner, 'Das Ende des christlichen Zeitalters oder die Stunde des Christentums', *Mennonitische Jugendwarte*, 17 (1937), 44–55, 46–7.

31 Günter Brakelmann, *Hans Ehrenberg: Ein judenchristliches Schicksal in Deutschland*, vol. 1 (Waltrop: Hartmut Spenner, 1997), pp. 191–3.

32 Hans Ph. Ehrenberg, *Deutschland im Schmelzofen: Gewalten, Fronten, Entscheidungen* (Berlin: Furche-Verlag, 1932), pp. 24, 36.

33 Ibid., pp. 25, 20.

34 As a founding member of the Confessing Church, Ehrenberg was among the first to protest in print against the 'zealotry' (*Schwärmerei*) and 'romantic piety' of the NSDAP. In the safer realm of private writing, he even compared the National Socialist state to an 'anti-God' (*Gegengott*) or 'antichrist'. Traugott Jähnichen, 'Von der "Schwärmerei" zur "Gegenreligion": Die Auseinandersetzung Ehrenbergs mit dem Nationalsozialismus als einer "politischen Religion"', in Manfred Keller and Jens Murken (eds), *Das Erbe des Theologen Hans Ehrenberg: Eine Zwischenbilanz* (Berlin: LIT Verlag, 2009), pp. 98–112, pp. 100–2.

35 Hans Ehrenberg, 'The Nazi Religion and the Christian Mission', *International Review of Mission*, 30 (1941), 363–73, 367, 371, 368.

36 Ibid., 370–1.

37 Hans P. Ehrenberg, *Autobiography of a German Pastor*, trans. Geraint V. Jones (London: Student Christian Movement Press, 1943), p. 111; Brakelmann, *Hans Ehrenberg*, vol. 1, pp. 23, 26–9, 42.

38 Historicist influences can also be detected in a follow-up article in which Ehrenberg declared that he used 'post-Christian' and 'post-totalitarian' in much the same way that words like 'post-capitalism' and 'post-Marxism' had entered political discourse in the 1930s. 'It is not implied that Capitalism, Marxism, Fascism are systems that have been overcome once and for all, but that these systems, which once had unrestricted dominion, have now passed their zenith and have entered on a period when their after-effects are working themselves out.' Hans P. Ehrenberg, 'After the Totalitarian World Revolution: Some Thoughts on Church and State in the World Church after the War', *International Review of Mission*, 36 (1947), 81–7, 81 n. 1.

39 W. J. Mander, *British Idealism: A History* (Oxford: Oxford University Press, 2011).

40 Arnold J. Toynbee, 'Christianity and Civilization' (1940), in Toynbee, *Civilization on Trial* (London: Oxford University Press, 1948), pp. 225–52, p. 236.

41 Ibid., pp. 236–7.

42 Ibid., p. 239. On totalitarian ideologies as 'neo-pagan' and 'ex-Christian', compare Arnold Toynbee, *Christianity Among the Religions of the World* (London: Oxford University Press, 1958), pp. 17, 19.

43 'Ex-Christian' as an equivalent of 'post-Christian' appears in Toynbee, *Christianity*, pp. 16–17.

44 Sam Brewitt-Taylor, 'The Invention of a "Secular Society"? Christianity and the Sudden Appearance of Secularization Discourses in the British

National Media, 1961–4', *Twentieth Century British History*, 24 (2013), 327–50.

45 Ibid., 332–3; Asa Briggs, *The BBC: The First Fifty Years* (Oxford: Oxford University Press, 1985), pp. 130–1, 294–5.

46 Arnold Toynbee, 'The World and the West: Russia', *The Listener*, 48 (1952), 839–41, 839. This passage is absent from the book version: *The World and the West* (London: Oxford University Press, 1953).

47 Douglas Jerrold, *The Lie about the West: A Response to Professor Toynbee's Challenge* (London: J. M. Dent & Sons, 1954), pp. 50, 53. See also '"Post-Christian" Era?', *The Listener*, 48 (1952), 1060; 'The World and the West', *The Listener*, 49 (1953), 50.

48 William H. McNeill, *Arnold J. Toynbee: A Life* (Oxford: Oxford University Press, 1989), pp. 186–7. Evelyn Charles Cary-Elwes, or Father Columba, as the Benedictine monk was usually called, referred to the 'post Christian' condition of the modern world in a letter to Toynbee, 9 February 1942, published in Christian B. Peper (ed.) *An Historian's Conscience: The Correspondence of Arnold J. Toynbee and Columba Cary-Elwes, Monk of Ampleforth* (Oxford: Oxford University Press, 1987), p. 106. In *The Sheepfold and the Shepherd* (London: Longmans, Green and Co., 1955), Columba would devote an entire chapter to 'the post-Christian' (pp. 72–87).

49 Toynbee, 'Christianity and Civilization', p. 239.

50 McNeill, *Arnold J. Toynbee*, pp. 187–9. To the surprise of historians and theologians alike, this became a central theme in the last volumes of *A Study of History*. See, e.g., Christopher Dawson, 'Toynbee's Study of History: The Place of Civilizations in History', *International Affairs*, 31 (1955), 149–58; Hayden V. White, 'Collingwood and Toynbee: Transitions in English Historical Thought', *English Miscellany*, 8 (1957), 147–78, 171–8.

51 Arnold Toynbee, 'The Cold War in the Roman Empire', *Pomona College Bulletin*, 48:4 (1950), 26.

52 Arnold J. Toynbee, *Democracy in the Atomic Age: The Dyason Lectures 1956* (Melbourne: Oxford University Press, 1957), p. 21.

53 Toynbee, 'Christianity and Civilization', pp. 249–51; Arnold Toynbee, *An Historian's Approach to Religion: Based on the Gifford Lectures Delivered in the University of Edinburgh in the Years 1952 and 1953* (London: Oxford University Press, 1956), p. 296.

54 Characteristic was his response to Oswald Spengler's *Der Untergang der Abendlandes* (The Decline of the West), 2 vols., 1918–23: 'Where the German *a priori* method drew blank, let us see what could be done by English empiricism.' Arnold J. Toynbee, 'My View of History' (1946), in Toynbee, *Civilization on Trial*, pp. 3–15, p. 10.

55 McNeill, *Arnold J. Toynbee*, pp. 223–4.

56 Ian S. Markham, *Plurality and Christian Ethics* (Cambridge: Cambridge University Press, 1994), pp. 29–43.

57 V. A. Demant, 'Christianity and Civilization', in W. R. Matthews (ed.), *The Christian Faith: Essays in Explanation and Defence* (London: Eyre and

Spottiswoode, 1944), pp. 191–204, p. 202. See also V. A. Demant, 'Our Culture: Its Religion', in Demant (ed.), *Our Culture: Its Christian Roots and Present Crisis: Edward Alleyn Lectures 1944* (London: Society for Promoting Christian Knowledge, 1947), pp. 97–113, p. 106. Dawson himself used the phrase 'post-Christian' as early as 1932 in *The Modern Dilemma: The Problem of European Unity* (London: Sheed and Ward, 1932), p. 29.

58 T. S. Eliot, *The Idea of a Christian Society* (London: Faber and Faber, 1939), p. 13.

59 Christopher Dawson, *Understanding Europe* (London: Sheed and Ward, 1952), p. 241.

60 Ibid., p. 26.

61 Ibid., p. 45.

62 Ibid., p. 252.

63 Ibid., p. 253. On the critical responses that Dawson's work elicited, see Christina Scott, 'The Vision and Legacy of Christopher Dawson', in Stratford Caldecott and John Morrill (eds), *Eternity in Time: Christopher Dawson and the Catholic Idea of History* (Edinburgh: T&T Clark, 1997), pp. 11–23, esp. p. 21.

64 Christopher Dawson, *The Historic Reality of Christian Culture: A Way to the Renewal of Human Life* (New York: Harper & Brothers, 1960), pp. 46, 30.

65 Dawson's American adventures are described in Christina Scott, *A Historian and His World: A Life of Christopher Dawson 1889–1970* (London: Sheed and Ward, 1984), pp. 178–203. Dawson's courses at Harvard resulted in *The Dividing of Christendom* (New York: Sheed and Ward, 1965) and *The Formation of Christendom* (New York: Sheed and Ward, 1967). On Catholic *ressourcement* more generally, see Gabriel Flynn and Paul D. Murray (eds), *Ressourcement: A Movement for Renewal in Twentieth-Century Catholic Theology* (Oxford: Oxford University Press, 2012).

66 Dawson, *Understanding Europe*, p. 24; Dawson, *Historic Reality*, p. 47.

67 Frank Petter, *Profanum et promissio: het begrip wereld in de missionaire ecclesiologieën van Hans Hoekendijk, Hans Jochen Margull en Ernst Lange* (Zoetermeer: Boekencentrum, 2002), pp. 75–116.

68 W. A. Visser 't Hooft (ed.), *The First Assembly of the World Council of Churches held at Amsterdam, August 22nd to September 4th, 1948* (London: SCM Press, 1949), p. 257.

69 J. C. Hoekendijk, 'Rondom het apostolaat', *Wending*, 7 (1952), 547–66, 556, 558, quoted in English translation from *The Church Inside Out*, trans. Isaac C. Rottenberg (London: SCM Press, 1967), pp. 48, 51.

70 Hoekendijk, 'Rondom het apostolaat', 555, 565–6.

71 Hoekendijk, *Church Inside Out*, p. 79.

72 Ibid., p. 81.

73 On the rise of these apocalyptic figures in mid-twentieth-century cultural criticism, see Mark Greif, *The Age of the Crisis of Man: Thought and Fiction in America, 1933–1973* (Princeton: Princeton University Press, 2014).

74 Alfred Weber, *Der dritte oder der vierte Mensch: Vom Sinn des geschichtlichen Daseins* (Munich: R. Piper, 1953).

75 Volker Kruse, *Soziologie und 'Gegenwartskrise': Die Zeitdiagnosen Franz Oppenheimers und Alfred Webers: Ein Beitrag zur historischen Soziologie der Weimarer Republik* (Wiesbaden: Deutscher Universitätsverlag, 1990), p. 273.

76 H. Berkhof, 'Tegen de bierkaai?', *In de Waagschaal*, 9 (1954), 37–9, 53–4, 71–2, to which Hoekendijk responded in 'Aanloop naar de evangelistiek V (slot): kleine boekenparade', *Woord en Dienst*, 3 (1954), 258–9. I analyse the Hoekendijk–Berkhof controversy in Herman Paul, 'The Sociological Myth: A 1954 Controversy on Secularization Narratives', *Journal of Religion in Europe*, 9 (2016), 179–203.

77 C. S. Lewis had popularized the phrase in his Cambridge inaugural, *De descriptione temporum* (London: Cambridge University Press, 1955), p. 7 and was credited with its invention by Philip Sherrard, 'A Post-Christian Epoch?', *Encounter*, 6:2 (1956), 25–9, 25.

78 Samuel H. Miller, 'Post-Christian Man', *The Christian Scholar*, 43 (1960), 265–8, 265; Loren E. Halvorson, 'The Secular: Threat or Mandate?', in James H. Burtness and John P. Kildahl (eds), *The New Community in Christ: Essays on the Corporate Christian Life* (Minneapolis, MN: Augsburg, 1963), pp. 169–86, p. 175; Howard Moody, *The Fourth Man* (New York: Macmillan, 1964), p. 115; Harvey Cox, *The Secular City: Secularization and Urbanization in Theological Perspective* (London: SCM Press, 1965), pp. 144–5, 148, n. 11. In *The Death of God: The Culture of Our Post-Christian Era* (New York: George Braziller, 1961), Gabriel Vahanian, by contrast, drew largely on Maritain, Dawson and Toynbee.

79 Paul J. Tillich, 'Protestantism in the Present World-Situation', *American Journal of Sociology*, 43 (1937), 236–48. A few years later, Tillich also introduced the phrase 'post-Protestant era': Ronald Henry Stone, *Paul Tillich's Radical Social Thought* (Atlanta, GA: John Knox Press, 1980), p. 101.

80 Martin E. Marty, *The New Shape of American Religion* (New York: Harper & Row, 1959), p. 32; Winthrop S. Hudson, *American Protestantism* (Chicago, IL: University of Chicago Press, 1961), p. 129; Will Herberg, 'God & the Theologians', *Encounter*, 21:5 (1963), 56–8, 57. See also Paul Goodman, 'We Are Post-Christian Men', *WFMT Perspective*, 10:11 (1961), 8–12, reprinted as 'Post-Christian Man', in Goodman, *Utopian Essays and Practical Proposals* (New York: Vintage Books, 1962), pp. 80–91. Helpful background is offered in Eugene McCarraher, *Christian Critics: Religion and the Impasse in Modern American Social Thought* (Ithaca, NY: Cornell University Press, 2000), pp. 147–81.

81 Sidney E. Mead, 'The Post-Protestant Concept and America's Two Religions', *Religion in Life*, 33 (1964), 191–204, 191.

82 Bruce Morgan, 'Is This the Post-Christian Era?', *Theology Today*, 18 (1962), 399–405, 399. Even critics like the theologian Georgia Harkness equated the 'post' with loss when they argued that American citizens were too much haunted by religious issues to deserve the epitaph 'post-Christian'. Georgia Harkness, 'Is Our Age of Anxiety a Post-Christian Era?', *Religion in Life*, 34 (1964), 42–9, 49.

83 Another outspoken critic was the American Jesuit Walter J. Ong, who denounced the 'post-Christian myth' for being Eurocentric and historically inaccurate. See Walter J. Ong, 'The Absurdity of the Post-Christian Myth', *WFMT Perspective*, 10:11 (1961), 13–17, reprinted as 'Post-Christian or Not?', in Ong, *In the Human Grain: Further Explorations of Contemporary Culture* (New York: Macmillan, 1967), pp. 147–64.

84 Jacques Ellul, *La technique ou l'enjeu du siècle* (Paris: Armand Colin, 1954), published in English as *The Technological Society*, trans. John Wilkinson (New York: Alfred A. Knopf, 1973).

85 Jacques Ellul, *Les nouveaux possédés* (Paris: Arthème Fayard, 1973), p. 62, quoted in English translation from *The New Demons*, trans. C. Edward Hopkin (New York: Seabury Press, 1975), p. 44.

86 Ellul, *Les nouveaux possédés*, p. 32, quoted in English translation from *New Demons*, p. 19.

87 Jacques Ellul, *Exégèse des nouveaux lieux communs* (Paris: Calmann-Lévy, 1966), pp. 79–84, 275–82.

88 Jacques Ellul, *Fausse présence au monde moderne* (Paris: Libraire protestante, [1963]), p. 33, quoted in English translation from *False Presence of the Kingdom*, trans. C. Edward Hopkin (New York: Seabury Press, 1972), p. 32.

89 As early as 1948, 'post-Christian civilization' figured in the subtitle of Ellul's *Présence au monde moderne: problèmes de la civilisation post-chrétienne* (Geneva: Roulet, 1948), though not in the book itself.

90 Georges Lasserre, 'Le christianisme et les mystiques sociales contemporaines', *La revue du christianisme social*, 49 (1936), 340–7, 343.

91 Ellul, *Les nouveaux possédés*, p. 38, quoted in English translation from *New Demons*, p. 24.

92 Andrew Goddard, *Living the Word, Resisting the World: The Life and Thought of Jacques Ellul* (Carlisle: Paternoster Press, 2002).

93 Ellul, *Fausse présence*, p. 13, quoted in English translation from *False Presence*, p. 8.

94 For Ellul's indebtedness to Barth, see Geoffrey W. Bromiley, 'Barth's Influence on Jacques Ellul', in Clifford G. Christians and Jay M. Van Hook (eds), *Jacques Ellul: Interpretive Essays* (Urbana, IL: University of Illinois Press, 1981), pp. 32–51; Jacob E. Van Vleet, *Dialectical Theology and Jacques Ellul: An Introductory Exposition* (Minneapolis, MN: Fortress Press, 2014).

95 Bruce L. McCormack, *Karl Barth's Critically Realistic Dialectical Theology: Its Genesis and Development, 1909–1936* (Oxford: Clarendon Press, 1995), p. 249.

96 Ellul, *Présence*, pp. 53, 63, quoted in English translation from *The Presence of the Kingdom*, trans. Olive Wyon (New York: Seabury Press, 1967), pp. 42, 49.

97 Ellul, *Fausse présence*, p. 23, quoted in English translation from *False Presence*, p. 21.

98 Sydney E. Ahlstrom, *A Religious History of the American People* (New Haven, CT: Yale University Press, 1972), p. 877.

99 Hugh McLeod, *The Religious Crisis of the 1960s* (Oxford: Oxford University Press, 2007), p. 16.

100 George A. Lindbeck, *The Nature of Doctrine: Religion and Theology in a Postliberal Age* (Louisville, KY: Westminster John Knox Press, 1984), pp. 8, 113. Note, however, the 'postliberal age' in the title. Peter Ochs even refers to 'the epoch of postliberal theology' in *Another Reformation: Postliberal Christianity and the Jews* (Grand Rapids, MI: Baker Academic, 2011), pp. 4–5.

101 Jürgen Habermas, 'Die Dialektik der Säkularisierung', *Blätter für deutsche und internationale Politik*, 53:4 (2008), 33–46. The extent to which Habermas actually dissociated himself from such a secularist position is subject to debate, however. See Luca Mavelli and Erin K. Wilson, 'Postsecularism and International Relations', in Jeffrey Haynes (ed.), *Routledge Handbook of Religion and Politics*, 2nd edn (Abingdon: Routledge, 2016), pp. 251–69 and, for further background, Jacob L. Goodson, 'Communicative Reason and Religious Faith in Secular and Postsecular Contexts', in Phil Zuckermann and John R. Shook (eds), *The Oxford Handbook of Secularism* (New York: Oxford University Press, 2017), pp. 316–32.

102 Howard Brick, 'The Postcapitalist Vision in Twentieth-Century American Social Thought', in Nelson Lichtenstein (ed.), *American Capitalism: Social Thought and Political Economy in the Twentieth Century* (Philadelphia, PA: University of Pennsylvania Press, 2006), pp. 21–46, pp. 25, 40–1.

103 Ernst Troeltsch, *Der Historismus und seine Probleme*, vol. 1 (Tübingen: J. C. B. Mohr, 1922). For background and context, see Otto Gerhard Oexle (ed.), *Krise des Historismus, Krise der Wirklichkeit: Wissenschaft, Kunst und Kultur 1880–1932* (Göttingen: Vandenhoeck & Ruprecht, 2007).

104 Bevir, 'Historicism', pp. 17–19 and, more generally, Mark Bevir (ed.), *Modernism and the Social Sciences: Anglo-American Exchanges, c. 1918–1980* (Cambridge: Cambridge University Press, 2017); Dorothy Ross (ed.), *Modernist Impulses in the Human Sciences 1870–1930* (Baltimore, MD: Johns Hopkins University Press, 1994).

105 David Myers, *Resisting History: Historicism and Its Discontents in German-Jewish Thought* (Princeton: Princeton University Press, 2003); Herman Paul, 'Who Suffered from the Crisis of Historicism? A Dutch Example', *History and Theory*, 49 (2010), 169–93; Herman Paul, 'Religion and the Crisis of Historicism: Protestant and Catholic Perspectives', *Journal of the Philosophy of History*, 4 (2010), 172–94; Liisi Keedus, *The Crisis of German Historicism: The Early Political Thought of Hannah Arendt and Leo Strauss* (Cambridge: Cambridge University Press, 2015), pp. 12–65.

2

The post-secular in post-war American religious history

K. Healan Gaston

Introduction

Anyone who has paid attention to post-secular discourse knows that the 1990s and early 2000s brought a veritable explosion of self-consciously 'post-secular' theorizing across a wide range of disciplines and moral communities. Religious thinkers increasingly latched on to poststructuralist critiques of scientific rationality and adapted them to their own purposes, while interest in religion also spread rapidly among secular philosophers and political theorists. Jürgen Habermas's post-secular turn and the debates around Charles Taylor's *A Secular Age* (2007) built on the developments of the 1990s and gave the burgeoning post-secular discourse additional momentum.

However, the 'post-secular' category itself has much deeper roots in American intellectual life. Like many early expressions of the postmodern, the post-secular can be traced back to an earlier generation of religious critics whose sensibilities were decisively shaped by American developments in the decades after World War II. In particular, the term emerged in the 1950s and early 1960s as interpreters of American religion clashed over the authenticity of the so-called 'post-war religious revival' and the shape of the religio-political future. Although many of these commentators argued that the moral shallowness and consumerism of much post-war religiosity reflected a secularizing impulse within the faith traditions themselves, other observers contended that what looked like secularization actually signalled the emergence of a new phenomenon, 'civil religion'. Still others viewed secularization itself positively, contending that religious groups could create more robust and fulfilling forms of faith by engaging this fruitful new social condition. As these divergent interpretations of the twentieth-century religious scene carried forward through the 1980s and 1990s, they continued to create discursive spaces wherein post-secular constructions flourished.

Like many of the other terms discussed in this book, the 'post-secular' construct often announced the impending arrival of a new age, even as it portrayed the era just ending in specific, controversial ways. Few of its users, moreover, were shy about their normative ambition to bring a post-secular world into being. This chapter illustrates those dynamics by examining a number of key moments in the early development of post-secular discourse, while keeping an eye on what they tell us about contemporary preoccupations with the category. The earliest post-secular constructions, like the broader discourse of 'secularism' itself, tended to identify both unbelief and theological liberalism as threats to genuine religion – and, in many cases, to challenge strict readings of the First Amendment's call for separation of church and state.

Early experiments:
Martin Marty, Andrew Greeley and Will Herberg

The earliest scholarly invocations of the term 'post-secular' came from the Lutheran pastor and historian Martin E. Marty and the Catholic priest, sociologist, and novelist Andrew M. Greeley. Born on the same day in 1928, Marty and Greeley shared a generational consciousness shaped by the crisis of World War II during their adolescent years.[1] Each made his career at the University of Chicago and in Chicago-area churches. Marty received his PhD from the University of Chicago in 1956 and then taught there from 1963 to 1998, while also leading a suburban church nearby from 1952 to 1967. Greeley grew up in Chicago, receiving his education at Catholic schools and St Mary of the Lake Seminary before doing his PhD work at the University of Chicago, even as he served a local parish from 1954 to 1964. Greeley continued to teach off and on at the university for decades, despite an infamous tenure denial in 1973 that he attributed in part to anti-Catholicism.

Despite the many similarities between Marty and Greeley, there were also significant differences between them that shaped their invocations of the post-secular. When Marty first floated that term, in 1958, he declared it empirically inadequate. By contrast, Greeley embraced a post-secular description of American public culture in 1966. Whereas Marty discerned a new form of what Robert Bellah would soon call 'civil religion' in the post-war United States, Greeley argued that secularizing projects had run their course and Americans stood ready to re-embrace the transcendent, albeit within the matrix of a complex, industrialized society. It was Greeley's work, then, that really launched the post-secular concept. Although Greeley himself switched over to 'unsecular' by 1972, his writings gave the term post-secular currency in American scholarly debates as the 1960s gave way to the 1970s.[2]

Nonetheless, Marty's earlier usage provides important clues about the context in which the post-secular discourse emerged: namely, debates over the meaning of the post-war revival. His 1958 *Christian Century* article, titled 'The Triumph of Religion-In-General', contended that 'religion-in-general' had replaced Protestantism as the nation's cultural lodestone since World War II, marking a fundamental break with its religious past. Americans, he explained, remained deeply devout – perhaps more so than ever. But the character of their devotion had changed decisively. 'Multi-faceted Protestantism', wrote Marty, 'once had a virtual monopoly in *forming* the religious aspect of American culture'. Now, 'religion-in-general' reigned: 'a temporalized national religion of which Protestantism, regarded in certain lights, is seen as a part'. The particularity of that transition, coupled with certain historical continuities, led Marty to label the post-war United States 'post-Protestant', while specifying that it was clearly 'not post-Catholic, post-Jewish, [or] post-secular'. America, he concluded, 'has created a God in its own image – a highly marketable, packaged God, first harbinger of life in post-Protestant times'. After again broaching and rejecting the post-secular description in his 1959 book *The Shape of American Religion*, Marty abandoned it altogether.[3]

The post-secular, summarily dismissed at its birth, appears to have lain almost entirely dormant until Greeley picked it up and gave it new life in his August 1966 presidential address to the American Catholic Sociological Society. The published version, 'After Secularity: The Neo-Gemeinschaft Society: A Post-Christian Postscript', declared that the Church and the modern world were moving from a 'post-Christian age' into a 'post-secular age'. A number of recent developments informed Greeley's analysis. As a liberal Catholic and a parish priest, as well as a sociologist, he was centrally concerned to make Catholicism relevant to the rising generation. Greeley welcomed many of the Vatican II reforms but worried that Catholic spirituality had also lost some of its richness as the Church had come to grips with 'the modern world' and thus become 'secularized'. Yet Greeley saw a post-secular sensibility emerging among the Catholic youth of the mid 1960s, with their deep hunger for mystical, personalized forms of religious experience.[4]

To capture this longing and the historical transition it portended, Greeley reached back to a conceptual distinction drawn by the late-nineteenth-century German sociologist Ferdinand Tönnies. Observing the processes of industrialization and urbanization first-hand, Tönnies distinguished the *Gemeinschaft* mode, symbolized by the rural village and structured by close, affective personal bonds and a perception of sameness, from the *Gesellschaft* of the modern world, with its impersonal, contractual relations. Greeley, from the vantage point of the mid 1960s, now discerned the emergence of what he called a '*neo-gemeinschaft* society'. The 'historians of the future', he wrote, would chronicle a move beyond modernization and secularization, through which Westerners had gained 'freedom and abundance', to a new phase, combining 'the freedom and affluence of a technological society with the warmth and fellowship of a tribal society'. In short, Greeley explained, a 'post-secularist' or 'post-post-Christian' society had begun to emerge.[5]

For Greeley, then, the post-secular concept captured the emergence of a new religious sensibility – what he termed the 'personalist revolution' – that expressed a 'hunger for new *gemeinschaft* in the post-secular world' and portended the emergence of a society combining the best of the modern world with key features of its premodern predecessor. Indeed, Greeley saw a broader 'revolt against the detribalized society', which strove to replace deep connections based on 'blood, land, and soil' with new bonds drawn from 'the human community' itself. Ascribing to humanity a 'desperate longing for community', Greeley expressed cautious hope that 'the post-secular community' could move beyond 'the oppression and tyranny of the old *gemeinschaft* society' to 'a more subtle and more sophisticated' means of forging meaningful and lasting human bonds. In doing so, he became the first American theorist to argue systematically that modern society was becoming – and should become – post-secular, in this case by combining the inner resources of the faith traditions with the external trappings of the industrialized world.[6]

Greeley's analysis of the nascent post-secular turn shared important features with the work of the post-war Jewish thinker Will Herberg. A former Marxist, Herberg spent the 1940s and most of the 1950s in the orbit of the Protestant theologian and ethicist Reinhold Niebuhr before ending up as the religion editor of William F. Buckley, Jr's conservative *National Review*. Through those years, he worked to bring themes from Niebuhr's writings into American Jewish thought, while adding the existentialist tenor of figures such as Martin Buber and Niebuhr's close colleague Paul Tillich. Like Niebuhr, but in a more pugnacious manner, Herberg rejected the longstanding tendency of Jews and theologically liberal Protestants to ally themselves with social scientists and other secular thinkers.

Herberg's writings, especially his iconic book *Protestant–Catholic–Jew* (1955), were key points of reference for Greeley, Marty and others of their generation as they grappled with the American religious scene in the late 1950s and early 1960s. As their scholarly identities took shape, each of the two took up Herberg's key themes: civil religion, pluralism, and the dynamics of suburban religious life. And each, like Herberg, saw something more than shallow conformity and consumerism at work in the post-war revival. Although historians typically remember Herberg's excoriation of spiritual celebrities such as Billy Graham and Norman Vincent Peale, he also expressed considerable hope about the spiritual longings that underpinned the revival. 'Within the general framework of a secularized religion embracing the great mass of the American people', he wrote *Protestant–Catholic–Jew*, 'there are signs of deeper and more authentic stirrings of faith'. Marty and Greeley agreed with Herberg that human beings were fundamentally religious by nature, and that the 1950s revival was both inauthentic and authentic at once. They also shared his interest in the suburbs, where Herberg believed that secularism was merely the most visible thread in a more complex religious tapestry. Despite their differences, Marty's post-Protestant analysis and Greeley's post-secular vision each held out the possibility that Americans would turn their attention from the Grahams and Peales of their day toward authentic forms of faith.[7]

Herberg seems not to have employed the post-secular concept in expressing this hope, or in analysing religion's role in the contemporary world more broadly. However, he repeatedly applied the parallel term 'post-modern' to an emerging religious sensibility that portended a move beyond secularism's dark reign. Indeed, Herberg is the earliest American thinker I have found using the post-modern category in this manner, which dovetailed closely with the meanings Greeley and his successors attributed to the post-secular. (Others, both in Herberg's circles and beyond, used 'post-modern' between the late 1940s and the early 1960s, but only Herberg imbued it with this particular anti-secular meaning.) Beginning with a 1950 article in Reinhold Niebuhr's journal *Christianity and Crisis*, and continuing through his 1951 theological tract *Judaism and Modern Man*, a 1952 *Judaism* article aimed at turning Jews away from secularism, and other writings, Herberg repeatedly applied the post-modern label to a dawning historical era after secularism. 'If secularism – believing and behaving as though man were sufficient unto himself – is the mark of the modern mind', he declared, 'I think we can say that there is already beginning to emerge a mind that is *post*-modern'. He described this emancipated, post-modern mind as 'free from the smug self-sufficiency of secularist humanism, keenly aware of the limitations and ambiguities of naturalistic science, and therefore at last open to the power of the word of God'. In the popular religious revival, as elsewhere, Herberg detected 'growing signs of a reaction against the pervasive secularism of the past century'.[8]

Of course, Herberg was best known for his 1955 classic *Protestant–Catholic–Jew*, which has profoundly influenced accounts of American religion ever since. That book reframed Herberg's hope for a post-modern turn in sociological terms, describing such a shift as well underway in the post-war United States. Whereas *Judaism and Modern Man* excoriated secularism for its utter failure as an interpretation of the human condition,

Protestant–Catholic–Jew stated flatly, as a matter of empirical fact, that avowed secularists were rapidly becoming extinct. 'The "village atheist" is a vanishing figure', Herberg declared. 'These still exist, of course, but their ranks are dwindling and they are becoming more and more inconspicuous', to the point where they failed to influence American public culture. In Herberg's rendering, '[s]elf-identification in religious terms' was 'almost universal' in 1950s America. Indeed, he continued, this sensibility was especially pervasive 'among the younger, "modern-minded" inhabitants of Suburbia', though it was 'rapidly spreading to all sections of the American people'. Although many saw Herberg's book as a scathing dismissal of the 1950s revival, those who read the book's closing theological chapter carefully could see that his narrative laid the sociological groundwork for religious change: an authentic revival of 'Jewish-Christian' faith.[9]

Herberg's hope for a move beyond secularism was hardly unique in the 1950s, but his sociological approach and adoption of the postmodern term found many reflections in the writings of Marty and Greeley. Marty's dissertation, later published as *The Infidel*, can be seen as an extended exploration of Herberg's 'vanishing atheist' theme. Meanwhile, his analysis of 'The God of Religion-In-General' resembled Herberg's assertion that the postwar revival currently reflected a divinization of the 'American Way', not a properly theistic outlook. A graduate adviser introduced Marty to Herberg near the end of his PhD work, and Marty later credited that encounter with turning him away from the usual practice of 'American religious history as a largely white Protestant preserve' toward 'the pluralist understanding of the Americans' spiritual journey'.[10]

Greeley's first study, *The Church and the Suburbs*, likewise reflected the influence of *Protestant–Catholic–Jew*, as well as his own pastoral practice. After invoking 'the American Way of Life' in the first line of his introduction, Greeley quoted at length from Herberg in a chapter on 'The Suburban Revival'. Like his elder, Greeley saw in the suburbs an entirely new mode of social existence that presented both unprecedented challenges and new opportunities – ideally, a kind of post-urban thinking with distinctive spiritual qualities. A few years later, commenting on a slightly modified version of Herberg's analysis, Greeley observed that 'nobody has yet proved Herberg wrong' and contended that the sociological research undertaken since 1955 had 'substantiated most of the things that he said'. Meanwhile, Greeley's 1966 analysis of a post-secular, *'neo-gemeinschaft'* society bore some resemblance to the generational dynamic Herberg had posited in *Protestant–Catholic–Jew*, wherein third-generation immigrants returned to their grandparents' religious traditions but sloughed off their ethnic dimensions. As Greeley developed his account of a post-secular impulse, he, like Marty and Herberg, contended that the crudeness of much post-war religiosity masked spiritual impulses far deeper and more authentic than those captured by the positive-thinking gurus. Herberg's underlying message, that American religious life could be redeemed, appealed to these young, suburban minister-scholars, who hoped to make the proverbial desert – America's 'crabgrass frontier' – bloom like a rose.[11]

Departures and convergences: Harvey Cox, Eugene Borowitz, Peter Berger and Richard John Neuhaus

Greeley's post-secular analysis appeared just as two other young figures, the Harvard theologian-ethicist Harvey Cox and the émigré sociologist Peter Berger, set in motion a wide-ranging debate about secularism and secularization that still reverberates today. Cox's *The Secular City* (1965) and Berger's *The Sacred Canopy* (1967) reveal less of Herberg's influence than did Marty and Greeley's works, although Berger had earlier identified both Marty and Herberg as theorists of America's 'vague religiosity' and would later assert that Herberg had anticipated Robert N. Bellah's 'civil religion' concept. Nor, to my knowledge, did Cox and Berger – each born in 1929, just a year after Marty and Greeley – employ the 'post-secular' construction. Indeed, both discerned a process of secularization in the United States, though they disagreed fundamentally about that dynamic's meanings, mechanisms and implications for religion. Still, the widely read works of Cox and Berger served as common points of reference for Greeley and other theorists who saw a post-secular turn on the horizon.[12]

These iconic books, like Greeley's address of 1966, also captured a growing perception that American public culture was undergoing dramatic changes in the 1960s. By 1970, the historian Sydney Ahlstrom discerned 'a fundamental shift in American moral and religious attitudes'. The proliferation of 'phrases such as post-Puritan, post-Protestant, post-Christian, postmodern, and even post-historical', Ahlstrom explained, reflected the disintegration of 'the old grounds of national confidence, patriotic idealism, moral traditionalism, and even of historical Judaeo-Christian theism'.[13]

In *The Secular City*, Cox caused a stir by framing secularization as liberation, not a direct assault on religion. Like so many American Baptists before him, he called for strict separation of church and state. In a 'post-Protestant' era, he wrote, Christians could finally 'stand free enough of their culture to be against it or for it selectively, as the guidance of the Gospel suggests'. Cox identified the true danger to religion as the backlash against secularization, not that process itself. He cautioned against 'the sly temptation of a new sacral society', in the form of Marty's 'American Shinto' or Herberg's tripartite 'American religion'. In truth, Cox argued, Americans did not share a single religious heritage of any kind. Rather, a 'Protestant sacral culture' had been imposed on all of them as they arrived. Indeed, he argued, the 'enforced Protestant cultural religion' had harmed Protestants too, such that secularization represented liberation for all religious communities. 'It would be too bad', he wrote, 'if Catholics and Jews, having rightly pushed for the de-Protestantizing of American society and having in effect won, should now join Protestants in reconstituting a kind of tripartite American religion with Americanized versions of Moses, Luther, and Saint Thomas sharing the haloes in its hagiography'. Cox thus set himself firmly against the likes of Marty, Greeley and Herberg, who agreed, despite their many interpretive and terminological differences, that secularization destroyed genuine faith.[14]

That was Berger's view as well. Indeed, his account of the depredations of secularization in *A Sacred Canopy* was so bleak that he felt compelled to issue a mea culpa two years later for what sometimes 'read like a treatise in atheism'. Writing in 1969, Berger now emphasized 'the rediscovery of the supernatural' in his time.[15] Yet neither Greeley nor Berger relied on the term 'post-secular' as the 1960s gave way to the 1970s. Rather, it made its way forward through the writings of the Reform Jewish theologian Eugene B. Borowitz, who repeatedly insisted that Jews were already post-secular, whereas Christians were still grappling with secularity.

In 1970, for example, Borowitz saw evidence that Christians were just coming to grips with modernity in a host of contemporary religious tendencies, including both 'Catholic calls to democratize the church and increase the role of the laity' and 'Protestant pleas to live out religion in the streets and through politics'. Although Borowitz agreed with Cox that 'urbanization and higher education are the keys to participating in the new secularity', he insisted that Jewish thinkers had engaged with such phenomena long ago and were now becoming 'fundamentally postsecular'. Jews, he explained, 'came through the alliance with secularity some time ago'. Now, 'a significant minority' recognized that 'beyond secularity lies the need for grounding in the transcendent. Being modern has made tradition a living option.'[16]

Borowitz's later writings carried the post-secular concept into the very different debates of the 1980s and 1990s. To be sure, Borowitz understood the appeal of secularity, especially from a Jewish perspective. 'Jews could be citizens', he noted, only 'when the state became secular'. As a result, Borowitz contended, secularism had become for liberal Jews a 'surrogate for traditional religion, indeed so great an improvement on it – so we believed – that we invested it with messianic power'. But in the present moment, he argued, secularism 'no longer holds much promise' to Jewish leaders, who recognized that it had 'eroded the stability and significance of our old values'. Borowitz remained a self-proclaimed 'religious liberal' in emphasizing 'the continuing virtues of secularism', but he sought 'to direct our attention to the general loss of a ground for our values' – a project, he explained, that 'firmly situates my liberalism on a religious foundation'. Absent 'a Judeo-Christian base', Borowitz declared, 'one cannot assume that the classical ethical concerns of our society and our social liberals will have any staying power'. As he summarized in 'Beyond the Secular City' (1985), '[o]ur problem is not how to defeat secularism, but how to tame it'. Like Cox, Borowitz believed that secularism could be redeemed.[17]

Ultimately, however, the true inheritor of Greeley's (and Herberg's) mantle was not Borowitz but Richard John Neuhaus, a Lutheran pastor who became a Catholic priest in 1990. Like Herberg, Neuhaus was a former leftist who moved steadily rightward over the course of his long career. By the time he published *The Naked Public Square* in 1984, he was one of the nation's best-known critics of secularism and a key architect of today's alliance of evangelicals, Catholics, and other theological conservatives on the religious right. He had also begun to argue that a 'post-secular' era was nigh.

The Naked Public Square may seem like a paean to civil religion, but an early article from 1970 found Neuhaus arguing that Herberg, Marty and Berger had revealed 'the dangers of being taken captive by society's demands for a utilitarian religion that sanctifies business as usual'. Although the laity had ignored the lesson, Neuhaus held out hope for a concerted push 'away from the cult of relevance' in the future and the opening of 'a new period of pastoral and theological seriousness in American religion'. In the mid 1970s, Neuhaus began to display a corresponding fascination with all things 'post-'. The opening pages of his 1975 book *Time Toward Home* cited a plethora of such formulations as evidence of the 'apocalyptic' sense 'that we live in a time that is post-everything': 'That there is a future we are not certain; that the past is finished there is no doubt.' Still, 'post-Christian' would have fit Neuhaus's portrait of American society in 1975 better than 'post-secular'. He discerned a thoroughgoing 'crisis in public morality', wherein many socially engaged Christians had 'lost their confidence in the explicit traditions that gave religious pertinence and plausibility to their witness'. These figures, he explained, 'became so enamoured with the secular order, forgetting its dependence upon moral assumptions and *their* sources, that they cut themselves off from the tree's roots in order to fondle, celebrate and affirm the grace of its leaves and branches'. Neuhaus linked that 'loss of confidence' in society's Christian foundations to the publication of Cox's *The Secular City*, though he hastened to specify that Cox had 'represented and *legitimated* that loss' rather than directly caused it.[18]

By the early 1980s, however, Neuhaus was confidently announcing the arrival of a 'post-secular America'. He declared authoritatively:

'We are witnessing the collapse of the 200-year hegemony of the secular Enlightenment over public discourse.' Neuhaus argued, in a populist vein, that ordinary citizens had never followed American political and religious leaders in seeking to thoroughly privatize religion. The 'worldview' of 'the great majority of Americans', he wrote, is 'tied to, and derived from, the Judeo-Christian tradition'. And that sensibility was beginning to reassert itself publicly in what Neuhaus now called a post-secular era.[19]

Although Neuhaus still distanced himself from the religious right in the early 1980s, he celebrated its impact on discussions of public morality. That movement, he explained, had 'triggered' a broad 'shift in American culture and politics' that was not inherently 'conservative and repressive' and could be 'turned to constructive and progressive purposes'. In Reagan's America, he argued, 'first principle questions are being asked for the first time in a long time'. (Neuhaus would go on to found the journal *First Things* in 1990.) Neuhaus sought 'a mediating language' that would reflect 'the Judeo-Christian tradition in which our discourse is historically rooted' but not 'leap from the Bible text to legislation or court decisions'. Even as Neuhaus decried what he soon dubbed 'the naked public square', he wrote that 'we seem to be moving into a post-secular period of American society', in which Americans were recapturing the religious and moral foundations of their social commitments.[20] Here, as elsewhere, Neuhaus argued that 'the post-secular character of American society tells us something about the likely prospects of world-historical change'.[21]

Communitarian legacies: Wilfred McClay

Today, post-secular discourse can be heard on all sides. Even left critics increasingly decry secularism as an assault on Islam, on women, on humanity itself. The famed critical theorist Jürgen Habermas has famously abandoned his secular stance and now stresses religion's contributions to public discourse. And Peter Berger, the doughty champion of secularization theory, reversed his stance in the 1990s and began to speak of 'desecularization'. Some of today's post-secular critics argue that secularization took place but is now being reversed; others say that it never occurred at all, or that secularization is actually impossible, because all human beings harbour religious beliefs and sentiments. And one theorist, Michael Novak, has argued – in Neuhaus's own *First Things* – that the post-secular era itself has already come and gone.[22]

But communitarians and neoconservatives in the vein of Herberg, Greeley and Neuhaus remain central to the contemporary discourse of post-secularity. Although Neuhaus himself seems to have stopped using the term regularly by the late 1980s, he noted with satisfaction in 2006 that the 'post-secular' now figured prominently in the national conversation. He cited in particular a recent review by the historian Wilfred M. McClay of Murray Friedman's *The Neo-Conservative Revolution*. McClay had just become a purveyor of post-secular discourse himself, but the issues at stake in his review would have been familiar to anyone reading Neuhaus in the 1980s – or Herberg in the 1950s. Indeed, McClay underscored the steep price that Jewish neoconservatives such as Herberg and Irving Kristol had paid for joining Christian conservatives to advance 'a post-secular, post-separationist ethos' that struck their secular and liberal counterparts as 'nothing short of madness'. In McClay, once again, we see the close link between anti-secularism and criticism of strict church-state separation that had propelled earlier discussions of secularization and the post-secular.[23]

From what I can discern, McClay first used 'post-secular' in 2004. Having recently co-edited a book called *Religion Returns to the Public Square*,[24] he was part of a round table on George Marsden's biography of Jonathan Edwards. Marsden was well known for insisting that Christian scholars deserved a 'place at the table' in the modern universities, because the first principles adopted by even the most secular scholars were matters of faith and the resulting forms of knowledge were equally plausible and rational. Among Marsden's critics, McClay listed 'post-secular thinkers, Christian and otherwise', as well as theological conservatives who deemed Marsden's approach inadequate. McClay did not explicitly locate himself within the latter group, but his subsequent analysis pointed in that direction. Christians, he argued, possessed cognitive resources and insights that actually made them *more* capable of understanding historical phenomena than their secular counterparts.[25]

Since then, McClay has continued to employ the post-secular idiom, usually to register his sense that secularism no longer dominates Western public cultures.[26] Most typically, McClay has used the term to announce the dawn of an age that finally saw through the pretensions of secularism. As he wrote in 2010, 'we now face a new era in Western history – an era in which the long-predicted obsolescence of religion is itself being rendered obsolete, and a fresh, post-secular understanding of the future is emerging into view'. This claim appeared alongside blurbs by the communitarian writers Michael Novak and George Weigel on the back of a book titled *The God That Did Not Fail*. The author, the conservative Catholic writer Robert Royal, had earlier sought to rehabilitate Christopher Columbus and now took on revisionist accounts of the founding generation, insisting that secularism was a recent innovation and 'all the main American Founders believed in a strong connection between religious belief and the health of the republican form of government'. Like Marsden and McClay, Royal contended that a state 'neutral among religions and irreligion' actually 'imposed a uniform *secularism* on the nation' and thus stamped out true pluralism.[27]

This remains the primary meaning of the post-secular for McClay, as for many others. In this usage, the term announces the onset of a new era of friendliness toward religion and scepticism toward secularism. In a 2008 essay on 'American Thought and Culture in the 21st Century', for example, McClay asked rhetorically: 'Who would have imagined, even two decades ago, the kinds of debates we would see roiling the post-9/11 world, at a moment when the immense motivational power of religion has roared back into view, as potent as a force of nature?' Indeed, he asserted that 'the secular worldview, whose triumph once seemed so inevitable, now seems stalled, and even to be losing ground, or being superseded'. Who, any more, could believe that 'the dream of a fully secularised public life, a condition that Richard John Neuhaus memorably labelled as "the naked public square"', was either plausible or desirable? Unusually, McClay here distinguished the post-secularity of the United States from the more secular climate of Europe and explained the religion's resurgence was not merely a matter of its own persistence but also the failure of secularism to provide 'an adequate framework for the great mass of Americans to lead meaningful, morally coherent lives'.[28]

Indeed, McClay presented his analysis in populist terms. He saw a dialectical process at work in American history, wherein the deep piety of the population acted as a brake on the claims of 'militant secularists', who had recently 'overreached' and produced the inevitable backlash. 'Atheists', he declared, had always found a broad American audience for their resistance to 'the coercions of any religious establishment, formal or informal'. Yet, 'when they take matters further, and insist that because religion "poisons everything" its public expression should be discouraged and ridiculed, if not actively suppressed, then their position becomes eccentric and marginal, and pushes the mainstream back toward a more religion-friendly centre'.[29]

McClay linked the homespun wisdom of the American people to a more universal, global perception of modernity's shortcomings: a growing realization that religion was crucial for asserting 'human dignity and moral order in a postmodern world dominated by voracious state bureaucracies and sprawling transnational business corporations'. In short, McClay summarized, religion offered 'a necessary corrective to the dehumanising effects of technocratic modernity, an avenue of escape from the iron cage'. McClay's analysis thus pointed in the same direction as Greeley's earlier concept of a '*neo-gemeinschaft* society'. Rebutting the claims of 'New Atheists' such as

Richard Dawkins and Sam Harris, he contended that 'in America it is secularism, rather than religion, whose power is ebbing away'.[30]

Like so many other communitarian and neoconservative contributors to the post-secular discourse, McClay referred back to the debates of the 1950s and 1960s over the post-war revival and civil religion, and beyond that to the writings of Rousseau and Durkheim. The 9/11 attacks, he wrote, 'reminded us of something that the best social scientists already knew – that the impulse to create and live inside of a civil religion is an irrepressible human impulse, and that this is just as true in the age of the nation state'. This was true, as both Durkheim and Robert Bellah had recognized, because 'the state itself is something more than just a secular institution': 'Because it must sometimes call upon its citizens for acts of sacrifice and self-overcoming, and not only in acts of war, it must be able to draw on spiritual resources, deep attachments, reverent memories of the past, and visions of the direction of history to do its appropriate work.' McClay thus aligned himself with Bellah's argument that American civil religion possessed substantive, authentic religious content. He contrasted this respectful, and in his view empirically grounded, approach to Herberg's dismissal of civil religion as simply nationalism and consumerism run amok.[31]

Yet McClay also adopted the sociologist Robert Wuthnow's claim that Americans actually possessed two civil religious traditions, one appealing to religious conservatives and the other to religious liberals. Emerging in the early twentieth century, Wuthnow explained, this split was largely smoothed over in the 1940s and 1950s but reasserted itself with a vengeance thereafter, leaving Americans deeply divided on whether their nation possessed a providential mission to spread 'traditional American values and institutions' or whether the Bible and the nation's founding documents alike called for progressive interventions in the name of equality. Amid this dispute, according to McClay, the post-secular era had dawned. Although religious belief had always been 'astonishingly pervasive' in the United States, the 'desecularisation' process had begun in earnest with the political maturation of the religious right. 'Ever since the election of Jimmy Carter as President in 1976', McClay explained, 'the taboos on public expression of religious sentiments by American political leaders seem to have been steadily eroding'.[32]

Still, McClay noted that the period before 9/11 had brought sharp, Herberg-style critiques of civil religion. Even Bellah had distanced himself from the concept, he noted. Meanwhile, believers of all stripes had joined Stanley Hauerwas in adopting a 'separationist' stance based on 'a growing sense that the American civil religion has become a pernicious idol, antithetical to the practice of their faith'. Yet 9/11 'changed all of that decisively', wrote McClay. He marvelled at 'how quickly the ailing civil religion seemed to spring back to new life', giving post-secular impulses a new 'urgency' and 'intensity': 'Coming at a moment when Americans had been gradually rethinking many settled precedents regarding religion and public life, the 9/11 attacks seemed to give a sharper edge to the questions being asked' and forced a 'choice between radically different perspectives on the proper place of religion in modern Western society'. In the wake of that catastrophe, McClay declared, it was less plausible than ever to describe the United States as a secular nation. Amid the polemics of fundamentalists and atheists, the American public in the wake of 9/11 did what it had always done, avoiding extreme positions and seeking 'something much simpler and more primal': 'Millions of Americans went to church, searching there for reassurance, for comfort, for solace, for strength, and for some semblance of redemptive meaning in the act of sharing their grief and confusion in the presence of the transcendent.' In short, '9/11 produced a great revitalisation, for a time, of the American civil religion'.[33]

Still McClay contended that the split between competing models of civil religion had quickly reasserted itself and hesitated to offer any firm predictions for the future. In the end, McClay concluded, one could never predict the future of religion with any certainty. 'The spirit bloweth where it listeth, and the paths taken by religious faith are not always obvious ones', he wrote. 'The only conclusions in which we can be entirely confident of our extrapolations are conclusions that warn us of the dangers of extrapolation', such as that undertaken by 'prophets of inevitable secularism'. Indeed, only one thing remained certain: '[T]hat, whatever some individual Americans may think, *religion* remains a powerful force that is not leaving the stage anytime soon.' If secularization were ever to actually occur, it would be in the distant future. For McClay, the central dynamics in post-secular America were a potent desecularizing impulse and an even older division between the religious left and right.[34]

McClay's formulation of the post-secular matters because of how influential his framing of the secular itself has been. His widely cited 2000 essay 'Two Concepts of Secularism' captured and codified an understanding of secularism that reverberated through innumerable American discussions in the twentieth century and tells us much about the tenor of the post-secular discourse. Like hundreds of American critics before him, McClay distinguished two forms of secularism. (Most of the earlier interpreters had identified these models as American and French, respectively, but McClay saved that charge of foreignness for a later essay.) One was 'a minimal, even "negative", understanding of secularism' that was 'almost identical to the language of the First Amendment' and was decidedly friendly to religion. This approach, 'equally respectful of religionists and nonreligion-ists alike', enforced 'the freedom of the uncoerced individual conscience' but showed 'a capacious understanding of the religious needs of humanity' and the inevitably social character of religion, which made 'the right of free association … just as important as the right of individual expression'.

On the other side, McClay continues, 'the more militant secularists, whom we can call the establishmentarian or "positive" secularists', viewed secularism as a 'crusading ideal' that required the establishment of 'unbe-lief' itself, by confining 'religion to a strictly private sphere, where it can do little public harm – and little public good'. Convinced of their own neutrality, McClay asserted, the advocates of positive secularism consid-ered themselves neutral but were actively 'creating and enforcing the naked public square'. As 'an ultimate and alternative comprehensive faith' rooted in the dogmatic 'ideal of self-mastery', McClay concluded, positive secular-ism directly threatened religion in a way that negative secularism, with its simple insistence on non-establishment, could never do.[35]

Post-secularism and the church-state question

McClay is hardly alone in equating the onset of post-secularity with the ouster of a 'positive secularism' – one that he believes contradicted the experience and institutions of the United States – and the restoration of a healthy, quintessentially American 'negative secularism' that allows all religions to flourish and ensures their equal status in the public eye. Post-secularism, in this vein, does not mean the total disappearance of secular worldviews. Rather, it means the reconfiguration of the public square as a space featuring robust, foundational arguments from the proponents of all worldviews, religious or secular.

Religion scholars have long noted that theories of religion and society, including theories of secularization, tend to discipline religious faith by distinguishing good religion from bad. As the post-secular discourse shows, such theories also delineate good secularism from bad and good pluralism from bad. It is incumbent upon scholars, then, to understand how advo-cates and other commentators have used terms such as 'post-secular'. In its communitarian and neoconservative guises – the guises it wore almost exclusively during its early years – the post-secular discourse goes beyond simple advocacy of religious faith. It implies a particular understanding of church-state relations, and of religion's centrality to public affairs, that many religious believers themselves – including Harvey Cox and his allies – rejected. Specifically, this version of post-secularism dovetails with the 'non-preferentialist' or 'accommodationist' argument that the state must be neutral between religions but cannot be neutral with regard to religion and irreligion. That understanding enshrines a particular definition of not only the term 'secularism' but also categories such as 'pluralism' and 'religious freedom', as well as the broader concept of religious authenticity itself.[36]

Indeed, such theorists often argue that secularism is sufficiently powerful and pervasive to snuff out the post-secular age in its infancy, should authentic believers fail to see and meet the existential threat it poses. In a 2020 article, McClay touted a historic rapprochement between 'believing Christians and believing Jews' who had joined hands in part to protect genuine, Judeo-Christian faith against the ultimate product of the Enlightenment: 'An ascendant secular nihilism, increasingly militant and seemingly intent upon sweeping away the moral, cultural and institutional norms that have defined our shared civilization for millennia.' This portrait of the contemporary world indicts not only unbelievers but also the prevailing forms of liberalism, both religious and political. And it underscores that delineating the good from the bad and the winners from the losers – as all debates around post-terms tend to do – can have striking implications in the real world.[37]

Notes

1 Beyond these commonalties, Marty also sat on the dissertation committee of Greeley's sister. Andrew M. Greeley, 'Andrew Greeley Replies to His Critics', *Journal for the Scientific Study of Religion*, 13:2 (1974), 229.

2 Andrew M. Greeley, *Unsecular Man* (New York: Shocken, 1972).

3 Martin E. Marty, 'The Triumph of Religion-in-General', *Christian Century*, 75:37 (1958), 1016–17 (italics omitted). In the 1959 book, based on the *Christian Century* articles, Marty again called the late 1950s 'post-Protestant times' – as opposed to, say, 'post-Catholic, post-Jewish, or post-secular times', *The New Shape of American Religion* (New York: Harper, 1959), p. 32. On the post-Protestant discourse, see Curtis Scott Drumm, 'Post-Protestant America? A Critique of Historiographical Models of Protestantism's Decline' (PhD dissertation, Southwestern Baptist Theological Seminary, 1999).

4 Andrew M. Greeley, 'After Secularity: The Neo-Gemeinschaft Society: A Post-Christian Postscript', *Sociological Analysis*, 27:3 (1966), 119–20. Greeley almost certainly drew on one precedent from the intervening years. He had reviewed a 1964 volume, co-edited by Marty, that featured a chapter on 'The Pastor and Social Conflict' by the Hungarian-born Presbyterian John R. Bodo. In his chapter, Bodo twice used the term 'post-secular': Robert Lee and Martin E. Marty (eds), *Religion and Social Conflict* (New York: Oxford, 1964), pp. 154, 160. Greeley deemed Bodo's essay 'undistinguished' but may have picked up the

post-secular category from it. Greeley, review of Lee and Marty (eds), *Religion and Social Conflict* (New York: Oxford, 1964), in *Sociological Analysis*, 27:1 (1966), 50–1.

5 Greeley, 'After Secularity', 125–6.

6 Ibid., 125.

7 Will Herberg, *Protestant–Catholic–Jew: An Essay in American Religious Sociology* (Garden City, NY: Doubleday, 1955), p. 288; K. Healan Gaston, 'The Cold War Romance of Religious Authenticity: Will Herberg, William F. Buckley, Jr, and the Rise of the New Conservatism', *Journal of American History*, 99:4 (2013), 1133–58.

8 Will Herberg, 'Secularism In Church and Synagogue', *Christianity and Crisis*, 10:8 (1950), 60–1; Herberg, *Judaism and Modern Man: An Interpretation of Jewish Religion* (Philadelphia, PA: Jewish Publication Society of America, 1951), p. 7 (and cf. p. 163); Herberg, 'Jewish Existence and Survival: A Theological View', *Judaism*, 1 (January 1952), 26. Union Theological Seminary president Henry P. Van Dusen, a colleague of Niebuhr and Tillich, casually invoked 'post-Modern' as an alternative to 'post-Christian' in a 1948 article, but he made no attempt to define it. 'It is sometimes loosely said today that we are living in the "post-Christian" era', Van Dusen wrote. 'That is a misstatement. But it may be said that we are moving into the "post-Modern" era. As has been often said, "it is the end of our time".' 'Revolution and Christian Response', *Anglican Theological Review*, 30:3 (1948), 145.

9 Herberg, *Protestant–Catholic–Jew*, p. 274; Gaston, 'The Cold War Romance of Religious Authenticity'.

10 Marty quoted Herberg at length in the earlier work, highlighting his claim that '"[r]eligion has become part of the ethos of American life to such a degree that overt anti-religion is all but inconceivable."' *The Infidel* (New York: Meridian, 1961), pp. 190–1.

11 Andrew M. Greeley, *The Church and the Suburbs* (New York: Sheed & Ward, 1959), p. xi, pp. 41–9; Greeley, review of *Religion and Social Conflict*, 50–1. Herberg figured prominently as a contributor in a volume that Marty and Greeley later co-edited with Stuart E. Rosenberg, *What Do We Believe? The Stance of Religion in America* (New York: Meredith Press, 1968). Rosenberg, too, may have been influenced by Herberg as a student at the Jewish Theological Seminary and Columbia University, two institutions within Herberg's orbit. Moreover, he knew Marty's work well and shared his interest in the suburbs. On his career, see Michael Brown, 'Platform and Prophecy: The Rise and Fall of Rabbi Stuart E. Rosenberg as Foreshadowed in His Early Toronto Sermons on Leadership', *Jewish History*, 23:2 (2009), 195–217.

12 Harvey Cox, *The Secular City: Secularization and Urbanization in Theological Perspective* (New York: Macmillan, 1965); Peter L. Berger, *The Sacred Canopy: Elements of a Sociological Theory of Religion* (Garden City, NY: Doubleday, 1967); Berger, *The Noise of Solemn Assemblies: Christian Commitment and the Religious Establishment in America* (Garden City, NY: Doubleday, 1961), pp. 41–2; Berger, *Religion in a Revolutionary Society* (American Enterprise

Institute for Public Policy Research, 1974). Cox invoked the term in the introduction to a 2013 reprint (Princeton, NJ: Princeton University Press) of his classic text.

13 Sydney E. Ahlstrom, 'The Radical Turn in Theology and Ethics: Why It Occurred in the 1960s', *Annals of the American Academy of Political and Social Science*, 387 (1970), 3.

14 Cox, *The Secular City*, pp. 118–19.

15 Peter L. Berger, *A Rumor of Angels: Modern Society and the Rediscovery of the Supernatural* (Garden City, NY: Doubleday, 1969).

16 Eugene B. Borowitz, 'Jewish Theology Faces the 1970's', *The Annals of the American Academy of Political and Social Science*, 387 (1970), 27, 22. Borowitz employed a chronologically narrower understanding of the post-secular than others, emphasizing secularity's broken promises to Jews since World War I. Eugene Borowitz, 'The Post-Secular Situation of Jewish Theology', *Theological Studies*, 31:3 (1970), 460. On Borowitz, see especially Hava Tirosh-Samuelson and Aaron W. Hughes (eds), *Eugene B. Borowitz: Rethinking God and Ethics* (Leiden: Brill, 2014).

17 Borowitz, *Exploring Jewish Ethics: Papers on Covenant Responsibility* (Detroit, MI: Wayne State University Press, 1990), pp. 96, 109, 39–40, 61.

18 Richard John Neuhaus, 'The War, the Churches, and Civil Religion', *Annals of the American Academy of Political and Social Science,* 387 (January 1970), 133, 138; Neuhaus, *Time Toward Home: The American Experiment as Revelation* (New York: Seabury Press, 1975), pp. 1, 85, 20. By the late 1960s, Berger and Neuhaus were locked in dialogue. Berger thanked Neuhaus for their lengthy discussions in the preface to *A Rumor of Angels*. In 1970, the pair co-wrote a book in which Berger called for gradual, ameliorative change while Neuhaus, then still a leftist, championed a revolution: *Movement and Revolution* (Garden City, NY: Doubleday, 1970). But the two Lutherans shared theological common ground and Neuhaus quickly moved away from his revolutionary politics. In 1975, they gathered a group of religious thinkers to craft the 'Hartford Appeal for Theological Affirmation', enumerating and repudiating various forms of 'capitulation to the alleged primacy of modern thought'. The group rejected humanistic and naturalistic understandings of religion, affirmed the rationality of religious language and the importance of religious institutions, and emphasized God's transcendence and the reality of 'hope beyond death'. 'An Appeal for Theological Affirmation', in Berger and Neuhaus (eds), *Against the World for the World: The Hartford Appeal and the Future of American Religion* (New York: Seabury, 1976), pp. 1–7.

19 Richard John Neuhaus, 'Educational Diversity in Post-Secular America', *Religious Education*, 77:3 (1982), 309–10. Neuhaus first used 'post-secular' in 'The Post-Secular Task of the Churches', in Carol Friedley Griffith (ed.), *Christianity and Politics: Catholic and Protestant Perspectives* (Washington, DC: Ethics and Public Policy Center, 1981), pp. 1–18.

20 Neuhaus, 'Educational Diversity in Post-Secular America', 313–14, 320.

21 Richard John Neuhaus, 'Moral Leadership in Post-Secular America', *Educational Freedom*, 11:7 (1982), 10. It should not surprise us by now to

find that Neuhaus drew on Will Herberg's writings and example, as a fellow Marxist-turned-conservative. Shortly after Neuhaus published *The Naked Public Square*, he declared his intellectual indebtedness to Herberg in 'Will Herberg: A Passion for Authenticity', *National Review* (31 December 1985), 83–4 and 'Will Herberg: Pluralist', *National Review* (22 January 1988), 54. The latter piece called Herberg 'the avant garde of a rebirth of vibrant pluralism'. In addition to serving as 'Bill Buckley's confessor', Neuhaus argued, Herberg stood 'alone among Jewish thinkers of his time' in rejecting 'the platitudes of mere tolerance' and becoming a 'true pluralist' – that is, 'a pluralist in his understanding of the connections between religion, moral judgment, and the social order'.

22 Michael Novak, 'Remembering the Secular Age', *First Things*, 174 (2007), 35–40.

23 Richard John Neuhaus, 'The Public Square: A Continuing Survey of Religion, Culture, and Public Life', *First Things*, 167 (2006), 63–80; Wilfred M. McClay, review of Friedman, *The Neo-Conservative Revolution*, in *Commentary* (February 2006), 74.

24 Wilfred M. McClay, *Religion Returns to the Public Square: Faith and Policy in America* (Baltimore, MD: Johns Hopkins University Press; Washington, DC: Woodrow Wilson Center Press, 2003).

25 Wilfred M. McClay, 'Completion or Revision', *Historically Speaking*, 5:6 (2004), 17–18.

26 For a more ambiguous rendering of the term, see Wilfred M. McClay, 'Winter Stories', *Commentary*, 132:5 (2008), 75–6.

27 Robert Royal, *The God That Did Not Fail* (New York: Encounter Books, 2006), back cover, 270–1. The earlier book is Royal, *1492 and All That: Political Manipulations of History* (Washington, DC: Ethics and Public Policy Center, 1992).

28 Wilfred M. McClay, 'Religion in Post-Secular America', in Martin Halliwell and Catherine Morley (eds), *American Thought and Culture in the 21st Century* (Edinburgh: Edinburgh University Press, 2008), pp. 127–8.

29 Ibid., p. 128.

30 Ibid.

31 Ibid., pp. 139, 134.

32 Ibid., pp. 139, 129.

33 Ibid., pp. 136–7, 130–1.

34 Ibid., pp. 138, 141.

35 Wilfred M. McClay, 'Two Concepts of Secularism', *Wilson Quarterly*, 24:3 (2000), 63–7. The French comparison appears in 'Secularism, American-Style', *Sociology*, 44 (2007), 160–3. McClay later dubbed these modes 'political secularism' and 'philosophical secularism' (Pew Research Center, 'Religion and Secularism: The American Experience', www.pewresearch.org/2007/12/03/religion-and-secularism-the-american-experience/, accessed 17 August 2020) but also continued to develop the positive-negative distinction, as in 'Secularism, American-Style'.

36 For a characteristic earlier statement of this church-state position, see Neuhaus, 'Educational Diversity in Post-Secular America', 314.

37 Wilfred M. McClay, 'What Christians See in Jews and Israel in 2020 of the Common Era', *Mosaic* (July 2020), https://mosaicmagazine.com/essay/history-ideas/2020/07/what-christians-see-in-jews-and-israel-in-2020-of-the-common-era/ (accessed 31 August 2020).

3

Defining the old, creating the new:
Post-ideology and the politics
of periodization

Adriaan van Veldhuizen

Introduction

It was in the late 1950s that the idea of a 'post-ideological era' made its first appearances. The German sociologist Helmut Schelsky, for instance, put forward the suggestion that German sociology had developed in a non-ideological direction, to the point of having reached a '*nachideologischen Epoche*'.[1] In a review of Schelsky's book, Raymond Aron argued that not only German sociology, but German society in general had entered this post-ideological phase. In this context, Aron referred to a debate that had started a few years earlier: the so-called 'end of ideology' debate.[2]

I argue that while annunciating a post-ideological age, many authors reasoned from the proposition that society was gradually developing from one stage to another. This often more implicit than explicit emphasis on the sequence of historical stages, paired with the urge to discuss them in their own historical context, hints at what I would call a 'historicist worldview'. Of course, there are many definitions of the term 'historicism' available, which makes this term prone to misunderstandings. The definition used in this chapter draws on the German historian Friedrich Meinecke. For him, historicism stood for the idea that the present should be understood as a product of long-term historical developments, that these developments have led to different stages or epochs over time, and that these stages all had their own zeitgeist. These stages and their zeitgeists should be studied and evaluated on their own merits, which leads to an individualizing approach of history that pays sustained attention to historical contexts and temporal situatedness.[3]

This chapter does not claim that everyone who employed the term post-ideological was or is a historicist in Meinecke's sense of the word. What I want to show, however, is that historicist modes of epochal thinking resonated in the use of the phrase 'post-ideological'. By highlighting traces of historicism in the works of European and American scholars after World War II, this chapter aims to present a twentieth century example of historicist reasoning. I argue that the 'post' in post-ideological is not just a descriptive term but has a performative capacity as well; it was used to establish a desired situation rather than to describe a current situation. The 'post' in post-ideological therefore 'breaks up time', declares an era ended, and starts a new one.[4]

The first section presents a *Begriffsgeschichte* of post-ideology in the 1950s and 1960s in which the first appearances of the phrase will be analysed. The second section presents a short historiographical overview of the 'end of ideology' thesis as it was debated in the 1950s and 1960s. The third section examines the relation between the end of ideology thesis and historicist reasoning. This will be done by exploring historicist modes of epochal thinking in three key texts on the end of ideology, written by three key authors: Raymond Aron, Edward Shils and Daniel Bell.

Post-ideological: A short conceptual history

This conceptual history focuses on the earliest use of the phrase 'post-ideological'.[5] I will determine when the phrase was used for the first time, which authors were using it, and how they used it.[6] My emphasis is on the question of whether people used the phrase 'post-ideological' to describe a phase, era, stage, age or epoch in history. This survey will stop around 1968, when more and more people started to use the concept – I will not take into account the rebirth of the concept in the 1990s.

It was probably in 1955 that the idea of a 'post-ideological era', 'epoch', 'age' or 'period' was mentioned for the first time. In a book review of Lionel Trilling's *The Opposing Self*, Paul Pickrel characterized Trilling as 'a true son of the age of ideology, feeling fully the appeal of the intellectual aggression we call ideology, the determination to make reality conform to the mind's reading of reality; yet the essence of what he has to say is that the universe speaks in a voice beyond ideology, and that man can realize the fullness of his being only by listening to that voice'.[7] Pickrel discussed Trilling's 'claim to intellectual leadership in this post-ideological age'.[8] He did not elaborate on what exactly he understood a 'post-ideological age' to mean. Although he stated that 'for the last century and a half, ideology has been the chief content of intellectual life', he did not elaborate on its current post-status.[9] Such offhand, largely descriptive uses of the phrase can be found in further book reviews and articles published between 1955 and 1958.[10] A precise definition of the 'post-ideological period', however, was lacking.

The emergence of a post-ideological period was not only debated in the United States. In 1959 Helmut Schelsky, as mentioned in this chapter's

introduction, advanced the idea that German sociology had developed in a
non-ideological direction, thereby entering a *nachideologischen Epoche*.[11]
Elsewhere in his book, Schelsky suggested that German sociology was not
the only place where ideology came to an end. In his assessment, ideology
was losing its importance for both Germany and sociology in general.[12] In
a 1960 review of Schelsky's book, Raymond Aron focused specifically on
this part of Schelsky's thesis, stating that 'post 1933 sociology could be
characterized by its non-ideological character, which corresponds with the
post-ideological character of the era we live in'.[13]

So around 1960 the phrase was used in several countries and languages,
in texts that assumed their readers to be able to grasp what it meant. These
readers were not necessarily academics: the term was used in political
magazines, newspapers and several other genres.[14] In 1963, for instance,
a United Nations paper on the development of Latin America, written by
José Medina Echevarría, explained why Europe and North America were
experiencing a post-ideological phase, whereas such a development could
not be detected in Latin America.

> To give a brief explanation for the 'post-ideological' phase in Europe and
> North America, it may be said that it is primarily due to the fact that on the
> spiritual plane Europe has to live on the ashes of the past, while on the mate-
> rial plane North America has to live on the affluency [sic] of the present. Of
> course this does not mean that the two cannot go together. But we should steer
> clear of any 'ideology of post-ideology', so reminiscent of the old 'philosophy
> of philosophy' or 'sociology of sociology'.[15]

Although authors did not agree on the geographical boundaries of this
post-ideological turn, the geographical element itself is important. Just like
Echevarría, most authors focused on the decline of ideology in the Western
world. Historian John Lukacs for instance believed that 'Europe (and to
some extent also the United States) seems to have entered the post-ideological
age'.[16] In 1959 Heinrich Gremmels, a German lawyer, was a lot more specific: 'West Germany has an advantage over the rest of the world today,
in so far, that we are already in the post-ideological situation in which we
have long since learned not to attempt to solve the world's mysteries.'[17] The
Canadian sociologist Léon Dion concluded something else, when he wrote:
'In short, American society has entered the post-ideological era because it
has achieved its goals.'[18] Some authors were even of the opinion that the
post-ideological age was a phenomenon also occurring in the communist
world. Philip Mosely wrote: 'Morally, though not politically, East-Central
Europe has been moving into a Post-Stalinist and post-ideological stage of its
development … To Soviet policy this new stage poses a complex challenge to
overcome its notoriously simplistic approach of the recent past.'[19]

Besides the geographical element there were other features of post-ideology on which intellectuals diverged. One of these was the question whether the new era had already begun, or was still to arrive. Irving Howe thought it was already there: he consistently used it as an adjective for his own times.[20] Konstanty Jeleński thought the post-ideological age was just about to start. Reuel Denney, on the other hand, seemed to take the post-ideological age for granted while concluding a book review with the statement that '[o]f all of the ways of saying that our own society is now living in a post-ideological age, this is the neatest'.[21] Others, such as Roy Pierce, were less sure about the post-ideological status of the present: 'If we are approaching, or are already in, a post-ideological age, it is proper to ask what is being offered in place of the ideologies which have disappeared (or may be disappearing).'[22]

Clearly, then, not all authors using the phrase were discussing the same thing. Post-ideological literature was something different from post-ideological politics or international relations. Moreover, authors were far from unanimous on where to locate the concept of post-ideology in place and time. The question whether post-ideological should be seen as a temporal signifier, however, can be answered with an unequivocal 'yes'. Many appearances of the phrase between 1955 and 1965 referred to a phase, period, stage, age or era.

Despite the variety in meanings of the concept, authors considered this post-concept something that should be easily understood by their audiences. This is not without reason because post-ideology was contextually understood, and its context is best explained by another phrase: 'the end of ideology'. Although there was no undisputed definition of this phrase either, most contemporaries would describe it as the thesis that fanatic political doctrines, Marxism in particular, were slowly vanishing from the Western world. According to some, this tendency was the outcome of profound political insight and modernization while others considered it the product of fierce repression.[23] In the next section I will elaborate further on how post-ideology became a signifier of the end of ideology debate.

The end of ideology: A survey

At the 1960 Congress for Cultural Freedom (CCF), Konstanty Jeleński sketched some 'Prospects for a Post-Ideological Society' in which he suggested that the post-ideological period would follow 'the end of ideology'.[24] The CCF was an international organization for poets, writers, historians, philosophers and scientists with divisions in several countries. It offered stages for fierce anti-communism on the one hand, and celebrations of a mild social democratic, slightly conservative welfare state on the other.

Although in 1966 it was revealed that the CCF had been financed by the CIA, it was initially considered a serious platform for the exchange of ideas and practices among intellectuals from all over the world.

From 1955 onwards, the phrase 'end of ideology' had become a recurring catchphrase at CCF conferences.[25] It appeared in the CCF journal *Encounter* and in CCF-sympathetic journals like *The Partisan Review* and *Dissent*.[26] As early as 1968, a first collection of essays on the topic appeared. It was titled *The End of Ideology Debate* and canonized some of the most important authors in the debate, including Shils, Aron, Bell and Seymour Martin Lipset.[27] The debate itself became object of academic study in the years after. Job L. Dittberner was the first to study the end of ideology thesis from a historical perspective. His 1976 dissertation 'The End of Ideology and American Social Thought: 1930–1960' presented Shils, Bell, Lipset and Aron as the key theorists of the debate.

Aron, indeed, wrote a chapter titled 'The End of the Ideological Age?' in the aftermath of the 1955 Milan CCF congress. Shils turned the phrase into a slogan against political fanaticism in general and communism in particular. In 1960 Bell had published *The End of Ideology: On the Exhaustion of Political Ideas in the Fifties,* a collection of essays that concludes with an essay on 'The End of Ideology in the West'.[28] Lipset in the same year observed that the 'characteristic pattern of stable Western democracies in the mid-twentieth century is that they are in a "post-politics" phase' (thereby casually introducing yet another post-concept).[29] Although the general theses of these authors revolved around themes such as modernization, decolonization, the end of socialism and developments in the Cold War, Dittberner and others stress that analyses and opinions differed from author to author.[30]

First of all, the concept of ideology has quite a kaleidoscopic character. To bring tangibility, Howard Brick identified its most striking features and asked what ideology meant to the authors.[31] Brick argues:

> From the various meanings of 'ideology', then, its 'end' could refer to the dismissal of totalitarian doctrines, or their waning appeal; to a realistic or pragmatic suspicion of all rigid formulas of ideas, that is, to fixed doctrines or 'isms', be they socially and politically destructive or seemingly benign, such as 'vegetarianism'; or to the elimination of all mental illusions clouding human cognition.[32]

Brick's account on the meaning of ideology in this context leads from Marx, via Mannheim, Adorno, Horkheimer, to the New York socialists in the 1940s, and the American liberals in the 1950s, all of whom left their traces in the debate.[33] Brick tracks how former Marxists started to explore the end of ideology in the 1940s and how the debate on the thesis gradually turned into a culturally conservative, anti-Soviet and anti-communist discourse. Like Dittberner, Brick emphasizes the importance of Edward Shils's 1955 essay 'The End of Ideology?', while also addressing Aron's chapter from the same year.[34] Brick emphasizes that most of the theorists of the end of ideology identified the turn from the 1950s to the 1960s as the beginning of a new era. Here Brick touches on something that is crucial for this chapter: the start of the debate on the end of ideology was not only a debate on what ideology was or should be, but also a debate about the demarcation of the present.[35]

In his 2016 PhD thesis Daniel Strand elaborates on this. He compares the end of ideology debate in the 1950s with a similar debate in the 1990s.[36] To unveil the differences between the two debates, he dissects the 'conceptualization of history' and the 'conceptualization of politics' of some of its major authors. Strand deduces how Aron, Bell, Lipset, Shils, H. Stuart Hughes and the Swedish political scientist Herbert Tingsten used historical narratives for politically legitimizing a Western way of living.[37] He asks how they assessed historical change and what forces they held responsible for the direction in which they saw history developing.[38] Strand doubts whether these authors had clear assumptions about the 'dynamics, directions and potential telos' of the historical process: was history a linear process; was it necessarily evolving towards a better social order; was it circular; was it driven by laws-like forces or by autonomous human beings; did it have a goal?[39]

Strand convincingly argues that most of the authors were adherents of 'modernization theory' as described by Nils Gilman.[40] In his *Mandarins of the Future*, Gilman links the 'search for a post-ideological age' – 'an age in which science trumps politics' – to the idea of an inevitable 'historical convergence between the West, the communist countries and the postcolonial world'.[41] Gilman studies how Lipset, Bell and Shils carried out the idea that all societies eventually transform into modern, post-ideological welfare states like the United States. He discusses the end of ideology thesis as a philosophy of history with a fascinating historico-geographical dimension: the opposition between industrial and non-industrial countries is not only an opposition in space, but also in time.[42] In line with Gilman, Strand argues that the end of ideology thesis depicted the welfare state as a phase in the historical process. Because it *succeeded* a stage of political quarrel and ideological bickering, Strand concludes with the remark that many theorists of the end of ideology had a teleological and deterministic view on history.[43]

Lastly, the subtlest reflection on the intentions of the key authors in the end of ideology debate comes from the historian Giles Scott-Smith, who stated that:

Bell, Lipset, Shils and Aron were later criticized for having *predicted* the end of ideology, such that the events of 1960s proved them wrong. But prediction was not the goal. End-of-ideology discourse had three principal poles. First, it was a prescriptive comment on the most practical approaches to socio-economic management for satisfying basic needs. Second, it represented a pluralist ideal that the interests of all sections of society could be represented in the democratic system. But third, and most important, it signified a social scientific method that emphasized how the conditions of modern industrial society had developed in ways that precluded any worthwhile analysis from Marxism.[44]

Following Scott-Smith, we could argue that the end of ideology debate was more than a widely shared descriptive statement. It formulated the ambition to go beyond the ideologies, Marxism in particular, that had dominated the West hitherto. In this sense, it was a political enterprise as well.

Politics of periodization: reading Aron, Shils and Bell

Adding to the literature discussed so far, I would like to draw attention to the historicist subtext of the politics of periodization and the traces of historicist reasoning and epochal thinking in three key authors on the end of ideology. The texts under consideration are not studied as exponents of classical historicism, and this section does not try to unmask the authors as historicists. I focus on historicist reasoning that aims not merely to describe a phase, period or era, but that is employed to *create* a new era, to express a desired situation and to contribute to the formation of a new world by elaborating on this new world.

Raymond Aron

Raymond Aron was much interested in the study of philosophy of history in general and that of historicism in particular.[45] However, the temptation to make this fascination for historicism the starting point of this section should be resisted. What is under scrutiny is the question of how and to what extent Aron used periodization as political tool. The concluding chapter of his *The Opium of the Intellectuals*, titled 'The End of the Ideological Age?', allows us to answer this question.

The fact that Aron's chapter, published just before the Milan conference of 1955, focuses on the end of an 'ideological *age*' is an obvious first indication for his mode of thinking. However, it might be helpful to say something about the book in general first. It argues that the binary political choice between the abstract idea of the market and the equally abstract idea of communism is not valid anymore. Although Aron rejects the errors of both absolutism and relativism, he first and foremost opposes political absolutism. Addressing his French colleagues, he states that '[t]he attitude of the French intellectuals is determined by national pride and nostalgia for a universal idea'.[46] What follows is an elaboration on the idea that ideology – Marxism in particular – has developed into a secular mode of prophecy.[47] Marxist religion offers a metaphysical wholeness in times of technical boundlessness and political desperation, and – hence the title of the book – serves as a playground for intellectuals. To understand how obsolete Marxism had become for Aron, it suffices to read one of his concluding remarks:

> The secular religions dissolve into politico-economic opinions as soon as one abandons the dogma. Yet the man who no longer expects miraculous changes either from a revolution or an economic plan is not obliged to resign himself to the unjustifiable. It is because he likes individual human beings, participates in living communities, and respects the truth, that he refuses to surrender his soul to an abstract ideal of humanity, a tyrannical party, and an absurd scholasticism.[48]

While breaking down Marxism, Aron referred to 'ages', 'epochs', 'periods' and 'stages' all the time, although not always in a negative manner.[49] While criticizing Marxism for the use of epochal concepts in speculative philosophies of history, he does not reflect on his own use of such concepts. Part two of the book, on 'The Idolatry of History', contains Aron's most elaborate contemplations on the meaning of history, the historical method, the use and abuse of history, and other relevant questions. Here Aron touches on the theme of 'historical-units', which brings him into conversation with Oswald Spengler and Arnold Toynbee. Aron states: 'Thus the historian, unlike the sociologist or the philosopher, seeks unity not so much in a privileged cause as in the singularity of the historical unit – epoch, nation or culture.' He then asks: 'What are historical units? Can one grasp unity through time and the individuality of the unit?'[50] But his answer is not as clear as his question. Again, Aron appears to be more interested in a critique of ideology than in developing a philosophy of history of his own.

Aron eventually argues that the ambition to predict or to steer the historical process is typical of ideological reasoning. This leads to an interesting observation. On the one hand, the book wants to avoid historical determinism and therefore criticizes ideological thinkers who are too strict in their epochal demarcations. Aron particularly condemns Marxism for its speculative character and rejects all metaphysical accounts of history and political theology. On the other hand, Aron himself points to an epochal transition from an age dominated by secular religions, at least in the West, to a new era of mild social democracy and conservative liberalism. About this epochal change Aron writes: 'That which characterizes the present period is no longer an excess of faith, but of skepticism.'[51] The same idea can be found in Aron's argument about the emergence of a 'phase *post-idéologique*' in his review of Schelsky's book on German sociology.[52] This review clearly shows that Aron is not without an agenda himself. For him, the post-ideological age is not a mere description, it is a preferred situation.

Edward Shils

Just like his friend Aron, Edward Shils was among the first to use the phrase 'the end of ideology'.[53] In 'The End of Ideology?' – often considered a starting point of the end of ideology debate – Shils gave an overview of papers presented at the 1955 CCF conference:

> Almost every paper was in one way or another a critique of doctrinairism, of fanaticism, of ideological possession. Almost every paper at least expressed the author's idea of mankind cultivating and improving its own garden, secure against obsessional visions and phantasies, and free from the harassment of ideologists and zealots. It was the intention of the conference's organisers to move thought further around the turning point to which we have come in the last years. This turning point might be described as the end of ideological enthusiasm.[54]

Shils was convinced that a Western way of living – non-ideological, scientific, rational, democratic, equalitarian and economically advanced – was about to defeat socialism.[55] As Daniel Strand analyses:

> In essence, Shils suggested that the modernized and industrialized Western democracies could be seen as being ahead of the decolonized countries which, due to their economic difficulties and absence of liberal democratic institutions, were still plagued by ideological conflicts. In this way, Shils's version of the end of ideology suggested that different countries were located in different historical times.[56]

Shils thought of ideologies not as subtle structures of belief, but as totalitarian systems. Just like Aron he strongly opposed Marxism for being 'obsessed with totality'.[57] Again like Aron, he connected ideologies with Millenarianism for their simplistic eschatological and teleological outlook.[58] Marxism was unable to deal with complexity and contingency because it thought in a static and timeless truth: 'It distinguishes sharply between the children of light and the children of darkness.'[59] Instead Shils preferred 'civil politics' based on traditional civil values and tradition – the theme on which he presented a paper at the 1955 conference. He encouraged 'depoliticized politics', as Stephen Turner puts it, and wanted people to engage with the 'workshop, neighborhood, club, church, team, family, friends, trade union, school, etc', not with political parties or grand narratives.[60] But as Turner adds: 'Civility is on the one hand highly particularized, with an identifiable series of self-understandings and a continuous sequence of transmission that varies from political tradition to political tradition, as manners vary; but is also a highly generic notion, for civility operates, analogously to Tocqueville's "equality", throughout advanced societies, and with similar consequences.'[61] This focus on historicity remained important throughout his career, for instance in 1966 when Shils pleaded for historical approaches in the social sciences. In his view, academia should not fall prey to one-size-fits-all models of the kind that could be found in both ideology and non-historical social science.[62]

Despite his emphasis on the importance of organically changing traditions, his sympathy for historicity and unicity, and his aversion of metaphysics, Shils never considered himself a historicist.[63] His judgement of 'German historical and philological scholarship in the nineteenth century' was far from positive, as he described it as being 'imbued with romantic hatred of the rational, the economic, the analytic spirit, which it castigated as the source and the product of the revolutionary, rationalistic trend of Western European culture'.[64] Nevertheless I would argue that Shils showed himself to be indebted to historicism, not because he thought of himself as a historicist, but because of traces of historicist reasoning that emerge in his work.[65]

In short, Shils did not dismiss every form of ideal-based politics. He even realized that, to a certain extent, ideology is part of the human condition. At the same time, he sketched an image of a world slowly developing into a place without ideology. His statement on the 'great tasks to be undertaken amidst the ruins of the ideologies' illustrates not only his belief in the beginning of a new epoch, but also that he was ready to help shape it.[66]

Daniel Bell

Daniel Bell's 1960 *The End of Ideology: On the Exhaustion of Political Ideas in the Fifties* is a rich, deeply historical volume about American society in transition. As a collection of essays – some written as contributions to the CCF – it touches upon a wide array of ideas, authors and developments. Looking back upon the volume in 1988, Bell argued that it was often mistaken for a monograph and better known for its title than for its content.[67] And indeed: only one chapter has the end of ideology as its central topic: 'The End of Ideology in the West: *An Epilogue*'. This title could obviously be understood as the epilogue to the book, but in a more daring mode, one could also argue that Bell himself wrote the epilogue to an era.

Bell first and foremost discussed the role and status of ideology. He analysed the roots and history of the concept and distinguished between interpretations of the concept of ideology as proposed by Bacon, de Tracy and Marx, but also noted that 'in popular usage the word *ideology* remains ... a vague term', which could encompass many things.[68] Clarifying things, Bell drew on Karl Mannheim's distinction between the *particular* and the *total* conception of ideology. When Bell discusses ideology, it is *total ideology* which is

> an all-inclusive system of comprehensive reality, it is a set of beliefs, infused with passion, and seeks to transform the whole of a way of life. This commitment to ideology – the yearning for a "cause," or the satisfaction of deep moral feelings – is *not* necessarily the reflection of interests in the shape of ideas. Ideology, in this sense, and in the sense that we use it here, is a secular religion.[69]

Although the chapter 'The End of Ideology in the West: *An Epilogue*' is not mainly about Marxism, the other essays in the book clarify that this is the secular religion Bell focused on. According to Bell, Marxism has lost its attractiveness in the West, after a strong consensus on the 'acceptance of a Welfare State; the desirability of decentralized power; a system of mixed economy and of political pluralism'.[70] A new kind of politics leads beyond traditional ideological outlooks and focuses on novel utopias that distinguish themselves from ideologies by being less categorical and less simplified because they 'specify *where* one wants to go, *how* to get there, the costs of the enterprise, and some realization of, and justification for the determination of *who* is to pay'.[71]

But Bell was not just analysing the end of a particular kind of politics, he also discussed the end of an era. His mode of reasoning is illustrated when he starts his chapter with references to 'a few periods in history when man felt his world to be durable, suspended surely, as in Christian allegory, between chaos and heaven'.[72] He states that at some moments in Ancient Egypt and in the Hellenistic period, just as in the years around the French Revolution, daily life changed so dramatically that there was a *before* and an *after*. Bell goes on that his own 'age, too, can add appropriate citations – made all the more wry and bitter by the long period of bright hope that preceded it'.[73]

The idea that Bell is writing the epilogue of an era finds some confirmation in the last pages of the chapter, where Bell writes that the 'end of ideology closes the book, intellectually speaking, on an era, the one of easy "left" formulae for social change'.[74] The book then closes with a somewhat dramatic quote from Alexander Herzen:

Do you truly wish to condemn all human beings alive today to the sad role of caryatids ... supporting a floor for others some day to dance on? ... This alone should serve as a warning to people: an end that is infinitely remote is not an end, but, if you like, a trap; an end must be nearer – it ought to be, at the very least, the labourer's wage or pleasure in the work done. Each age, each generation, each life has its own fullness.[75]

It is not without reason that Brick characterizes Bell mentality as 'clearly a utopian one'.[76]

In 1988, Bell retrospectively described the last chapter of his book as a text that 'noted, in melancholy fashion, a new phase'. Describing himself as 'a participant in these intellectual wars', Bell admitted that he had been particularly critical of the totalitarian ambitions of Marxism.[77] That Bell was perhaps more than just 'a participant in the debate', is apparent from the fact that he fuelled the debate about the end of ideology in more ways than by merely writing a book. He not just participated in the CCF but was one of the first who knew that the CIA supported this intellectual endeavour too.[78] For Bell, Marxism stood for an ideology that – at least in certain circles – had been dominant for a period of time. It therefore is not just the end of Marxism that Bell advocated, it is not even the end of ideology as such. What he does declare ended, however, is the age in which ideology is a noteworthy factor to consider in the Western world. As said, this chapter does not want to suggest that Bell should be seen as a full-blown historicist. At other times he even appeared to be an anti-historicist.[79] But the fact that there is a tendency to epochal thinking in his work, unmistakably shows a residual historicist element.

Conclusion: Politics of periodization

This chapter has argued that the phrase 'post-ideological' as it appeared in the 1950s was mostly used as an adjective to a period, era, phase or stage that was considered to be over – or one that should come to an end. Although the adjective could be combined with a broad variety of nouns – such styles, politics and ways of living were considered post-ideological – the majority of the authors used the concept to propose a delineation of historical time.[80] In this context, post-ideology appeared together with other post-concepts such as post-political and post-industrial, often in work by the same authors, such as Daniel Bell. The end of ideology debate provided a context for them all.

Further analysis of this end of ideology debate reveals that its key contributors did not aim to declare all forms and manifestations of ideology to be passé, they first and foremost sought to relegate Western modes of 'dogmatic' Marxism to the past. Shils most explicitly emphasized this uniquely Western element in his endeavour, but Bell and Aron similarly pointed to the primacy of the Western world. All authors initially expected ideologies to remain or flourish in Asia and Africa. Bell for instance, expected a dominant role for ideology in Africa and Asia, however he was not expecting a revival of Marxism there. He pointed at new ideologies of 'industrialization, modernization, Pan-Arabism, color, and nationalism'.[81]

Following Scott-Smith and Lipset, we might say that the end of ideology was not a 'prediction' of the future, and more than a striving for the end of ideology in general.[82] The authors discussed in this chapter longed for a new era, a fresh start in several ways; they longed for a change in the sociopolitical situation. As Dennis Wrong characterized the end of ideology debate in 1968: 'All of these writers … tend to favor the development they describe, although their precise attitudes differ, some taking a "tragic" view of politics and the human condition while others are complacent.'[83] Their shared political ambition to change the Western world was given form with words. The concept 'post-ideological' helped shape a new era.

Although all authors noted a tension between the rejection of ideology on the one hand and their teleological, sometimes even utopian, appeal to a post-ideological age on the other, they continued in their endeavour because, as Aron said, 'the post-ideological phase is not a symptom of exhaustion, but, on the contrary, a mark of a progress in scientific consciousness'.[84] The post-ideological was not just a description, it was a sign of a political programme, too. Authors used this language to declare Marxism irrelevant at a time when a great part of the world was still under its spell.

By emphasizing this applied form of epochal thinking, the historicist tendencies in the politics of periodization, and the use of historicist utterings that could be read as speech-acts trying to go beyond the current epoch, this chapter argues that even among American and French intellectuals in the 1950s, in the social sciences and the humanities some elements of classic historicism were kept alive. Even though the authors I discussed can hardly be called historicists, and sometimes even took anti-historicist positions, there was a residual historicism at work in how they wrote about stages, ages and eras. They drew on a historicist tradition, a mode of thinking, that, through authors like Mannheim, had travelled from Europe to the US, and remained topical in post-war debates.

Notes

1 Helmut Schelsky, *Ortsbestimmung der Deutschen Soziologie* (Düsseldorf: Eugen Diederichs Verlag, 1959), p. 35.

2 Raymond Aron, 'Sociology allemagne sans idéologie?', *Archives européennes de sociologie*, 1:1 (1960), 170–4, 170.

3 Friedrich Meinecke, *Die Entstehung des Historismus* (Munich: Carl Hinrichs, 1965), p. 2.

4 This metaphor is borrowed from Chris Lorenz and Berber Bevernage (eds), *Breaking Up Time: Negotiating the Borders between Present, Past and Future* (Göttingen: Vandenhoeck & Ruprecht, 2013).

5 Although the term has been used by many authors, research on the development of the concept is scarce. Only more recent uses of the concept have been subjected to critical scrutiny, for instance by Michael Freeden, 'Confronting the chimera of a "post-ideological" age', *Critical Review of International Social and Political Philosophy*, 8:2 (2005), 247–62.

6 It is hardly possible to prove that a phrase or word was *not* used before a certain date. However, no earlier uses of the phrase 'post-ideological' and its equivalents or conjugations in French, German, English and Dutch have been found. Searches have been conducted in databases such as Google Books, EBSCO, JSTOR, Springer, WorldCat, ProQuest, Gallica, Delpher, Germanistik im Netz and in newspapers like *The Washington Post*, *The New York Times*, *Die Zeit*, *Die Frankfurter Allgemeine Zeitung* and *Le Monde*. Unfortunately, *Le Figaro* has been digitized only until 1942. Since Raymond Aron was an editor to this newspaper and one of the first to use the phrase, it might be that earlier mentions can be found there.

7 Paul Pickrel, 'The Opposing Self: Nine Essays in Criticism, by Lionel Trilling', *Commentary Magazine* (1955), 398–400, 398. Daniel Bell considered Lionel Trilling as one of his 'intellectual nesters': Daniel Bell, *The End of Ideology: On the Exhaustion of Political Ideas in the Fifties* (Cambridge, MA: Harvard University Press, 2nd edn, 2001), p. 300.

8 Pickrel, 'The Opposing Self', 399.

9 Ibid., 398.

10 Irving Howe describes Wallace Stevens as 'a forerunner of post-crisis, post-ideological man' in Irving Howe, 'Another Way of Looking at the Blackbird', *New Republic* (4 November 1957), 16–19, 17. Amiya Chakravarty writes that 'Prime Minister Jawaharlal Nehru's oft-repeated faith in a rapidly evolving, post-ideological period (postpresent ideologies, that is) in a changing world, and his insistence that we not only help the meliorative forces but prepare our minds for the larger freedoms could be further amplified'. A. Chakravarty, 'India and America by Phillips Talbot and S. L. Poplai', *Saturday Review* (26 April 1958).

11 Schelsky, *Ortsbestimmung*, p. 35.

12 Ibid., pp. 55–6. To Schelsky 'post-ideological sociology' first and foremost was a discipline in which big ideas and overarching theories had disappeared.

13 Aron, 'Sociologie allemande sans idéologie?', 170–5, 170. Original: 'la sociologie d'après 1933 se caractérise par son caractère non idéologique, qui répond d'ailleurs au caractère post-idéologique de l'époque que nous vivons'. Aron was not the only one who used the term 'post-ideological' in a review of this book; it can also be found in the review of Kurt Wolff: Kurt H. Wolff, 'Review', *American Sociological Review*, 25:4 (1960), 586–7, 586.

14 For example: Reuel Denney, 'Review: Less is More', *The Virginia Quarterly Review*, 38:3 (1962), 513–17, 516.

15 José Medina Echevarría, *Economic Development in Latin America: Sociological Consideration* (Mara del Plata: United Nations Economic and Social Council – Economic Commission for Latin America, 1963), p. 71.

16 John Lukacs, *Decline and Rise of Europe: A Study in Recent History, with Particular Emphasis on the Development of a European Consciousness* (Westport, CT: Greenwood Press, [1965] 1976), p. 261.

17 Heinrich Gremmels, *An der Milvischen Brücke: Europäische Gesinnung und politische Bildung* (Stuttgart: Deutsche Verlags-Anstalt, 1959), p. 91. Original: 'Westdeutschland hat heute der Welt gegenüber insoweit einen Vorsprung, als wir bereits in der postideologischen Situation sind, in der wir längst auf die Lösung irgendwelcher Welträtsel grundsätzlich zu verzichten gelernt haben.'

18 Léon Dion, 'Les origines sociologiques de la thèse de la fin des idéologies', *Il Politico*, 27:4 (1963), 788–96. Original: 'Bref, la société Américaine serait parvenue à l'ère post-idéologique parce qu'elle aurait réalisé ses buts.'

19 Philip E. Mosely, 'Ideological Diversities and Crisis within the Communist Area', *Modern Age*, 9:4 (1965), 343–53, 353.

20 Howe, 'Another Way of Looking', 17; Irving Howe, 'In Fear of Thinking', *New Republic* (28 May 1962), 25–6, 25; I. Howe, 'The Negro revolution', *Dissent*, 10:3 (1963), 205–14, 207.

21 Denney, 'Review: Less is More', 516.

22 Roy Pierce, 'Liberalism and Democracy in the Thought of Raymond Aron', *Journal of Politics*, 25:1 (1963), 14–35, 14.

23 This definition is inspired by a longer definition given by Howard Brick, 'The End of Ideology Thesis', in Michael Freeden and Marc Stears (eds), *The Oxford Handbook of Political Ideologies* (Oxford: Oxford University Press, 2013), pp. 90–112, p. 90.

24 Konstanty Jeleński, 'Introduction', in Jeleński (ed.), *History and Hope: Tradition, Ideology, and Change in Modern Society* (New York: Congress for Cultural Freedom; Books for Libraries Press, 1962), pp. 1–13, pp. 11–13.

25 The phrase appeared for the first time in 1946 in Albert Camus, 'The Confusion of Socialists', in Camus, *Between Hell and Reason: Essays from the Resistance Newspaper Combat 1944–1947* (Hanover, NH: Wesleyan University Press, 1991), pp. 124–5. The first time a comparable phrase was used in the context of the CCF was in 1951: H. Stuart Hughes, 'The End of Political Ideology', *Measure*, 2:2 (1951), 146–58. Several conceptual histories have been written

about this concept. Lipset starts his with Friedrich Engels, while others start with the 1951 article 'The End of Political Ideology' (on the Berlin CCF) from Stuart Hughes or even the Frankfurt School. These are plausible points of departure, but since I focus on the connection with post-ideology, I take the period around the 1955 CCF as my point of departure. Cf. Seymour Martin Lipset, 'A Concept and Its History: The End of Ideology', in Lipset, *Consensus and Conflict: Essays in Political Sociology* (New Brunswick, NJ: Transaction Publishers, 1985), pp. 81–109, p. 82; Hughes, 'End of Political Ideology', 146–58.

26 Max Beloff, 'Discussion', *Encounter*, 6:2 (1956), 71–4, 73; J. H. Goldsmith, 'Paris Letter', *Partisan Review*, 23:1 (1956), 81–90, 83; Raymond Aron, 'Coexistence: The End of Ideology', *Partisan Review*, 25:3 (1958), 230–40; Harold Rosenberg, 'Twilight of the Intellectuals', *Dissent*, 5:3 (1958), 221–8, 222.

27 Chaim I. Waxman (ed.), *The End of Ideology Debate* (New York: Funk and Wagnalls, 1968). Later a few other articles and essays appeared on this topic. See, for example, Lipset, 'A Concept and Its History'.

28 Bell, *End of Ideology*, pp. 402–3.

29 Seymour Martin Lipset, *The Political Man: The Social Bases of Politics* (New York: Doubleday, 1960), p. 92.

30 Job L. Dittberner, *The End of Ideology and American Social Thought, 1930–1960* (Ann Arbor, MI: UMI Research Press, 1979), pp. 130–6; Christopher Adair-Toteff, 'Mannheim, Shils, and Aron and The "End of Ideology" Debate', *Politics, Religion & Ideology*, 20:1 (2019), 1–20, 1.

31 Brick, 'End of Ideology Thesis', pp. 90, 102.

32 Ibid., p. 91.

33 Ibid., pp. 94–5.

34 Edward Shils, 'The End of Ideology?', *Encounter*, 5:5 (1955), 52–8, 53.

35 Brick, 'End of Ideology Thesis', pp. 99–100.

36 In the early 1990s a new debate on the end of ideology emerged, in which authors like Anthony Giddens, Francis Fukuyama, Jaques Rancière, and Chantal Mouffe discussed 'post-politics', among other things. A good overview of the debate can be found in Japhy Wilson and Erik Swyngedouw (eds), *The Post-Political and Its Discontents: Spaces of Depoliticisation, Spectres of Radical Politics* (Edinburgh: Edinburgh University Press, 2014).

37 Daniel Strand, *The End of Ideology in the 1950s and the Post-Political World of the 1990s* (Stockholm: Department of Culture and Aesthetics Stockholm University, 2016), p. 100.

38 Strand quotes Hermansson Adler and Peter Osborn to clarify his ideas on 'concepts of history' (Strand, *End of Ideology*, pp. 16–17).

39 Ibid., p. 17.

40 Nils Gilman, *Mandarins of the Future: Modernization Theory in Cold War America* (Baltimore, MD: Johns Hopkins University Press, 2003).

41 Ibid., p. 56; Strand, *End of Ideology*, p. 49.

42 Gilman, *Mandarins of the Future*, pp. 58–61.

43 Strand, *End of Ideology*, pp. 26, 41–51, 58–60, 182–4.
44 Giles Scott-Smith, 'The Congress for Cultural Freedom, the End of Ideology and the 1955 Milan Conference: Defining the Parameters of Discourse', *Journal of Contemporary History*, 37:3 (2002), 437–55, 443.
45 Raymond Aron, *Dimensions de la conscience historique* (Paris: Plon, 1961), p. 24; Raymond Aron, *Introduction à la philosophie de l'histoire* (Paris: Gallimard, 1939); Raymond Aron, *Memoirs: Fifty Years of Political Reflection*, trans. George Holoch (New York: Holmes & Meier, 1990).
46 Raymond Aron, *The Opium of the Intellectuals*, trans. T. Kilmartin (New Brunswick, NJ: Transaction Publishers, 2001), p. 318.
47 Steinmetz Jenkins argues that Aron did not only reject Marxism, but neo-liberalism as well. I think this thesis does not contradict what I argue in this chapter, but discussion of the parallels is beyond the scope of this chapter. Daniel Steinmetz Jenkins, 'The Other Intellectuals: Raymond Aron and the United States' (PhD dissertation, Columbia University, 2016).
48 Aron, *Opium of the Intellectuals*, pp. 323–4.
49 Over a hundred hits include historicist arguments like: 'Let man in history regard his own epoch in the perspective which the passage of time allows to the historian: our grandsons will accept, perhaps with gratitude, so why not follow their example in advance?' (ibid., p. 113).
50 Ibid., p. 146.
51 Ibid., p. xxiii.
52 Aron, 'Sociologie allemande', 170, 175.
53 Shils, 'End of Ideology', 52–8.
54 Ibid., 53.
55 Strand, *End of Ideology*, pp. 72, 130.
56 Ibid., p. 104.
57 Edward Shils, 'Ideology and Civility: On the Politics of the Intellectual', *Sewanee Review*, 66:3 (1958), 450–80, 452.
58 Ibid., 459.
59 Ibid., 460.
60 Stephen Turner, 'The Significance of Shils', *Sociological Theory*, 17:2 (1999), 125–45, 138; Edward Shils, *The Torment of Secrecy: The Background and Consequences of American Security Policies* (Glencoe, IL: The Free Press, 1956), p. 226, as cited in Strand, *End of Ideology*, p. 127.
61 Turner, 'Significance of Shils', 141.
62 Edward Shils, 'Seeing it Whole', *Times Literary Supplement* (28 July 1966), 647–8.
63 Shils did use the word historicism mainly to choose sides with Karl Popper in his battle against what he considered historicism. Pooley reflects on the problematic use of the concept 'historicism' in Shils's work, but does not elaborate on the question whether Shils himself should be called a historicist. See Jefferson Pooley, 'Edward Shils' Turn Against Karl Mannheim: The Central European Connection', *American Sociologist*, 38:4 (2007), 364–82, 378–9. Although the relation between Shils and Karl Mannheim is very interesting in this context,

there isn't scope to discuss it satisfactorily in this chapter. Cf. Edward Shils, 'Karl Mannheim', *The American Scholar*, 64:2 (1995), 221–35; David Kettler and Volker Meja, *Karl Mannheim and the Crisis of Liberalism* (New Brunswick, NJ: Transaction Publishers, 1995), p. 239 and Stephen Turner, 'The Young Shils', *Tradition & Discovery: The Polanyi Society Periodical*, 39:3 (2012), 43–51.

64 Edward Shils, 'The Intellectuals and the Powers' in Shils, *The Intellectuals and the Powers and Other Essays* (Chicago, IL: University of Chicago Press, [1958] 1972), pp. 3–41, p. 20.

65 Shils did not develop a theory on the stage-like development of society, though at a few moments (while reflecting on the development of social sciences) he hinted on how traditions developed in stages. At other moments he rejected thinking in stages for being too simplistic. His struggle with this theme can be found in many places in his work, for instance in Edward Shils, *Tradition* (Chicago, IL: University of Chicago Press, 1981), pp. 131, 140; Edward Shils, *The Calling of Sociology and Other Essays* (Chicago, IL: University of Chicago Press, 1980), pp. 228, 232.

66 Shils, 'End of Ideology', 57.

67 Bell, *End of Ideology*, p. 409.

68 Ibid., p. 399.

69 Ibid., p. 399–400.

70 Ibid., pp. 402–3.

71 Ibid., p. 405.

72 Ibid., p. 393.

73 Ibid., p. 393.

74 Ibid., p. 405.

75 Ibid., p. 407.

76 Howard Brick, *Daniel Bell and the Decline of Intellectual Radicalism* (Madison, WN: University of Wisconsin Press, 1986), p. 210.

77 Bell, *End of Ideology*, p. 413.

78 Frances Stonor Saunders, *Who Paid the Piper?* (London: Granta Books, 2000), p. 395.

79 Bell was for instance reluctant on what 'modernity' should mean. He later referred to modernity as an 'attitude' that 'is not necessarily one element of time or a period but a more general element of human behaviour'. So here he appears to step away from the historicist notion. Peter Beilharz, 'Ends and rebirths: an interview with Daniel Bell', *Thesis Eleven*, 85:1 (2006), 93–103, 101.

80 Judith Shklar, for example, spoke about the 'post-ideological state of mind': J. Shklar, 'The Political Theory of Utopia: From Melancholy to Nostalgia', *Daedalus*, 94:2 (1965), 367–81, 378. A year later, though, she wrote about the 'post-ideological age': J. Shklar, *Political Theory and Ideology* (New York: MacMillan, 1966), p. 19.

81 Bell, *End of Ideology*, p. 403.

82 Lipset, 'Concept and Its History', p. 81.

83 Dennis Wrong, 'Reflections on the End of Ideology', in Waxman (ed.), *End of Ideology Debate*, pp. 116–25, p. 116.

84 Aron, 'Sociologie allemande', 172. Original: 'La phase post-idéologique n'est pas un symptôme d'épuisement mais bien au contraire la marque d'un progrès de la conscience scientifique.'

4

The death and rebirth of 'postcapitalist society'

Howard Brick

Introduction

Among post-constructions, the notion of 'postcapitalist' society may be unusual – first, because the way of looking at mid-twentieth-century social reality it implied was more widespread than the number of its explicit uses would suggest, and second, because the idea clearly died away by the end of the twentieth century only to be reborn in the second decade of the twenty-first. The term 'postcapitalist society' had been used by a few European writers in the 1950s (particularly Anthony Crosland in Britain and Ralf Dahrendorf in Germany) and at best very rarely, or sceptically, in the United States. Nonetheless, the general mode of thought I call 'the postcapitalist vision' held sway among significant US social theorists and political observers for a few decades after World War II, whether they said so or not.[1] That sway persisted, paradoxically, precisely in the age that we have come retrospectively to call 'the golden age of capitalism', 1945–75, the 'Glorious Thirty' years of boom. It was *after* the 'golden age' that this post-construction faded from view, especially as the end of the Cold War ushered in a triumphalist spirit regarding capitalism itself to be permanent and unalterable. The post-construction's second birth since around 2010 has recapitulated some features of mid-twentieth-century postcapitalist discourse while also significantly altering its tenor.

This much should be obvious about a 'post-prefix' term: it can never be understood apart from the name of the existent phenomenon it presumes to have surpassed, and a good deal of the fascination with and perplexity aroused by post-constructions stems from the uncertain definition of the root term itself. A great part of what makes 'postmodern' so elusive a concept lies in the vague and varied meanings of 'the modern'. So it goes with 'capitalism', whose origins and history of usages pose a preliminary puzzle.

Mainstream observers of social and economic affairs in the industrializing West did not always easily embrace the term 'capitalism', and even dissenters were slow to embrace it. In nineteenth-century America, early workers' protests decried the depredations of lordly 'capitalists' but did not necessarily define the existing order of things by the noun 'capitalism'. Marx himself, though he described the mechanisms of 'capitalistic accumulation', preferred the term 'bourgeois society' to 'capitalism'. Nevertheless, once the practices of the capitalist became generalized as 'capitalism', the negative connotations suggested by these protest traditions made the term anathema to those who defended the status quo and considered the economic and social norms of the day merely the product of social evolution, the outcome of progress, or better yet, the revelation of natural 'principles of political economy'. In 1883, William Graham Sumner sneered at those who 'have been found to denounce and deride *the modern system* – what they call the capitalist system'. The scholarly eleventh edition of the *Encyclopedia Britannica*, published in 1911, lacked an entry on 'capitalism', and devoted less space to defining the economic category of 'capital' (considered a universal, i.e., the savings or reserve fund that all human societies relied upon) than it did to the variety of 'capitals' that topped architectural columns.[2]

The term gained wider acceptance in the social sciences in turn-of-the-century work by the 'younger' German historical economists-cum-sociologists, Werner Sombart and Max Weber, and then by the 1920s in French-language historiography (work by Henri Pirenne and followers) as well as Anglo-American social thought. By 1930, marking the distance travelled since the eleventh *Britannica*, volume III of the New York-based *Encyclopedia of the Social Sciences* featured a thirteen-page double-columned essay on capitalism by Sombart himself.[3] Of course, only when 'capitalism' seemed in this fashion to designate a real phenomenon was it possible for some social theorists to imagine its supersession in a 'postcapitalist' (NB: *not* 'socialist') order.

The new-found respectability of 'capitalism' in academic circles (though not, for the most part, among economists, who still had little use for it) did not have a great effect on common usage. To be sure, a few business publications used the term in the 1920s, and some exponents of the business-community Right employed it in the 1940s and 1950s, but alternative phrases such as 'free enterprise' still held pre-eminence for much of the twentieth century.[4] Joseph Schumpeter and John Kenneth Galbraith felt comfortable with the term, but 'capitalism' in the vernacular retained its hint of animosity. Viewed from the Left, *avoidance* of the term thus always appeared to be an exercise in euphemism, as if it were necessary to deny that the going system bore the exploitative and inegalitarian marks many people had learned to associate with capitalism. Thus, when *Forbes* magazine began advertising itself in the 1970s as 'Capitalist Tool', it did so to poke fun at the revived leftist rhetoric of the 1960s while assuming a brash, unapologetic demeanour. *Forbes* set a new tone: by the 1990s the system's defenders showed no embarrassment in using the name.[5]

Here was the paradox: although generally avoided by defenders in the late nineteenth century because it was deemed unnecessary (or obnoxious) to give a distinctive name to something that right-minded people considered simply the natural condition of the economic world – for if it were acknowledged as something historical, as having arisen in time, it could pass away in time as well – by the 1990s it was possible both to name the capitalist phenomenon and claim its permanence at the same time. Moreover, the now-ubiquitous habit (on both Right and Left) of judging contemporary society 'capitalist' meant that by this time the *post*capitalist vision, which had judged the present to be a drawn-out transition beyond simple capitalist norms, had for all intents and purposes vacated the scene. I date the end of its first run in Western social thought to the 1970s.

Discerning the postcapitalist vision

The keynote for the current I see in the mid twentieth century came from Western Europe in the 1950s, though as we will see its origins can be traced back roughly to the era of World War I. In post-World War II Britain, Anthony Crosland, intellectual leader of the Labour Party's 'new right', described the emergence of 'postcapitalist society', confident that a new 'statist' order – decidedly not a 'socialist' order *yet* – had displaced 'capitalism'. Given partial nationalizations and a substantial measure of social provision, Crosland saw an end to 'the absolute autonomy of economic life'. Furthermore, he wrote, 'the dominant emphasis ceases to be on the rights of property, private initiative, competition, and the profit motive; and is transferred to the duties of the state, social and economic security, and the virtues of cooperative action'. 'Postcapitalist society' was also adopted by the German liberal Ralf Dahrendorf, for whom the separation of ownership and control in the corporation as well as the proliferation of public bureaucracies meant that 'capital – and thereby capitalism – has dissolved and given way, in the economic sphere, to a plurality of partly agreed, partly competing, and partly simply different groups'.[6]

In Western Europe, the demands and the promise of reconstruction fostered hope for a new world dawning, as the political left gained new-found strength from the defeat of Europe's far right and the accompanying embarrassment of its conservatives. I aim to demonstrate that a 'postcapitalist' reformist current appeared in American no less than European thought and that even those less bold than Crosland and Dahrendorf in naming a new order can reasonably be included among its adherents or proponents. In fact, both Crosland and Dahrendorf called upon some prominent figures of American social thought in making their arguments, and they regarded the trends they cited as marks of America's future too. For their part, American liberals at war's end were also conscious of witnessing some kind of epochal renewal, as they looked across the Atlantic at left-leaning political developments and as they contemplated the near future in a society coming to terms with a raft of recent (New Deal) welfare-state legislation and a central state seemingly empowered by the demands of war mobilization. Arthur Schlesinger wrote in 1949, 'Britain has already submitted itself to social democracy ... and the United States will very likely advance in that direction through a series of New Deals.'[7]

Amidst such expectations, we can recognize in American intellectual life a particular way of looking at contemporary Western societies and their logic of development – a postcapitalist vision – that held some sway among intellectuals mainly in the left-liberal orbit, though it cannot be said to dominate either academic life or popular consciousness. It advanced one or more of the following, related arguments: that these societies were no longer adequately understood as 'capitalist', were witnessing the steady decline in the social salience of capitalist institutions, or had moved beyond the characteristic structures and processes of capitalism. Those who made the last (boldest) claim – that Western society had passed a boundary *beyond* capitalism or was about to – cited various markers of change: the appearance of new institutional forms for organizing enterprise that were not entirely 'private'; the rise of the regulatory state that increasingly limited the sway of market mechanisms and ultimately deprived them of the power to determine social affairs; the role played in motivating social change by noneconomic forces such as the scientific estate, organized knowledge or egalitarian values of civic inclusion, participation and social provision; the apparently collectivizing impact of advanced technology; and perhaps the waning of economics as the privileged sphere of social action and analytical understanding.

The idea that capitalism was obsolescent filtered through post-war intellectual culture in various ways. Writing in an American magazine in 1953 on the alpine sanitorium, the Berghof, depicted in his 1924 novel, *The Magic Mountain*, Thomas Mann cast 'capitalism' – in fullest health identified with an old bourgeois way of life – as a fading order:

> Such institutions as the Berghof were a typical pre-war [World War I] phenomenon. They were only possible in a capitalistic economy that was still functioning well and normally. Only under such a system was it possible for patients to remain there year after year at the family's expense. *The Magic Mountain* became the swan song of that form of existence.[8]

Americans, too, thought 'capitalism' no longer adequate for understanding the forms modern society was taking at mid-century – that a 'normal' capitalism, as Mann put it, no longer existed. The leading sociologist of the day, Talcott Parsons had begun his career in the 1920s fascinated by Sombart's and Weber's work on the nature of capitalism, and he declared that understanding 'capitalism as a social system' was the key to building a modern social science – precisely because that concept rightly construed modern society as an integrated order of institutions, beyond the level of individual, rational choice posited by the old-fashioned social theory of Anglo-American economics. Yet, by the early 1940s, Parsons had concluded that 'the capitalism/socialism dichotomy' no longer applied, for American society was not *simply* capitalist, and in certain profound ways – bound to grow in significance as time went on – had already surpassed the norms of capitalism.[9]

Immediately, it is clear that such 'postcapitalist' views dealt both with conceptual issues (whether the concept of 'capitalism' was defined precisely enough to be analytically useful) and with empirical judgements of contemporary social change. These two dimensions could hardly be disengaged. Definitions had always been problematic and never resolved into a clear consensus. From the start, observers had debated whether capitalism was defined primarily by the norms of 'economic individualism' (self-interest in the pursuit of wealth, freed of limiting, communal norms); by the social and geographic expansion of market exchange; by a policy of laissez-faire (essentially autonomous markets) or by the monopolistic practices of great financiers ('capitalists'); by the perpetual accumulation of private wealth in the form of capital, based on the generalization of wage labour; or by an *attitude* toward accumulation and an associated behavioural disposition (*Geist*, spirit, or 'ethic', as Weber and Sombart proposed). Uncertainty over how to apply the term only grew as post-war writers perceived one or another of these defining traits to be altered or undermined by reforms of the mid twentieth century: a boost in state intervention that either manipulated the market through fiscal (Keynesian) means or limited its operations in certain respects by regulation; changes in the meaning of private property as capital ownership apparently moved its base from individuals and families to corporate organization; and reorganization of occupational groups, such as the rise of professional and technical ranks that fit easily into neither bourgeois nor proletarian (wage-labour) classifications.

Given such intertwined theoretical and empirical concerns, one mode of argument addressed the scope of the concept, capitalism: if it were agreed that capitalism defined an *economic* system, did it make sense to name a whole *society* 'capitalist', or did such a designation prejudge (and perhaps misjudge) the relative weight of different elements – besides the economic sphere, the political, cultural, familial and psychological aspects that make up a complex social order? Empirical observers wondered whether the mechanisms of capitalism – let us say, accumulation of profit in private hands by means of competitive enterprise acting in an open market – any longer dominated social life as they once had. In this mode of the post-capitalist vision, then, doubts about the analytical adequacy of the concept specifically questioned the *centrality* of capitalism in contemporary society.

The new mood in social analysis also entailed questions about the *distinctiveness* of capitalism. Writers at mid-century might show some hesitation in using the term 'capitalism' as if they were perplexed about the proper terms of social criticism in the contemporary world. William J. Goode of Columbia University, who defined himself as a 'critical soci-ologist' influenced by the example of radical iconoclast C. Wright Mills, referred in passing to 'the capitalist use (for the modern scene, read "indus-trial use") of machinery' – as if the limited case of capitalism no longer sufficed as a target of social polemic.[10] Goode did not fully explain his substitution, which might have implied either that the 'modern scene' had somehow surpassed capitalism, or simply that the modern scene included communist or social-democratic regimes whose industrial machinery bore much the same consequences as the capitalist use of it did. If, however, capitalist societies seemed less distinctive to some observers ready to widen the target of their criticism, capitalism appeared to some others as more indistinct, blurred both by 'mixed' systems or by prospects for 'conver-gence' of capitalist and anticapitalist orders on some new, third term. The idea of a 'mixed economy' often meant more than a homeopathic dose of government regulation in a private market economy, but rather an admix-ture of features that created something new: even the hard-nosed realist of French sociology, Raymond Aron, wrote in 1954, with reference to the post-war order encompassing regulation, state enterprises and limited planning, that 'socialism has ceased in the West to be a myth because it has become a part of reality'.[11]

The postcapitalist vision was not a socialist one, though its genealogy owed something to styles of socialist thought typically known as 'revi-sionist' in the early twentieth century, associated with the 'evolutionary' perspectives of the German Social Democrat Eduard Bernstein. The kind of gradualism signalled by Bernstein's notion of capitalism 'growing over into' socialism – opposed to the expectation of a critical revolutionary break between the old order and new – lent to the postcapitalist vision its char-acteristic understanding of change: that the present marked a transitional moment where no clear divisions or boundaries were marked. This notion of a very porous boundary may make this post-construction different from others that emphasize the notion of a decisive shift beyond an old category.

The conception of change signalled by the postcapitalist vision had been suggested earlier in the twentieth century by the grand old man of French social democracy, Jean Jaurès: moderns, he wrote, would experience the advent of socialism as navigators 'crossed the line of a hemisphere – not that they have been able to see as they crossed it a cord stretched over the ocean warning them of their passage, but that little by little they have been led into a new hemisphere by the progress of their ship'.[12] Latter-day socialists might still hold forth such a vision. A visiting Polish lecturer told American students in 1960 that 'socialism is not a system based on opposition to capitalism and separated from capitalism by a clear line of distinction, but a method of steady improvement and progress in a democratic, industrial nation', something to grow out of Western welfare states in time. Most postcapitalist theorists, less certain of naming the result, nonetheless borrowed this developmental imagination: gradual changes in degree could usher in world-shifting transformations barely sensed until they had come to pass. Social change was persistent, perpetually reinventing society, tending to elude old labels and old practices.

Yet, precisely because of the subtle and elusive character of change, what I call the postcapitalist vision was also characterized by a great deal of ambivalence and uncertainty, a characteristic hesitancy that resulted at times in apparent self-contradiction. Even the boldest advocate of an explicit 'postcapitalist' interpretation, Anthony Crosland, seemed on occasion to undercut his own claims: as the British Labourite reviewed the tasks of socialist politics in the 1950s, he noted that 'since [the 1930s], alas, the mischievous enemy [capitalism] has retreated, and gone into disguise as well'.[13] Was it part of 'postcapitalist' theory to assert that capitalism had both surrendered to a successor regime – some kind of state-directed quasi-social economy – and yet still held the stage in a 'disguised' form? It was as if contemporary social structure, for the postcapitalist theorist, was a kind of shape-shifter, appearing at one moment as an updated form of modern capitalism and at another as a new-fangled order where private property, markets, business cycles, bourgeois prestige, class inequality and the like had lost their determinant force in social relations. Here, at least, there appears linkage with another, somewhat later post-construction: self-conscious proponents of 'postmodernism' would erect a principle of 'uncertainty, an insecurity, a doubt' at the heart of that sensibility.[14] Indeed, liberal social analysts at mid-century had already adopted a posture of measured scepticism about even their own definitions of the going system and its future. Nonetheless, for most advocates of the postcapitalist vision – imagining a future difficult to name except in relation to what it moved beyond – their scepticism or modesty regarding the name of the emergent order was linked to a remarkable progressive confidence in some sort of evolution toward a 'social economy' or a society that had moved past the unalloyed supremacy of markets and private wealth.

The postcapitalist vision, then, was a rather capacious mode of discourse. A fair number of American scholars and intellectuals from the 1940s to the 1960s were prepared to believe that American society had moved, was moving, or would soon move beyond the boundaries of capitalism as such. Some others, who were reluctant to make such a strong claim, would still affirm that they were witnessing the steady reduction in the salience of such distinctively capitalist institutions as the private corporation, a diminution in the scope of market processes (and the expansion of a social sphere of public goods, collective resources, and welfare provision), and hence a decline in the centrality or privileged status of economics. Even those social and political critics who saw the new shape of post-war society and politics as a matter more threatening than promising – those who perceived a new, centralized state having ominous powers of war-making and social control – were inclined to credit some kind of recent sea-change in the structure of social life, a move beyond old capitalist standards of market autonomy and class conflict to the highly organized order of a politically managed economy. For them, the new stage of social development called for a new kind of opposition no longer wedded to an old left-wing critique of capitalism. By no means do I propose the postcapitalist vision as the *main* current or the sum total of American social thought in this period. It was largely limited to left-liberal intellectuals and some of their more radical critics. Yet this vision constituted one of the prevalent moods among post-war Western intellectuals. A sense that something dramatic about contemporary social structure had changed in recent years typically trumped alternative and more traditional left-wing arguments that the lineaments of bourgeois society had survived intact the constant alterations of modernity and the stresses of twentieth-century wars and depressions. As a matter of positioning, advocates of a postcapitalist vision certainly set themselves off from orthodox Marxists and communists.

A rough notion of genealogy provides the best way to conceive the long linkages constituting the postcapitalist vision over the broad middle of the twentieth century – beginning already in fact by the end of the century's first quarter. Constructed in retrospect in terms of descent, the postcapitalist vision appears as the sum of a limited set of themes, motifs, terms, expectations and arguments handed down in time from one intellectual cohort to another – at each step replicated, deployed in new ways, or reshuffled, recast and supplemented by new additions. This set included characteristic notions regarding the changing nature of economic organization and of property, 'silent revolutions' transforming the old order, the cultural malady of competitive individualism and the expanding scope of social solidarity, the decay of ruling classes, the emergence of new forces of productivity and new motives to economic dynamism, the perpetual rein-vention of modernity, a break with economistic standards of public policy and of conceiving social order, the declining imperatives of scarcity, and the coming centrality of social rights in the definition of citizenship.

Such arguments appeared in the early work of Walter Lippmann, who wrote in 1914 that the separation of ownership from management in the great corporation meant that 'most of the rights of property [have] already disappeared' and the time was 'sure to come when the government will be operating the basic industries'.[15] Meanwhile, Lippmann's superior at the *New Republic* Herbert Croly forecast 'the day ... when citizens can forget the economic aspects of life' as society moved beyond 'a fear economy'.[16] The institutional economist Rexford Tugwell, who promoted the virtues of 'planning' industrial development in order to avoid gross social disruptions and uphold standards of human welfare, regarded such terms as 'capitalism' and 'socialism' as nothing more than reifications of theoretical notions that mistook the actual fluidity of social reality. Anthropologists and psycholo-gists in the 1930s saw the capitalist, competitive individualist drive toward 'success' as pathological, so that the post-war observer David Riesman could welcome what he perceived as the ongoing demise of the 'inner-directed' man and the rise of non-pecuniary motivations and more col-laborative work styles. Very much part of this perception of a mid-century value shift was Talcott Parsons' view that the real locus of social analysis in the future had to focus on phenomena that political economy per se couldn't understand: namely, the phenomena of socialization whereby cul-tural norms became 'internalized' to shape the personality for social roles. In the late 1940s, as he led the reorganization of Harvard's social sciences in the creation of a new interdisciplinary Department of Social Relations – combining sociology, cultural anthropology and social psychology – he cel-ebrated what he called the coming 'shift of emphasis away from economics' both in the priority of the disciplines and in the nature of social reality.[17]

A broad sense of passing a boundary infected observers in other quar-ters as well. In *The Church and Contemporary Change* (1950), Methodist bishop G. Bromley Oxnam wrote that the present generation was witness-ing 'a new beginning ... as significant as was the passage from slavery to feudalism, and from feudalism to capitalism'.[18] More modestly but still suggestive, political scientists Robert Dahl and Charles Lindblom in 1953 argued that Western societies now featured plural forms of property and enterprise – from the private corporation to the regulated utility, the public authority under tripartite governing boards, cooperatives, national health services, and so forth, all 'attest[ing] the inventiveness of our times' and dooming the relevance of old 'isms' such as 'capitalism' and 'socialism'.[19]

Within this general field of social thought, particular arguments or phrases echoed each other uncannily all the way from roughly 1914 through the 1950s and 1960s. Along the way, events variously quickened or chastened the reformist spirit of the times, and visions of a new order came forth boldly or modestly, depending on circumstances. Indeed, a telling shift occurred almost exactly at the mid-century point in close association with the onset of the Cold War, which played a complex, even paradoxical role in shaping the postcapitalist vision. Emerging as it did from late-Progressive and interwar reformist currents, that vision did not *originate* in a euphemistic defence of American life against Soviet broadsides or against radical critics at home whose critique of capitalism was deemed subversive under the lowering cloud of McCarthyism – though its arguments were not infrequently deployed for such ends. There was an elective affinity between the postcapitalist vision and pro-Western Cold War polemics, facilitated by the fact that the reformist heritage that gave rise to it had always been non-revolutionary and largely anti-communist. The remarkable feature of that time was not that the Cold War fostered postcapitalist thought, but rather that the Cold War's conservative imperatives left much room at all for a reformist view that looked forward to a major transformation, however smoothly it glided across Jaurès's hemispheric line, in the social and economic ways of bourgeois order. The onset of the Cold War no doubt dampened and modulated the grandest hopes of reform that flourished in Europe and the United States right at the end of the war against fascism. As a result, the vision of postcapitalist reform grew more subdued, even fugitive. Yet it survived to flourish again in the 1960s.

In many ways, the closely aligned notion of 'postindustrial society' marked the culmination of the mid-century postcapitalist vision. At its inception in the late 1950s and early 1960s, the core of postindustrialism lay in the notion that economic dynamics as traditionally understood – namely the primacy of market exchange and economic calculation in terms of efficient allocation – were giving way to new principles of organization as social development came to depend more on 'social goods', notably science and higher education. Postindustrial advocates tended to assume that since productivity gains now relied on scientific knowledge and scientifically trained workers, public funding of research and education became the central motive force of economic development, calling forth a more socialized order. Daniel Bell, who long insisted that postindustrial society did *not* mean 'postcapitalist' society, nonetheless claimed that the university as a public resource would replace the corporation as the central institution of postindustrial society.[20] This order was to be government-centred, future-oriented and dependent on planning the cultivation of knowledge and expertise in terms of social needs rather than (solely) old economic norms of efficiency.

Meanwhile, Columbia University sociologist Amitai Etzioni, in a 1968 book dedicated to his radical students in New York and Berkeley, described what he called an 'active society', reforming itself in order to approximate more closely its most cherished ideals of equality, liberty and belonging. Such ongoing processes grew from the prevalence of self-conscious individuals with flexible ego boundaries who were open to change and fellowship (another echo of the interwar social-psychological critique of competitive individualism), and from the growing capacities of centralized government to control resource use and social development. According to Etzioni, particularistic economic interests were bound to play ever less of a role in governance, and the trend of the future moved toward declining inequalities of wealth and income as bounds of inclusion in social citizenship widened.[21]

It is perhaps ironic that the theory of postindustrial society – replete with its connotations of an increasingly social economy – reached its widest audience in the 1970s, just as the postcapitalist vision was entering a precipitous decline. Bell's major work, *The Coming of Post-Industrial Society* appeared in 1973, followed three years later by *The Cultural Contradictions of Capitalism*. Critics at the time asked (sometimes jeeringly) why 'capitalism' now came back into focus as an object of analysis. Bell protested that the second book represented no shift, no surrender of his postindustrial theory, since the two publications were really companion volumes, both drawn from a common manuscript drafted in 1969. I have argued elsewhere that the moods of the two books indeed fit as part of a whole, though profoundly ambivalent, perspective on modernity.

Yet Bell's decision to dwell a bit on the concept of 'capitalism' at this time said a great deal. In the spirit of the reformist age of the post-war years, Bell still regarded capitalism as a decadent system, though its lingering standards and consequences (viz., an acquisitive consumer ethos that eroded obligations to the commonweal) might prove to be the spoiler obstructing or aborting the hoped-for postindustrial transition.[22] In this sense, recognition of the limits or inhibitions of profound social-structural change spelled trouble in the field of postcapitalist vision. The deepening of economic crisis in the 1970s helped accelerate the waning of that vision, not so much because the postcapitalist vision depended on growth but because the most severe recession since World War II made crystal clear how recalcitrant the economic realm remained and how mistaken Crosland and others had been in asserting its autonomy had ended. The tendency of Talcott Parsons' 'new social sciences' to trumpet their ascendancy and promote a noneconomic concept of civil society was embattled by a revival of political economy, a reassertion that matters of property, wealth, and exchange, economic development, inequality, and the uses of power, stood close to the centre of social structure. This revival appeared both on the Left, in the renewal of academic Marxism, and on the Right in the return of new varieties of Smithian market ideology. Needless to say, the shift back, away from the post-war liberal noneconomic concept of society, was accompanied by a rapid decline in confidence that Western society had *already* entered a transitional phase of development leading *beyond* capitalism. In the wake of the 1970s crisis, commencing a policy shift toward deregulation, privatization and open market practices, it became increasingly commonplace and unobjectionable to recognize Western society as capitalist indeed. And by the 1990s, with the 'end of the Cold War', liberal and conservative prophets both claimed that this order was interminably fixed in place.

The new postcapitalism

A few years before the 2008 financial collapse, I wrote: 'The present peculiar conjunction of naming [capitalism] and claiming permanence [for it] may pass ... as the triumphalist post-cold war mood of the booming 1990s fades from memory, as more familiar patterns of conflicting interests return, and as capitalist development continues to incite speculation about the course of change.'[23] That is to say, 'postcapitalist' visions could very well revive. Indeed now in the past ten years, this 'post-' term has re-emerged in a flurry of new publications with titles such as *Does Capitalism Have a Future?*, *How Will Capitalism End?*, and *Inventing the Future: Postcapitalism and a World Without Work*. *The Nation* magazine devoted a special issue in 2017 to the theme of getting 'out from under capitalism'.[24] Among all these, Paul Mason's *Postcapitalism: A Guide to Our Future* gained a good deal of attention as an engaging, forceful argument that another world is not only possible but indeed in the offing.[25]

Most immediately striking in this new crop is precisely the common attempt to reawaken a future-orientation deemed oppositional to that sensibility we might identify with Margaret Thatcher and with Francis Fukuyama of 1992: 'there is no alternative' to the culminating 'end of history' identified with free-market capitalism.[26] These new works are generally on the Left – and compared to the mid-century vision, more radically so. That is to say, this 'new' postcapitalism is more self-consciously oppositional to the existing social conditions. Although Paul Mason and James Livingston (in *No More Work*), as in the older vision, describe trends that are immanent and emergent, occurring all around us in the present, the new postcapitalism makes clearer that the envisioned future will be, in some fashion, profoundly at odds with inherited capitalist norms.[27] *This* postcapitalist vision, then, is more decidedly *anticapitalist*: rather than the coming postcapitalist order understood as an evolutionary product of the uncertainly 'capitalist' character of today, it is in some fashion about the 'supplanting of capitalism'.[28] By and large, these works are more willing than were the mid-century social liberals to tap a Marxian critique of capitalism. Still, the designation 'postcapitalist', much like in the mid-century tradition, connotes some measure of uncertainty regarding the character of what comes 'after' – or at least its use suggests that these authors typically find older definitions of 'socialism' unhelpful in describing the future they anticipate. Clearly, they all have dispensed with any notion of a clear teleology of the sort typically tied to a 'vulgar' Marxist 'determinism'. Peter Frase, in *Four Futures: Life After Capitalism*, employs 'postcapitalist' primarily in the sense of anything that might come after the 'end of capitalism,' marking out several alternative futures of various desirable or injurious outcomes.[29] For others, 'postcapitalist' implies more definitely some kind of egalitarian, quasi-collectivized order that can be imagined as a break from, and passage beyond, the class-differentiated market model of privatized exchange and profit accumulation. The preference for 'postcapitalist' thus signals some combination of these two postulates: the coming order will not replicate anything like the centralized, command-economy of the Soviet (or other early socialist 'planning') model, and the anticipated future entails a rather prolonged process of change, experimentation and institution-building not really conceivable as insurrectionary revolution or new state-building.

For more detail on this new postcapitalist vision, compared with the old, let us turn to look at Paul Mason's in particular. Hidden in today's information technology and 'networked' knowledge, Mason argues, lies the promise of a grand social transition toward a collaborative mode of production surpassing the price system of bourgeois markets, a transition made absolutely imperative in our time by the coming, combined threats of climate disaster, aging populations and the gargantuan growth-killing overhang of debt the world over. The great crisis of 2007–08 and its enduring effects have not only demonstrated the failure of the 'neoliberal' project of the 1980s and 1990s (that is, the construction of an unbridled free-trade, low-wage and financialized order) but also provided a hint of further trends eating away at the old mechanisms of market society. Neoliberalism, that is, proved unable to build a viable growth engine on the basis of our time's new technology ('info-tech'), for the networked, digital world cannot be assimilated to the cost-accounting methods and value-added processes of capitalism. Digitized, networked knowledge is so shareable and enduring that its 'marginal cost' tends toward zero.[30] The value of goods and services built by digital means thus steadily declines – despite the attempts of new monopolists (Apple, etc.) to prop them up by enforcing intellectual property rights. The motor of capital accumulation peters out.

The neoliberal employers' offensive was successful, however, in rendering the working class and the old labour movement almost entirely atom-
ized, having no prospects of assuming a vanguard role in social change. But
no worry: the productive force of info-tech itself already bears within it the
incubus and proponents of a new order. Not only does info-tech's potential for skyrocketing productivity and cost reductions make available an
abundance of 'free stuff', but the behavioural models of shared knowledge,
collaborative creativity, and casual attitudes that 'blur' the boundaries
of work and leisure point the way forward. The 'networked' generation
of the young who are accustomed to mobile connectivity, Mason writes,
expects lots of 'free stuff' (why should cost-free file-sharing of pop music
be prohibited?) and they act productively for the sake of the work without
pay (viz., the power of Wikipedia's contributors, or the computer geeks
who make modular improvements to 'open source' software). New models
of 'peer-to-peer' exchanges and services outside the marketplace, cooperative workshops, and the collective provisioning that emerged in popular
insurgent movements like the urban assemblies that protested neoliberalism from Greece to Spain to Turkey (and more modestly in Occupy Wall
Street in the United States) early in the 2010s. These forces will goad
government and business to make way, as we embark on the postcapitalist 'project', for a long, gradual shift to a new mode that will increasingly
displace the marketplace, private productive property, and compulsive
profit-making.

Mason's history of capitalist development as well as his crisis-oriented
analysis offers a sharp contrast to the confident, gradual evolutionism of the
old postcapitalism. Yet much of his argument is also all too familiar. His
claims regarding the immanent transformative effect of info-tech echo not
only Walter Lippmann's 1914 claim that 'a silent revolution is in progress'
as corporate combination 'is sucking the life out of private property' but
also the original 'postindustrial' claim that a shift away from market abso-
lutes stemmed from the inevitably *public* good of knowledge. Moreover,
the debate over 'automation' (the term coined in the early 1950s to refer
to computer-controlled continuous-flow production processes capable of
displacing great amounts of living labour) arose in the early 1960s to make
many of the same arguments that Mason and other 'end-of-work' theorists
offer today: the prospect of mass redundancy meant either a social disaster
of mounting, permanent unemployment (and coercive means of controlling
a superfluous underclass) *or*, more promisingly, the radical reduction of the
work week and a break between work and wage accomplished by a publicly
provided basic income.

Clearly, however, no automatic mechanism of social reason came to
play in the late twentieth century to meet productivity gains with scaling

back labour and building new means of social provision. Despite the 'post-industrial' confidence that knowledge resources could not be commodified, business, legislatures and courts have managed to go rather far in that direction, even if Mason is correct that the intellectual-property regime is in the long run a losing battle against the free flow of tech knowledge. Along with Mason's fond optimism that info-tech is by nature the incubus of a new society, he counts on the modes of 'spontaneous' collectivity and collaboration evident in the worldwide protests of 2010–13 (all too evanescent, in fact) as the source of social energy: 'The 99 per cent are coming to the rescue,' he states simply in the book's next-to-last line. 'Postcapitalism will set you free', is the last.

Would that it were so. But the key elements of the old socialist and labour movements that Mason leaves behind as putatively obsolete represent precisely the kind of thing we need to think much harder about in imagining 'transition' – and that is, what new forces of *solidarity* (agents who imagine collectivity and act to realize it as an alternative to illusory, marketized individualism) and *organization* (a base for persistent, long-run and vision-driven agitation) can be built in our time to put his kind of 'postcapitalist project' into effect, in opposition to the terribly powerful forces we know are arrayed *against* that project. For it isn't at all clear that the ninety-nine per cent of networked millennials 'spontaneously' generate those forces. The new postcapitalist speculation, which I am prepared to welcome, still needs, in addition to forecasts like Mason's, a hard-headed new politics of social movements and new strategies of mobilization for change – some practical picture of and preparation for the struggles to come that could, under some sort of conditions, take us from here to there.

Notes

1 Howard Brick, *Transcending Capitalism: Visions of a New Society in Modern American Thought* (Ithaca, NY: Cornell University Press, 2006).

2 William Graham Sumner, *What Social Classes Owe to Each Other* (Caldwell, ID: Caxton Printers, 1952), p. 56; 'Capital', *Encyclopedia Britannica*, 11th edn, new form, vols 5 and 6, p. 278.

3 Werner Sombart, 'Capitalism', *Encyclopedia of the Social Sciences*, vol. 3 (New York: Macmillan, 1930), pp. 195–208.

4 James Warren Prothro, *The Dollar Decade: Business Ideas in the 1920's* (Baton Rouge, LA: Louisiana State University Press, 1954), pp. xiv–xv, 216, 219, 225, 232; Francis X. Sutton, *The American Business Creed* (Cambridge, MA: Harvard University Press, 1956), p. 28, 32, 46; Lisa McGirr, *Suburban Warriors: The Origins of the New American Right* (Princeton, NJ: Princeton University Press, 2001), pp. 99, 224.

5 The slogan, '*Forbes*: capitalist tool', appeared in occasional double-page ads in the magazine (to recruit new subscribers) starting January 1967. It appeared regularly from November 1976, and by February 1980, it became a registered trademark.

6 Anthony Crosland, *The Future of Socialism* (London: J. Cape, 1956); Crosland, 'The Transition from Capitalism', in R. H. S. Crossman (ed.), *New Fabian Essays* (New York: Praeger, 1952), p. 42; Ralf Dahrendorf, *Class and Class Conflict in Industrial Society* (Stanford, CA: Stanford University Press, 1959), p. 261.

7 Schlesinger, quoted in Nelson Lichtenstein, *State of the Union: A Century of American Labor* (Princeton, NJ: Princeton University Press, 2002), pp. 151–2, ellipses added.

8 Thomas Mann, 'The Making of The Magic Mountain', *Atlantic Monthly* (1953), reprinted in Mann, *The Magic Mountain*, trans. H. T. Lowe-Porter (New York: Vintage, 1969), p. 719.

9 Talcott Parsons, '"Capitalism" in Recent German Literature: Sombart and Weber', *Journal of Political Economy*, 36 (1928), 641–4; and '"Capitalism" in Recent German Literature: Sombart and Weber – Concluded', *Journal of Political Economy*, 37 (1929), 31–51; Parsons, 'On Building Social System Theory: A Personal History', *Daedalus*, 99 (1970), 838, 852, 858.

10 William Josiah Goode, *World Revolution and Family Patterns* ([New York]: Free Press of Glencoe, 1963), p. 16.

11 Raymond Aron, *The Century of Total War* (London: Verschoyle, 1954), p. 355, quoted in Crosland, *Future of Socialism*, p. 63.

12 Jean Jaurès, quoted in Daniel T. Rodgers, *Atlantic Crossings: Social Politics in a Progressive Age* (Cambridge, MA: Belknap Press of Harvard University Press, 1998), p. 18.

13 Crosland, *Future of Socialism*, p. 5.

14 Judith Stacey, *Brave New Families: Stories of Domestic Upheaval in Late Twentieth Century America* (New York: Basic Books, 1990), p. 17.

15 Walter Lippmann, *Drift and Mastery: An Attempt to Diagnose the Current Unrest* (New York: M. Kennerley, 1914), pp. 36, 51, 57–8.

16 David W. Levy, *Herbert Croly of the New Republic: The Life and Thought of an American Progressive* (Princeton, NJ: Princeton University Press, 1985), p. 171, ellipsis added.

17 Brick, *Transcending Capitalism*, pp. 65–73, 108–14, 135–45, 172–80.

18 G. Bromley Oxnam, *The Church and Contemporary Change* (New York: Macmillan, 1950), quoted in Robert Wuthnow, *The Restructuring of American Religion: Society and Faith since World War II* (Princeton, NJ: Princeton University Press, 1988), p. 38, ellipsis added.

19 Robert A. Dahl and Charles Edward Lindblom, *Politics, Economics, and Welfare: Planning and Politico-Economic Systems Resolved into Basic Social Processes* (New York: Harper & Brothers, 1953), pp. 4–5, 7, 16, 46.

20 Daniel Bell, 'The Post-Industrial Society', in Eli Ginsberg (ed.), *Technology and Social Change* (New York: Columbia University Press, 1964), pp. 44–59.

21 Amitai Etzioni, *The Active Society: A Theory of Societal and Political Processes* (London, New York: Collier-Macmillan; Free Press, 1968), pp. 198, 211, 516, 528.

22 Howard Brick, *Daniel Bell and the Decline of Intellectual Radicalism: Social Theory and Political Reconciliation in the 1940s* (Madison, WI: University of Wisconsin Press, 1986), pp. 199–210.

23 Brick, *Transcending Capitalism*, pp. 269–70, ellipsis added.

24 Immanuel Wallerstein et al., *Does Capitalism Have a Future?* (Oxford: Oxford University Press, 2013; Wolfgang Streeck, *How Will Capitalism End? Essays on a Failing System* (London: Verso, 2016); Nick Srnicek and Alex Williams, *Inventing the Future: Postcapitalism and a World Without Work* (London: Verso, 2015); *Nation* 304: 16 (22/29 May 2017).

25 Paul Mason, *Postcapitalism: A Guide to Our Future* (New York: Farrar, Straus and Giroux, 2015).

26 Francis Fukuyama, *The End of History and the Last Man* (New York: Free Press, 1992).

27 James Livingston, *No More Work: Why Full Employment Is a Bad Idea* (Chapel Hill, NC: University of North Carolina Press, 2016).

28 Srnicek and Williams, *Inventing the Future*, p. 75.

29 Peter Frase, *Four Futures: Visions of the World after Capitalism* (New York: Verso, 2016).

30 Mason, *Postcapitalism*, p. 115.

Part II

'Post' rising to prominence (1970s–1990s)

5

Post-Keynesian:
A rare example of a post-concept in economics

Roger E. Backhouse

Introduction

For John King, author of *A History of Post Keynesian Economics since 1936*, post-Keynesian economics is 'a dissident school of thought in macro-economics'.[1] His book traced post-Keynesian economics back to 1936, the year when *The General Theory of Employment, Interest and Money*, by John Maynard Keynes, was published. This was important to establish the legitimacy of the dissenting tradition he represented, demonstrating that the economists who formed the subject of his book were the true heirs of Keynes and that the dominant interpretation of Keynesian economics, which he chose to call the 'Grand Neoclassical Synthesis', was 'a travesty of Keynes'.[2] Such histories often overlook the fact that the term post-Keynesian has a much more complicated history.[3] When first used, in the early 1940s, it had a strictly temporal connotation. For the next two or three decades the term was generally used to denote ideas that had been developed on the basis of the theories found in Keynes's book, with no implication that these were in any way unorthodox. The term was embraced by architects of the 'Grand Neoclassical Synthesis' rejected by King and other modern post-Keynesians. It was not until the middle of the 1970s that the term was used to denote a newly emerging school of thought dissenting from the main body of economics.

At this point it is worth noting that one source of dispute among economists who identify as post Keynesian has been whether the term should be hyphenated, the presence or absence of a hyphen being used to denote different meanings of the term. In quotations, I have preserved whatever the author wrote, but in my own writing I have chosen to treat 'post' as an adjective and to use a hyphen where the term 'post-Keynesian' is used as an adjective, and to omit the hyphen where it is used as a noun, unless I am talking specifically about someone who identified as a Post Keynesian (without the hyphen).[4]

The frequency with which the term was used is indicated by Figure 5.1. It was first used in the early 1940s and gradually became more common (note that the graph cites only uses in a set of journals, not in books and other publications) until, at the end of the 1970s, use of the term trebled. There were two reasons for this. One is that the term 'Keynesian' was more frequently used and the other is that there was a rise, shown in Figure 5.2, of the proportion of articles using the term Keynesian that also used the term post-Keynesian (or post Keynesian). From the mid 1950s to the late 1970s, roughly 10 per cent of articles using the term Keynesian also used the term post-Keynesian, whereas from the late 1970s onwards roughly 20 per cent did so.

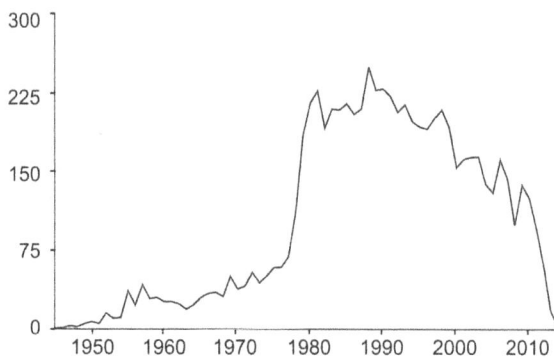

Figure 5.1 Uses of the term 'post-Keynesian' or 'post Keynesian', in JSTOR, 1945–2014. It is not completely accurate (for example, a 1942 article is not included, possibly because a line break separated the two words), and no attempt has been made to take account of the increased number of articles during the period. The sharp decline in 2010 is probably due to some technical reason relating to JSTOR's journal coverage.

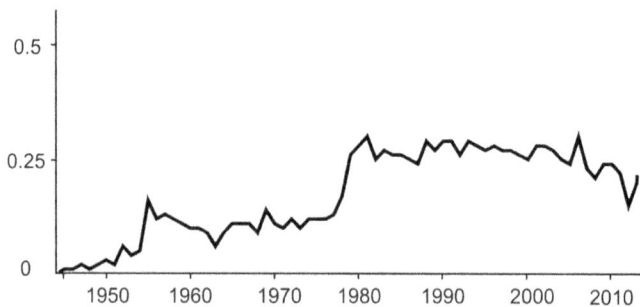

Figure 5.2 Ratio of uses of 'post-Keynesian' to uses of 'Keynesian'. Data as Figure 5.1 but with additional search for 'Keynesian'. For the reason previously cited, 2014 is omitted.

Keynesianism and Post-Keynesianism, 1936–71

What may be the first use of the term 'post-Keynesian' in a journal article could hardly be clearer in attributing to it a purely temporal meaning. Everett Hagen wrote that something was 'written in the post-Keynesian period': it had been written since 1936 but failed to use the theory of saving and investment proposed by Keynes.[5] From this, echoing the widespread use of the term 'pre-Keynesian' to denote ideas that had been superseded by Keynesian economics, the term 'post-Keynesian' came to refer to work that did not merely come after the *General Theory* but drew on Keynes's ideas. Thus, Gottfried Haberler could write 'the post-Keynesian, Keynes-inspired literature'.[6] Another writer implied that the two meanings were effectively synonymous in that, since Keynes's book, his assumptions had been generally accepted, writing, 'Post-Keynesian literature seems to take the parallelism of investment and employment for granted. This suggests that the correctness of Keynes's basic assumptions is tacitly accepted.'[7]

This was the sense, denoting work that came after Keynes and built on his work, in which Hans Neisser used the term in a course 'Keynesian and post-Keynesian Economics' taught at the New School, probably for at least a decade.[8] The course discussed Keynes's *General Theory* but it also covered the growing literature on macroeconomic problems inspired by Keynes, notably works that took dynamics into account, Keynes's own theory being considered too static.[9]

The term was used in the same sense in books. The publisher described the elementary textbook, *Introduction to Economics* by Theodore Morgan as 'a post-Keynesian text', claiming:

> This recently published book integrates the significant Keynesian develop-
> ments of recent years into the traditional body of economics. Only the por-
> tions of Keynes' contributions that have stood up, as modified by discussions
> of 1936–1948, have been included.[10]

The notion that some Keynesian ideas had been dropped as not standing up to subsequent critical examination served to differentiate modern economics from Keynesian, giving clearer meaning to the term post-Keynesian.

A significant development in 1954 was the appearance of the term post-
Keynesian in a book title: Kenneth Kurihara's *Post-Keynesian Economics*.[11] Reviews of this book are one reason for the sharp rise in mentions of 'post-Keynesian' in the journals. This collection of essays prompted Alvin Hansen, one of the major figures in propagating Keynesian ideas in the 1940s, to muse on what it meant to be post-Keynesian:

> Does the volume live up to its title *Post-Keynesian Economics?* Yes and no. It is post-Keynesian in the sense that most of the discussion is cast in terms of the Keynesian tools of analysis. It is post-Keynesian in that the endeavor is made here and there to improve on Keynes, but the result in this respect is far from impressive. It is post-Keynesian in the sense that a part of the volume is devoted to 'filling the empty boxes' of the Keynesian analysis with empirical data. [...] It is post-Keynesian in the respect that it seeks in two chapters ... to assess the Keynesian stream of thinking against the background of earlier traditions. It is post-Keynesian in the respect that it takes a fresh look in a number of chapters at policy programs stemming from the Keynesian system.[12]

Hansen specifically rejected the idea that this amounted to a survey of modern developments in the subject, for there was much literature that was not cited. He distinguished between post-Keynesianism as building upon Keynes and as writing in the period after Keynes. Others still used the term with a purely temporal connotation.

Use of the term post-Keynesian had political implications. Morgan's textbook, cited above, was advertised as adopting a viewpoint on employment that was 'middle-of-the-road, yet post-Keynesian'.[13] This statement was challenging the notion, clearly believed to be widely held, that to be a Keynesian, and by extension a post-Keynesian, was to be on the left. This came out most explicitly in the attacks on another textbook, *The Elements of Economics*, by a young Canadian, by then a professor at Stanford, Lorie Tarshis.[14] An anonymous reviewer writing for an organization called the National Economic Council, accused the book of being propaganda for Keynesian theory, containing many lies of omission and distortion.[15] Its danger, so it was argued, lay in its emotional effect:

> [It] plays upon fear, shame, pity, greed, idealism, hope, to urge young Americans to act upon this theory [Keynesian economics], as *citizens.* This is not an economic text at all. It is pagan-religious and political tract. It inspires an irrational faith and spurs it to political action. From cover to cover there is not a suggestion of any action that is not political – and Federal.[16]

The review was sent to 15,000 banks, urging them to donate to the cause of purifying textbooks, and to all the trustees of all colleges using the book.[17] There is no evidence that the campaign was successful.

Sales of Tarshis's book did fall dramatically but this was likely to have been the result of the appearance in the following year of another textbook, which came to dominate the market for introductory textbooks: Paul Samuelson's *Economics: An Introductory Analysis.*[18] This was also attacked on account of its Keynesianism, by businessmen many of whom were associated with the Dupont chemical company, which was strongly represented on the Corporation of the Massachusetts Institute of

Technology (MIT), where Samuelson was a professor.[19] Samuelson has written of having responded to these attacks by writing his textbook as though a lawyer were looking over his shoulder. He did not use the terms Keynesian or post-Keynesian, preferring to refer to 'the new economics' but this did not stop the book being identified as Keynesian which, in the eyes of some, was tantamount to being Communist. Frank Chesterman, of the Bell Telephone Company, wrote:

> It is perfectly obvious that the young man is socially minded if not strictly communistic. It would be a terrible reflection on MIT if the book in its present condition were published. [...] I question whether Samuelson is a member of some of the subversive societies we hear so much about because his line of reasoning and method of expressing his thought are those of that group.[20]

Such remarks were to resonate with the rising anti-Communist mood of the Cold War. However, with the strong support of MIT President Karl Compton and Vice President James Killian, the book was published, and thrived.

The facts that the book was recommended in most leading universities and in *all* military academies, institutions unlikely to be hotbeds of communism, and that it reflected the thinking of most of the younger generation of economists, did not persuade critics, appalled by its message that government intervention might sometimes be needed to stabilize a capitalist economy. Conservative attacks continued throughout the 1950s, though with a changed emphasis, for Samuelson increasingly represented the establishment view. He was no longer, as he had been for his pre-publication critics on the MIT Corporation, a young scholar who was thought to need guidance. The tone of the attacks in the 1950s was set by William Buckley who, in *God and Man at Yale*, widely considered a seminal text for modern conservatism, criticized the Keynesian textbooks used at Yale for their unqualified belief in the ability of government to improve on what the private sector could achieve.[21] However strongly Samuelson and other Keynesians might express their commitment to the free enterprise system, Buckley read their statements about the need for government intervention as implying an omniscient state that needed to be much larger. His conclusion was that '[i]ndividualism is dying at Yale, and without a fight'.[22]

One of the reasons that Samuelson's textbook is important for the history of the term post-Keynesian is that in its third edition (1955) he proposed the phrase 'neoclassical synthesis'. The term remained in the book until the seventh edition (1967), before being dropped completely in the eighth edition (1970). If the government pursued policies to maintain full employment, he argued, then the traditional supply-and-demand theory of how individual markets worked ('neoclassical' theory) would come into its own.[23] This was an idea found in Keynes's *General Theory* but it was Samuelson who made it more precise and gave it a name. When groups of economists began to criticize orthodox Keynesianism in the 1970s, they typically picked out Samuelson's neoclassical synthesis, or some variation on it, as their target. Samuelson's Keynesianism had come to represent the orthodoxy.

A significant feature of Samuelson's neoclassical synthesis was that it was not a purely theoretical synthesis. It embodied a set of beliefs about how demand management policy could be used to ensure full employment. It was a Keynesian idea, developed by economists who came after Keynes, who had died in 1946, which meant that it was legitimate to speak of 'the post-Keynesian preoccupation with full employment'.[24] Thus Samuelson could include a section on 'The Post-Keynesian Thinking of Our Times' in an article on economic policy under the Eisenhower administration.[25] Neither the 'neoclassical synthesis' nor 'post-Keynesian' referred purely to a body of economic theory.

Post-Keynesianism as heterodoxy, since 1975

In the mid 1970s a new way of using the term emerged, made prominent in an article by two young economists, Alfred Eichner and Jan Kregel, 'An essay on post-Keynesian theory: a new paradigm in economics'.[26] This article was prominent because it was published in the *Journal of Economic Literature*, one of the journals included in the American Economic Association's membership package. They introduced the term in the following words: 'This generalization [of Keynes's theory] may be said to represent, in Thomas Kuhn's sense ... a new paradigm; and since it extends the analysis set forth in Keynes's *Treatise on money* (1930) and *The general theory*, it can be termed post-Keynesian.'[27] Like earlier users of the term, they used the term post-Keynesian (hyphenated) to denote an extension of Keynes's ideas, but unlike earlier users, they confined it to a specific extension, sharply distinguished from the standard approach. It became the label for a dissenting tradition, represented by the *Journal of Post Keynesian Economics*, established in 1978. For the founders of the JPKE, the absence of a hyphen in the term 'Post Keynesian' signalled their difference from the post-Keynesianism of Kurihara and the economic mainstream.

King argued that the use of the term to denote a particular approach to economics, had precursors.[28] However, though economists such as Nicholas Kaldor and Joan Robinson, considered to be among the giants of the post-Keynesian tradition, had used the term earlier, and though they had argued that their approach to the subject was both a legitimate extension of Keynesian ideas and superior to other approaches to the subject, their use of the term was still in the traditional mould. For example, when Kaldor had used the term in 1955, it was confined to a footnote, and he bracketed Keynesian and post-Keynesianism analyses together.[29] Even in the late 1960s, it had been hard to see any difference between the way the term was used by someone who later became a prominent post Keynesian (Paul Davidson) and someone whose work helped to lay the foundations for mainstream macroeconomics (Edmund Phelps). Consider first Davidson's use of the term:

> Is the finance motive really as significant as Keynes believed? And if it is, why has it been given short shrift and almost vanished by neglect in the post-Keynesian literature? ... From the argument above it seems to follow that the disappearance of the finance motive from the post-Keynesian literature has led to some omissions and some confusions.[30]

The term clearly has a purely temporal connotation, for Davidson was claiming that the post-Keynesian literature had abandoned an idea considered important by Keynes. This was also the way Edmund Phelps, whose work was influential in changing macroeconomic theory in the 1970s, used the term, referring to 'the post-Keynesian analysis of inflation', talking about how, 'in post-Keynesian economics' unexpected inflation could 'buy' an increase in output and employment.[31] He was describing the Phillips curve, a key component of the orthodox theory, which he was developing in ways to which those who later labelled themselves as post-Keynesians (and post Keynesians), took exception. The suddenness with which the new usage of the term emerged is shown by its absence from Joan Robinson's Ely Lecture, 'The second crisis in economic theory', delivered to the American Economic Association in December 1971, that is widely credited with stimulating the organization of a new grouping of post-Keynesian economists.[32] What was necessary for post-Keynesian economics to emerge in this way? The main factor behind the movement was that groups of economists in Britain and the United States had become convinced that modern economics had taken a wrong turning and that it was actively misleading as a guide for policy and for understanding modern economies. Returning to certain Keynesian ideas was believed to be the way forward. The article by Davidson, quoted above, titled 'Keynes's finance motive' illustrates this. His argument was that Keynes attached importance to a particular theory of the demand for money that could not be found anywhere in the contemporary literature, and that Keynes had been right and modern economists were wrong.[33]

Although he was not involved in the organization of post-Keynesian economics, an important foundation had been laid by Axel Leijonhufvud in *On Keynesian Economics and the Economics of Keynes*.[34] In this substantial book that was very widely cited by orthodox and unorthodox economists Leijonhufvud used the term 'Keynesian economics' to refer to contemporary work that was described as Keynesian but which, he argued, was significantly different from the economics found in Keynes's own work. What went under the label of 'Keynesian economics' was no longer the economics of Keynes.

However, the creation of a post-Keynesian movement probably required more than this. One factor fomenting dissent from the mainstream was that economics was becoming more mathematical. This process can be dated back at least to the 1930s, when the *Econometric Society* was formed, but for many years, mathematical economists remained a minority. By the 1970s it had become accepted that graduate students needed to learn some mathematics and mathematical rigour had become more important as a criterion by which good and bad work were distinguished. Along with this increased use of mathematics was a focus on models of rational individual agents and efficient, competitive markets. Work that did not meet these standards, perhaps because it was attempting to analyse situations that could not be reduced to simple maximizing behaviour, was widely deemed to be of lower quality. Thus although the great names of post-Keynesian economics – Kaldor, Robinson, Davidson and Sidney Weintraub – had, during the 1950s and 1960s, regularly published in the leading journals, engaging in debate with leading exponents of other viewpoints, this was becoming much harder for those who did not accept the emerging rules of the game.[35] The result was that economists espousing certain types of unconventional theory felt excluded.[36] The lack of mutual understanding between groups of economists could be rationalized by Thomas Kuhn's theory that science involved competing paradigms. This argument was presented in Kregel's *The Reconstruction of Political Economy: An Introduction to Post- Keynesian Economics* as involving a gestalt shift, complete with an illustration that could be either a vase or two faces.[37] He argued that the post-Keynesian and orthodox perspectives were mutually incompatible.

The post-Keynesian departure from the mainstream was accentuated because this was the time when many economists were moving away from Keynesianism, both in theory and in policy advice. The emergence of 'stagflation' (simultaneously rising inflation and unemployment) was considered by many to undermine Keynesian economics, and anti-Keynesian ideas became much stronger. The so-called 'age of Keynes' – the three decades after the Second World War – ended abruptly. For Robert Lucas and Thomas Sargent, two of its leading critics, the Keynesian era had become an interesting historical episode when economists had adopted a flawed framework. This shift in mainstream attitudes towards Keynes, contributed to the marginalization of those who were coalescing under the 'post-Keynesian' label.

The emergence of post-Keynesian economics as a dissenting school of thought and, with it, the changed meaning of the term post-Keynesian, was also stimulated by factors external to the discipline. The 1960s and 1970s were a turbulent period, politically and economically. Towards the end of the 1960s, the acceleration of the Vietnam War provided a focus for radical ideas, leading to the establishment of the Union for Radical Political Economy (URPE), accusing the mainstream in economics of neglecting issues such as class, power, gender and race. Post-Keynesianism was separate from Radical Economics, but there were significant overlaps. Radicals might not look back to Keynes, but there were shared political goals and a shared distrust of orthodox economics. These reasons for being open to a reconstruction of economics were compounded by the economic problems of the 1970s which caused many economists, even those with no inclination to form dissenting groups, to complain about the state of the discipline.

The final stage in the consolidation of post-Keynesian economics was a reconstruction of the past, a process of which King's *History of Post Keynesian Economics* forms a part. In that history, a line of descent is traced from Keynes (including, in some accounts, not only his *General Theory* but also his earlier work) to modern post-Keynesians, focusing on the contrast with those whom Robinson called 'bastard Keynesians' who misrepresented Keynes's ideas. The reason why the term post-Keynesian could acquire its specific meaning only with the construction of such narratives is that post-Keynesian economics was never defined by a single theory but was seen to comprise a family of doctrines, raising questions about the coherence of the term.[38]

Economists' use of labels and identities

The use of post-prefixes is not common in economics. The only other example listed in the contents of the *New Palgrave Dictionary of Economics*, a major reference work, the first edition of which filled four large volumes and the second edition eight volumes, is postmodernism, a concept clearly brought in from outside the discipline.[39] It seems likely that the reason for this is that, irrespective of the reality that lies behind this, most economists see themselves as scientists. For scholars in the humanities, concepts such as postmodernism, post-imperial or post-Christian play an analytical role: they form important components in accounts and analyses of literature, history or religious practice. In contrast, as with the natural sciences, economics does not work with concepts to which the post-prefix could be attached. Terminology such as 'post-Darwinian' in biology or 'post-Newtonian' or 'post-Einsteinian' in physics may be a useful shorthand for talking about the histories of disciplines, but they play no significant role in biology or physics. The same is true of Post-Keynesian, which accounts for why the history of this term is so different from that of the other concepts discussed in this volume.

Part of the reason for the rarity of post-prefixes in economics may be that economists are much more sympathetic towards the prefixes 'neo' and 'new'. The two editions of the *New Palgrave* contain entries for 'neo-classical', neoclassical synthesis, neoclassical growth theory, neo-Ricardian economics, new classical macroeconomics, new economic geography, new institutional economics, new Keynesian macroeconomics, and new open economy macroeconomics. The prefixes 'new' and 'neo' can even be combined, as in the 'new neoclassical synthesis'. It is terminology that can be very confusing for students.

Possibly the most widely used of these terms is 'neoclassical'. The term was coined by Thorstein Veblen in 1899, as a label for the economics of Alfred Marshall and his contemporaries, based on a theory of individual maximizing agents, often analysed using mathematics. Criticizing both approaches for failing to recognize the implications of evolutionary ideas, Veblen sought to link 'neoclassical economics' to the 'classical' economics of Jeremy Bentham and John Stuart Mill, arguing that neoclassical economists and their classical predecessors were guilty of adopting a teleological approach, failing to see that Darwinian evolution had no goal. The term neoclassical re-emerged in the late 1920s and during the 1930s it was adopted as a label for economic theories based on economizing scarce resources and involving utility or profit maximization. In the hands of many economists, 'neoclassical' economics was associated with support for laissez-faire and free trade.[40] The term was needed because of the growth of 'institutional economics', which sought to develop an approach more firmly grounded in facts about the world.[41] Although 'neoclassical' economics was typically not mathematical in the interwar period, the term came to be associated, above all, with the mathematical theory of optimizing consumers and firms provided in Paul Samuelson's *Foundations of Economic Analysis* (1947).[42] When Samuelson introduced the term 'neoclassical synthesis' in 1955, he was trying to link Keynesian economics to this older tradition which was more congenial to conservatives.

In contrast, the 'new classical macroeconomics' is the approach to macro-economics developed in the 1970s by Robert Lucas and others, reviving certain policy conclusions often attributed to classical economists, though developing them using very different methods. This was strongly criticized by supporters of the neoclassical synthesis, who were increasingly identified as Keynesians rather than as neoclassical, even if they did not seem that way to those who identified as post Keynesian. The term 'new Keynesian' was adopted as label for those who wanted to defend Keynesian policies whilst adopting many of the theoretical innovations of the new classical economics. When, around the turn of the century, there was a convergence between new Keynesian and new classical ideas, the term 'new neoclassical synthesis' was introduced to denote the new, generally accepted, approach to the subject.

For the most part, these terms serve no analytical function.[43] They serve to identify different theories or groups of theories and as a convenient shorthand. 'New Keynesian economics', 'new classical macroeconomics', 'neoclassical growth theory' or 'neoclassical development economics' identify families of models based on certain sets of assumptions. However, even if such terminology is used to alert the reader to the broad approach an economist is or is not following, in any article, much more specific assumptions will then be made in order to construct the model from which conclusions are drawn. As is the case with 'post-Keynesian economics' such labels identify both groups of theories and groups of economists advocating those theories. Thus, article titles such as 'A post Keynesian theory of health-care' or 'A post Keynesian analysis of the financial crisis' do little more than identify the provenance of the article, serving to tell some economists that they will find the paper congenial and others that it is probably not for them.

Part of the rhetoric of modern mainstream economics is that there is simply economics, or that there is good economics and bad economics. Most economic arguments centre on mathematical theory and statistical analysis or, in the past twenty years or so, experimental results. Verbal arguments are typically subservient to the mathematics. The implication is that doctrinal labels should be unnecessary in the same way as they are unnecessary in most natural science. Thus James Tobin, considered to be one of the leading Keynesian (neoclassical synthesis) economists of the post-war era, was typical when he argued that, in his youth, he objected to being identified as a Keynesian, not because of any hostility to Keynes but because he objected to being identified with any school of thought: he wanted to be identified simply as an economist. However, after the rise of 'monetarism' and the new classical economics in the 1970s, he took pride in being described as a Keynesian because he took issue with the way the field was developing.

Tobin's position illustrates how, despite this rhetoric of everyone being just an economist, economists do identify with different positions and with different groups. The reason why the term 'neo' or 'new' is used more commonly than 'post' is presumably to indicate both that an approach has roots in the past and that it is modern and innovative, connotations that are weaker with the term 'post'. The function of labels such as 'new Keynesian' or the 'new trade theory' is typically to differentiate the work described by the label from older, possibly discredited work. Thus, in the 1980s, the term new Keynesian was used to denote work that conformed to what were believed to be higher standards of rigour than the 'old' Keynesian economics, implicitly asserting that new classical strictures against theory that was not based on formal microeconomic theoretical foundations did not apply to the 'new Keynesian' theories.

Though most groups wishing to assert their identity are on the fringes of the discipline, is common for mainstream economists to use geographical markers to identify different approaches to the subject. For example, there is the Chicago school (associated with free markets and monetarism), MIT economics (the Massachusetts Institute of Technology, associated with more liberal politics and formal modelling), and the Virginia school (associated with public choice theory through the series of universities with which James Buchanan and his associates were involved). Economists might associate Harvard with left-leaning economics and Minnesota or Rochester with more conservative policy positions. The terms 'saltwater' (universities near the east coast, including Harvard, MIT and Yale) and 'fresh-water' (Chicago, Rochester and Minnesota, near the Great Lakes or inland on big rivers) have been used as broader labels for different approaches to macroeconomics associated with those universities. This may be an important part of economists' rhetoric, such terms being used to denigrate or dismiss opponents, but they fit poorly with the rhetoric of economists being simply economic scientists, free of ideological commitments.

Although dissenting economics may use the term 'neoclassical' to refer to the dominant approach in economics – to what they see as the orthodoxy emphasizing utility-maximizing consumers, profit-maximizing firms and clearly defined market structures such as perfect or monopolistic competition – few economists would apply the term to themselves.[44] They may talk of the 'neoclassical' growth model as a shorthand for a class of model but, most of the time they have no need for any such label. Dissenting traditions, such as post Keynesians, are simply ignored.

Dissenters, on the other hand, do argue in terms of schools of thought: their identity matters much more. One feature of dissenting schools of thought that emerged in the 1970s was that several of them looked back to past economists whose work was believed to have been unjustly neglected. 'Austrians' focused on a tradition that traced back to the late-nineteenth-century Austrian economist, Carl Menger; post Keynesians looked back to Keynes and some of them, the neo-Ricardians, to the early-nineteenth-century British economist David Ricardo. All of these schools can be identified with a particular ideology, Austrians on the right or libertarian end of the political spectrum, post Keynesians, neo-Ricardians,

Radical Economists and Marxists on the left. Sometimes identity in relation to other heterodox economists matters, as when, in the 1970s, the founders of the *Journal of Post Keynesian Economics* used the label 'Post Keynesian' (capital P and space between the words) to indicate something broader than the 'post-Keynesian' approach (lower-case p and hyphen between the words) advanced by Eichner and Kregel as well as differentiating themselves from the mainstream.[45]

Concluding remarks

Use of the term post-Keynesian can be linked to the changing fortunes of Keynesian economics. In the 1950s and 1960s, Keynesian ideas dominated the relevant parts of academic economics – those dealing with the determination of employment, output and inflation – even though for the early part of the period Keynesians were sometimes the subject of vicious attacks. 'Post-Keynesian' initially had a purely temporal meaning. Whilst the McCarthyite political climate may have influenced the use of the term, providing one more reason for some economists to favour alternatives such as 'the new economics' or 'national income analysis', there is no hard evidence that it had a significant effect. Post-Keynesian economics remained closely identified with Keynesian economics and was never a way of distancing from Keynes. Distance was achieved instead by not mentioning his name, something encouraged by the rhetoric of turning economics into a science. By the early 1970s, the situation changed in that more economists were arguing that, to use Leijonhufvud's terminology, Keynesian economics was not the economics of Keynes. Shortly afterwards, the label post-Keynesian was taken up to denote what its proponents argued was a new paradigm in economics. At the same time, other economists, usually called the new classical economists, argued that Keynesian ideas had been found wanting, both theoretically and empirically. Mainstream Keynesians embraced the label new Keynesian, leaving the embattled dissenting minority, searching for an identity, to coalesce around the 'post-Keynesian and 'Post Keynesian' labels. Post-Keynesianism therefore acquired a meaning very different from the one it had in the 1950s.[46]

Notes

1 John E. King, *A History of Post Keynesian Economics Since 1936* (Cheltenham: Edward Elgar, 2002), p. 1.
2 Ibid.

3 It is important to acknowledge that King (ibid., pp. 9–10) makes the same point that I make here about how usage of the term post-Keynesian changed. However, his emphasis differs because whereas my concern is with the term itself, he is concerned with the body of ideas that it is used to denote. Thus, he argues that economists who did not use the term but whose work became central to the work of those economists who later self-identified as post Keynesian should be described as post Keynesian.

4 I note the ease with which errors can slip in when some people attach meaning to something that is taken by others to be a point of grammar that can be left to a copy-editor.

5 Everett Hagen, 'Saving, Investment and Technological Unemployment', *American Economic Review*, 32 (1942), 553–5.

6 Gottfried Haberler, 'The Place of the General Theory of Employment, Interest, and Money in the History of Economic Thought', *The Review of Economics and Statistics*, 28 (1946), 187–94.

7 L. Albert Hahn, 'Wage Flexibility Upwards', *Social Research*, 14 (1947), 148–67, 151.

8 The exact dates when he taught the course are not known. We know only that he was teaching in in 1947–48 and for some years after. 'Back Matter', *Social Research*, 14 (1947). His papers contain a syllabus (Hans Neisser, 'Keynesian and Post-Keynesian Economics') which includes a reference to a book published in 1956.

9 K. E. Boulding, 'In Defense of Statics', *The Quarterly Journal of Economics*, 69 (1955), 485–502, 501 uses post-Keynesian as a label for dynamic theories of the business cycle that built on, but went beyond, Keynes's static theory.

10 'Back Matter', *The American Economic Review*, 40 (1950).

11 Kenneth K. Kurihara, *Post-Keynesian Economics* (New Brunswick, NJ: Rutgers University Press, 1954; London: George Allen and Unwin, 1955).

12 Alvin H. Hansen, 'Post-Keynesian Economics', *The American Economic Review*, 45 (1955), 360–72, 360.

13 'Back Matter', *American Economic Review*, 38 (1948).

14 Lorie Tarshis, *The Elements of Economics: An Introduction to the Theory of Price and Employment* (Boston, MA: Houghton Mifflin, 1947). See O. F. Hamouda and B. B. Price (eds), *Keynesianism and the Keynesian Revolution in America: A Memorial Volume in Honour of Lorie Tarshis* (Cheltenham: Edward Elgar, 1998).

15 Untitled review, *National Economic Council Review of Books*, 4 (1947), 1–8.

16 Ibid., 5.

17 Paul A. Samuelson to James Killian, 22 August 1950, Paul A. Samuelson Papers, Duke University, Box 45, quoted in Roger E. Backhouse, *Founder of Modern Economics: Paul A. Samuelson,* vol. 2 (Oxford: Oxford University Press, 2017), p. 569, note e.

18 Paul A. Samuelson, *Economics: An Introductory Analysis* (New York: McGraw Hill, 1948).

19 See Yann Giraud, 'Negotiating the "Middle-of-the-Road" Position: Paul Samuelson, MIT and the Politics of Textbook Writing, 1945–55', *History of Political Economy*, 46 (2014), 134–52; Backhouse, *Founder of Modern Economics*.

20 Ibid., 560–1.

21 William F. Buckley, *God and Man at Yale: The Superstitions of 'Academic Freedom'* (Washington, DC: Gateway Regnery, 2002). The first edition was 1951. The textbooks he attacked included those by Morgan, Tarshis and Samuelson. He also attacked teachers in other disciplines, including sociology, for failing to promote traditional Christianity.

22 Ibid., p. 101.

23 The term 'neoclassical' is discussed below.

24 Alexander Eckstein and Peter Gutmann, 'Capital and Output in the Soviet Union, 1928–1937', *The Review of Economics and Statistics*, 38 (1956), 436–44.

25 Seymour E. Harris et al., 'The Economics of Eisenhower: A Symposium', *Review of Economics and Statistics*, 38 (1956), 357–85, 373.

26 The term had been used in unpublished materials since 1971, and Kregel had used it as the title of a book in 1973. See Tiago Mata, 'Dissent in Economics: Making Radical Political Economics and Post Keynesian Economics, 1960–1980' (PhD dissertation, London School of Economics and Political Science, 2005). But none of this was as prominent as an article in the *Journal of Economic Literature*.

27 Alfred S. Eichner and J. A. Kregel, 'An Essay on Post-Keynesian Theory: A New Paradigm in Economics', *Journal of Economic Literature*, 13 (1975), 1293–314, 1293.

28 King, *History of Post Keynesian Economics*, p. 9.

29 'In fact the whole of the Keynesian and post-Keynesian analysis dodges the problem of the measurement of capital': Nicholas Kaldor, 'Alternative Theories of Distribution', *The Review of Economic Studies*, 23 (1955), 83–100, 98, n. 2.

30 Paul Davidson, 'Keynes's Finance Motive', *Oxford Economic Papers*, 17 (1965), 47–65, 49, 61.

31 Edmund S. Phelps, 'The New Microeconomics in Inflation and Employment Theory', *The American Economic Review*, 59 (1969), 147–60, 147.

32 Joan Robinson, 'The Second Crisis of Economic Theory', *The American Economic Review*, 62 (1972), 1–10. On the early history of the post-Keynesian movement, see Frederic S. Lee, 'The Organizational History of Post Keynesian Economics in America, 1971–1995', *Journal of Post Keynesian Economics*, 23 (2000), 141–62. E. R. Weintraub 'Sidney Weintraub and American post Keynesianism: 1938–1970', *Journal of Post Keynesian Economics*, 37:1 (2014), 31–42, argues that the American branch of post-Keynesianism developed largely independently of the British.

33 For our purposes, the details of this theory do not matter.

34 Axel Leijonhufvud, *On Keynesian Economics and the Economics of Keynes* (Oxford: Oxford University Press, 1968).

35 A good example is the theory of capital, mentioned in the quotation from Kaldor. In the mid 1950s, Robinson had challenged the coherence of a key concept in orthodox theory, the aggregate production function. She argued that, in a world where goods were produced by different production processes, involving different combinations of capital and labour, it was logically impossible for a single measure of capital to perform the functions required by orthodox theory. The significant point for the present argument is not whether Robinson or her main opponents, including Samuelson, were correct (she was) but that the debate could take place in the pages of the leading journals even though her initial papers did not formulate the problem using any mathematical notation.

36 This is well illustrated by the correspondence between Eichner and Robinson, published in Frederic S. Lee, 'On the Genesis of Post Keynesian Economics: Alfred S. Eichner, Joan Robinson and the Founding of Post Keynesian Economics', *Research in the History of Economic Thought and Methodology*, 18C (2000), 1–258. Eichner exchanged letters with the editor of the *American Economic Review*, in which charges of discrimination in the journal were met with the argument that the work in question did not meet the required standards for publication.

37 J. A. Kregel, *The Reconstruction of Political Economy: An Introduction to Post-Keynesian Economics* (London: Macmillan, 1973).

38 Defining post-Keynesian economics, a subject on which there is a large literature, usually involves identifying three traditions: (1) A focus on uncertainty that cannot be reduced to numerical probabilities (i.e. uncertainty that cannot be reduced to risk), which is central to the work of American post-Keynesians such as Weintraub and Davidson and Hyman Minsky; (2) The Cambridge (UK) critique of the theory of capital and the aggregate production function, associated above all with Robinson; (3) The 'classical' theory of price-determination (going back to the early-nineteenth-century economist, David Ricardo), associated with Piero Sraffa and other Italian economists with strong Cambridge (UK) links. An influential example of this literature is O. F. Hamouda and G. C. Harcourt, 'Post Keynesianism: From Criticism to Coherence?', *Bulletin of Economic Research*, 40 (1988), 1–33.

39 John Eatwell, Murray Milgate, and Peter Newman (eds), *The New Palgrave: A Dictionary of Economics* (4 vols, London: Palgrave, 1987). Steven N. Durlauf and Lawrence A. Blume (eds), *The New Palgrave Dictionary of Economics*, 2nd edn (8 vols, London: Palgrave, 2009).

40 However, this identification was not universal, for 'neoclassical' theories were also used by market socialists such as Oskar Lange.

41 Defining institutionalism is beyond the scope of this chapter. For the definitive account, see Malcolm Rutherford, *The Institutionalist Movement in American Economics, 1918–1947: Science and Social Control* (Cambridge: Cambridge University Press, 2011).

42 Paul Samuelson, *Foundations of Economic Analysis* (Cambridge, MA: Harvard University Press, 1947).

43 Readers may think that 'post-capitalist' discussed by Howard Brick, stands as a counter example. However, such language is much more common in history, sociology and political science – often under the label 'political economy' – than in economics. Students taking a degree in a mainstream economics department may well never encounter the term 'capitalist', let alone 'post-capitalist', in their entire degree programme. In the 1970s and 1980s they might have encountered such terms in courses on comparative economic systems but such courses fell out of favour with the fall of European communist regimes in Eastern Europe and the Soviet Union.

44 It is debatable whether this approach still represents the orthodox approach, and whether there still exists anything that could be considered orthodoxy. See Roger E. Backhouse and Béatrice Cherrier (eds), *The Age of the Applied Economist: The Transformation of Economics since the 1970s* (Durham, NC: Duke University Press, 2017).

45 See Mata, 'Dissent in Economics', chapter 8.

46 I am grateful to Tiago Mata, Roy Weintraub and to participants at the post-prefixes conference for helpful comments on an earlier draft. Responsibility for any remaining errors is my own.

6

Lost in the post: (Post-)structuralism between France and the United States

Edward Baring

Introduction

Today, the term 'post-structuralism' designates a stage in the intellectual history of modern France. According to a familiar narrative, post-war French thought is divided up into a number of moments that can conveniently structure an American college course. The great success of existentialist ideas in the 1940s, propounded by figures like Jean-Paul Sartre and Simone de Beauvoir, who emphasized the free and acting subject, was followed by a 'structuralist' reaction, when Claude Lévi-Strauss and Roland Barthes foregrounded anonymous structures that transcended and determined the self. Moving on at pace, so the narrative goes, these ideas were challenged by a range of post-structuralists, most prominently Jacques Derrida but also Gilles Deleuze, Luce Irigaray and Julia Kristeva. The 'post-structuralists' added a dash of Nietzsche to the staid structuralist mix, which tended to dissolve certainties and unsettle the structures that earlier scholars had described.

Despite the attractive simplicity of this narrative, it quickly runs into difficulties. Several figures are hard to place. Are Jacques Lacan and Louis Althusser structuralists or post-structuralists? It is generally assumed that we can distinguish between an early and late Michel Foucault. But in a 1983 interview that is well beyond his putative break with structuralism, Foucault rejected 'post-structuralist' as a description of his work.[1] Even the archetypal post-structuralist, Jacques Derrida, refused the label.[2]

To a certain extent, such refusals should be understood as a salutary suspicion of -isms. Intellectuals are often reluctant to let their ideas be reduced to slogans, or to be seen as just one of a group. And certainly, if we take post-structuralism to be a school with a rigid set of doctrines that have to be accepted without question, it is clear that there is no such thing. But the French aversion to 'post-structuralism' cannot be attributed solely to intellectual self-assertion. Foucault's rejection is telling on this point. The 1983 interview opened with a query about the origin of 'post-structuralism'.[3]

Foucault, however, simply ignored the question, only returning to the term in passing later on. Instead, he focused his analysis on 'structuralism'. For him, this latter term, though equally objectionable as a label for his work, at least had a meaning one could discuss.

That Foucault was more familiar with 'structuralism' than 'post-structuralism' is instructive. At the time, the term *post-structuralisme* was hardly ever used in France.[4] Rather it found traction predominantly in America, when a range of academics began to grapple with a new generation of French thinkers. As the historian of ideas Vincent Descombes noted in 1991, 'it so happens that what goes in France under the label "structuralist philosophy" is known in the U.S.A. as "post-structuralist philosophy". Just by crossing the Atlantic, the very same book that was still considered of structuralist vintage when it left Saint-Germain-des-Prés would be recategorized as poststructuralist.'[5] The form of the word 'post-structuralism' thus sits uneasily with its referent. The relationship of post-structuralism and structuralism is not one of supersession but of translation. To understand the emergence and meaning of 'post-structuralism', therefore, we first need to analyse the French word it was meant to render in English.

Structuralism in France: a polemical unity

Unlike *post-structuralisme*, the term *structuralisme* had considerable currency in 1960s France. In July 1967, the influential magazine, the *Quinzaine Littéraire*, published an essay by François Châtelet, 'Où en est le structuralisme?' which featured a now famous cartoon by Maurice Henry: 'The Structuralists' Lunch Party'. The cartoon depicted Foucault, Lacan, Lévi-Strauss and Barthes sitting in a circle amidst palm trees and dressed in grass skirts, a reference to the type of society many associated with Lévi-Strauss's anthropology.[6] The resonance of the word *structuralisme* cannot simply be seen as an effect of vulgarization in the popular press. Some of the most important French-language philosophy journals – such as *Esprit* (1963), the *Revue Internationale de Philosophie* (1965) and *Les Temps Modernes* (1966) – published special editions on structuralism in the 1960s, and that decade saw the appearance of a range of books that sought to define the movement, from Jean Piaget's idiosyncratic 'Que sais-je' volume to the more substantial *Qu'est-ce que le structuralisme?* edited by the philosopher François Wahl.

Despite the widespread use of the term, few thought that the structuralist movement cohered. The *Quinzaine Littéraire* article began by acknowledging its variety and complexity and reached the conclusion that 'only a very hasty reading, one can see, can constitute a doctrinal body called "structuralism"'.[7] The divergences were foregrounded in Henry's cartoon, which was hardly the picture of a genial get-together. Foucault is trying to speak, but he is confronted by Barthes's stony expression and Lacan's defensive scepticism; Lévi-Strauss does not appear to be listening at all. The worry that 'structuralism' might involve a number of scholars talking past each other pervades the literature. In the introduction to his edited volume, Wahl felt compelled to ask the question, 'Does structuralism exist?' and was sceptical that one could identify a common approach.[8] Others were equally unconvinced. Foucault complained in the pages of the *Quinzaine Littéraire* on 1 March 1968 that 'structuralism is a category which exists for other people, people who aren't in it ... We ourselves don't see any unity.'[9]

If there was a unity to structuralism then, it was a weak or thinly coherent one. Rather than a school, it is better to consider structuralism as a diverse appeal to a shared set of sources, the most important of which was Ferdinand de Saussure's 1916 *Course on General Linguistics*. In that text, Saussure had made a number of claims whose implications would be enthusiastically debated almost half a century later. First, he had shifted analytic focus from linguistic reference to linguistic structures. A word's meaning arose not from the relationship between a 'signifier' (the sound pattern 'tree') and a 'signified' (the concept of a tree), but rather thanks to a homology between the differences between signifiers (the word 'tree' sounds different from 'plant' and 'leaf') and the differences between the signified objects (tree, plant and leaf). The upshot of this argument was that the sign was 'arbitrary', and a different signifier could take its place as long as the structure of differences was maintained.[10] Second, these structures had to be understood 'synchronically'. Since meaning was produced according to the set of relations between signifiers, the history of a language (diachronic change) was irrelevant to its meaning. Saussure argued his point by comparing language to a game of chess. Certainly it was interesting to understand how a game had developed up until a particular point, but that history was irrelevant to the next move.[11] Third, Saussure's structures exceeded and determined the individual. It was not possible for any single person to shape his or her language. Rather the structure of a language constrained what an individual could say and how.[12]

The Saussurian revival can be traced back to the anthropologist Lévi-Strauss. Fleeing France in 1941, he had learnt about Saussure in New York from the Czech linguist Roman Jakobson.[13] Saussure's structuralism then informed Lévi-Strauss's 1949 thesis, the *Elementary Structures of Kinship*, where he argued that marriage choices were not entirely free or determined by individual preferences. Rather they were the effects of a shared set of structures that distinguished appropriate from inappropriate partners. Lévi-Strauss based his work on the study of non-Western societies, which he quickly came to present not as inferior or undeveloped, but as privileged means for grasping the universal structures of human thought.[14] Though Lévi-Strauss rejected the idea that there was any natural logic to these structures – for instance, he argued that the incest taboo could not be explained by biology, just as Saussure argued that words could not be explained by their referent – he did think that these social structures could be explained by the architecture of the human brain.[15]

Lévi-Strauss introduced Saussure to his friend, the psychoanalyst Lacan, who incorporated Saussure's ideas in his famous 'Rome Report' from 1953. There he posited what he called the 'symbolic' realm as the foundation of psychoanalysis. When Lacan argued that the unconscious was 'structured like a language' he meant language understood in Saussure's sense, one that preceded and shaped the ego.[16] The literary critic Barthes picked up structuralist ideas in his 1957 book *Mythologies* in order to redirect attention from the manifest meaning of cultural products to a latent and often ideological one. In his famous example, the cover of *Paris-Match* depicted a young black soldier saluting the tricolour flag, but it also carried the mythological signification of a colour-blind French Empire, which was all the more powerful because it was implicit, and thus shielded from rational scrutiny.[17] Finally, in his 1962 *History of Madness*, Foucault suggested that human reason was not a reflection of the world, but rather a result of the suppression of madness.[18] Foucault expanded the scope of this argument in his *Order of Things* from 1966, where he laid out a stadial history of different epistemic structures that were independent and determinative of the subject.[19]

Whatever the parallels between these projects, it was clear that structuralism was more a set of debates and questions than a coherent set of ideas. One of the major divides was disciplinary. The early structuralists worked in a variety of fields: anthropology, psychoanalysis, literary criticism and the history of ideas. In the 1960s, structuralism started to make inroads into philosophy. In 1964, Lacan began to teach a seminar for philosophy students at the École Normale Supérieure, one of the most important institutions of higher learning in France.[20] He had been invited by Althusser, the director of studies in philosophy, who also embraced a 'structuralist' approach in his reading of Marx.[21]

The transfer was not without its problems. Althusser and his students were savagely critical of Lévi-Strauss for seeing primitive societies as windows into men's souls, and thus naturalizing certain social forms, a classic gesture of ideology. Moreover this contravened structuralist principles, they thought, because it led Lévi-Strauss to think that social structures were rooted in brain biology.[22] Similarly, they resisted Foucault because they thought that his appeal to a foundational suppression of madness came close to being an 'origin' of rational structures.[23] For them, the whole point of structuralism was that it eschewed the idea of an origin or 'centre' in the same way that it eschewed the idea that signifiers could be explained by their referents.

It was in this context that Derrida first came to read and think through structuralist ideas. We should note the contingent nature of Derrida's engagement. Before 1963 he had been interested primarily in phenomenology, but the rapid rise of structuralist ideas in the 1960s made them unavoidable, and several of Derrida's early essays engaged with structuralism, challenging the idea that structures were atemporal and fixed, often through an appeal to Nietzsche.[24] The pressure to grapple with structuralism intensified when Derrida entered the École Normale Supérieure in 1964 to teach the history of philosophy. There he confronted Althusser's reading of structuralism, which, coupled with Lacan's, had left its mark on a generation of students. The structuralist enthusiasm at the École lends context to Derrida's most extensive engagement with structuralist ideas: his essays and then book *Of Grammatology* from 1965–66 and 1967, which included long treatments of both Saussure and Lévi-Strauss.

As I have shown elsewhere, Derrida's position in these essays is complicated, and is best understood as a critical engagement with the Althusserians, his colleagues and students at the ENS, rather than with Lévi-Strauss, a scholar working at another institution.[25] It is true that Derrida follows Althusser and his students in criticizing Lévi-Strauss's nostalgia for the 'primitive'.[26] But for Derrida that nostalgia manifested itself in the drawing of a sharp line between primitive and advanced societies, and by extension nature and culture, and thereby skated over the deficiencies of the former that had encouraged the development of the latter. That is why, in contrast to the Althusserians, Derrida praised Lévi-Strauss's desire to ground cultural structures in the brain. Here, Lévi-Strauss worked to deconstruct the ideological nature/culture distinction, to which Derrida thought Althusser and his students remained beholden.[27] Rather than exclude all appeals to nature, Derrida argued that we should fold that nature into our analyses. This argument leads up to Derrida's most famous catchphrase. Because a supposedly original and pristine speech (like a supposedly original and pristine nature) was wracked with the same tensions as writing (or culture), Derrida could argue that 'there is nothing outside of the text'.[28]

As the triangular attacks between Althusser, Lévi-Strauss and Derrida show, intellectual life in France was riven by a number of debates where the very meaning of structuralism was in question. And yet these divisions should not be seen as weaknesses. Rather they allowed structuralism to become the unsurpassable philosophy of its time. It was sufficiently capacious to encompass a vast range of thinkers, and amorphous enough to resist easy refutation. There could be no 'post-structuralism' in France, because it was unclear what it would mean to leave structuralism behind.

Reading Derrida in America

The intellectual effervescence in France raised the profile of structuralism in America. France had amassed significant cultural capital in the United States since the end of the Second World War, thanks to the international reputations of Sartre and other existentialists, whose work had attracted the interest of literary scholars.[29] Americans were so caught up in the thrall of existentialism that the more academic philosophical developments of the French 1950s registered little in the American imagination. But the rise of new structuralist criticisms of existentialism made French thought relevant again, especially in literary circles. Moreover, Lévi-Strauss's account of human difference and attempt to move beyond ethnocentrism resonated in American society, which was in the throes of the civil rights and the anti-war movements. When the *New York Times Magazine* published a profile on Lévi-Strauss in January 1968, it bore the title 'There are No Superior Societies'.[30]

In the summer of 1965, René Girard, a historian and literary critic, who was at that time a professor at the Johns Hopkins University, wrote a letter to the director of the Humanities and Arts section of the Ford Foundation. Girard bemoaned the fact that structuralism had not found a foothold on this side of the Atlantic, and attributed this failure to the lack of inter-disciplinary institutions. For this reason, Girard sought funding for a 'structuralist section' at the newly founded Johns Hopkins Humanities Center and proposed two conferences as well as a 'Distinguished Visiting Professorship in Structuralism'.[31] With $36,000 in funds forthcoming, the first conference was planned for October the following year. The thirty-five-year-old organizer, Richard Macksey, hoped to include a range of younger scholars in addition to established voices, and (probably on the advice of Hegel scholar Jean Hyppolite), reached out to Derrida in April 1966.

Derrida's presentation at the conference, 'Structure, Sign, and Play', had a dual and only apparently contradictory effect: it foregrounded Derrida's engagement with structuralism at the expense of his other intellectual interests, and it tended to reduce his ambivalent treatment to a simple critique. The very fact that Derrida was included in the conference reinforced the impression he was a member of the structuralist family. Given the goals of the conference organizers, Derrida chose to present on Lévi-Strauss, and he formulated his paper in structuralist terms. Thus, what was in fact only a passing interest for Derrida – after the paper he never engaged with Lévi-Strauss at length again – came to shape the American reception of his work.

At the same time, the American context of the conference gave Derrida's critique a sharper edge. In his 'Structure, Sign, and Play', Derrida made a set of arguments that were very close to the ones he had made in the almost contemporaneous 'Grammatology' articles: he criticized Lévi-Strauss's nostalgia for primitive societies, and yet praised his breakdown of the nature/culture division, which counted as an attack on the Althusserians.[32] In Baltimore, however, Althusser was not yet well known and so the latter intervention was illegible. Participants focused rather on Derrida's challenge to Lévi-Strauss's nostalgia, seeing it as a criticism of structuralism in general, even though, as we saw, it had been first deployed by Althusser to impugn Lévi-Strauss's structuralist credentials. Derrida encouraged the idea that he was breaking with Lévi-Strauss and structuralism in the closing moments of his paper: he described the 'as yet unnameable which is announcing itself and which can do so, as is necessary whenever a birth is in the offing, only under the species of the nonspecies, in the formless, mute, infant, and terrifying form of monstrosity'.[33] Derrida might have been riffing off the way he had been presented in the conference programme. Derrida's paper was scheduled for the final day, and, due to his late inclusion, it did not yet have a title. The programme merely offered the promissory note: 'to be announced'.[34]

Thanks to the Baltimore conference, Americans saw Derrida as both more and less of a structuralist than was possible in France. Initially the former impression dominated. After the conference, Macksey continued to refer to Derrida as one of the 'structuralist gang'.[35] American academics approached Derrida through his relationship to structuralism, and they tended to overlook his phenomenological work. Even when American scholars focused on Derrida's criticism of structuralism, they considered him significant to the extent that he participated in and 'deconstructed' the structuralist tradition. In his 1971 essay, 'Abecedarium culturae: Structuralism, Absence, Writing', Edward Said presented Derrida as a structuralist, and indeed shaped his reading of structuralism in terms that foreshadowed the discussion of Derrida's work. As he wrote, 'at bottom structuralism is a set of attitudes to and of writing: grammatology'.[36] Conversely, Derrida merited mention 'in an essay on structuralism because his work is a critique, by grotesque explication, of the structuralists'.[37] Even Gayatri Chakravorty Spivak, in her enormously influential introduction to the English translation of *Of Grammatology* (1976), posed the question: 'Can Derrida – substituting the structure of writing (the sign "sous rature") for the structure of the sign – simply be dubbed a grammatological structuralist historian of philosophy, and there an end?' To which she answered, 'no doubt', before going to suggest that in replacing the sign by writing, the sign 'under erasure', his work would 'deconstruct structuralism'.[38] As late as 1979, in his popular book on structuralism, John Sturrock presented Derrida as a member of the movement, even if he admitted that Derrida refused the label.[39]

Over time, however, the latter impression of Derrida's work predominated, in large part because American scholars were all too willing to consign structuralism to the past. Indeed, the American reception of structuralism was, from the beginning, marked by a critical distance and caution. In the introduction to the 1966 edition of *Yale French Studies*, the first American volume dedicated to structuralism, the Yale professor Jacques Ehrmann chose a rather contrary epigraph: a line from the Polish writer Witold Gombrowicz, 'reality is not about to let itself be completely enclosed in form. Form for its part does not agree with the essence of life.' Ehrmann admonished his readers not to forget what eluded structuralism's grasp. In so far as the volume could be seen as an endorsement of structuralism, it was structuralism as a '*living* question', which encouraged 'a series of interrogations' that might even come to 'question structuralism itself'.[40]

Given this caution amongst its proponents, structuralism did not make significant inroads into English-speaking academia. As late as 1972, in their anthology *The Structuralists*, Fernande M. de George and Richard T. de George could present the future of structuralism only in aspirational terms. As they wrote, 'structuralism promises an intellectual revolution in the social sciences, the humanities and the arts. Whether the revolution will be successful, only time will tell. It is at present a promise in search of its fulfilment.'[41] At the same time other scholars were foretelling its demise. In his 1972 book *The Prison-House of Language*, Fredric Jameson argued that 'a genuine critique of Structuralism commits us to working our way completely through it so as to emerge, on the other side, into some wholly different and theoretically more satisfying philosophical perspective', one that would 'reopen text and analytic process alike to all the winds of history'.[42]

In his book, Jameson followed the consensus at the time and presented Derrida as a structuralist, even arguing that Derrida's triple publication of 1967 marked structuralism's 'zenith'.[43] Jameson did argue that Derrida had come to discern the limits of structuralism and thus had engaged in a 'structuralist critique of structuralism'. This was, however, by no means a break from it. Derrida's work, Jameson wrote, 'feels its way gropingly along the walls of its own conceptual prison, describing it from the inside as though it were only one of the possible worlds of which the others are nonetheless inconceivable'.[44] Derrida might have realized that he was caught in the structuralists' prison-house of language, but he had lost hope of ever escaping.

For others, however, growing misgivings about structuralism encouraged them to take Derrida's reading of Lévi-Strauss as a critical breakthrough. We can follow this changing understanding of Derrida's relationship to structuralism by examining the titles of the Baltimore conference and its proceedings. The conference was originally given the title 'Languages of Criticism and the Sciences of Man'. By the time the papers were published in 1970, however, and in large part due to the growing fame of Derrida's contribution, the editors Macksey and Donato added the subtitle 'The Structuralist Controversy', which was promoted to the title for the 1972 paperback edition. In the new preface, '1971: The Space Between', the editors suggested that the republication of the volume deserved a word of explanation because by then 'the very existence of structuralism as a meaningful concept' was in question.[45] They noted that linguistics had been dislodged from its earlier dominant position, and a resurgent Nietzscheanism had upset structuralism's scientific pretensions. By 1971, at least according to the editors of the volume, structuralism was dead, and something new had taken its place.

The idea that structuralism was now a thing of the past guided Donato's 1973 essay for *SubStance*: 'Structuralism: The Aftermath'. According to Donato, Derrida had undermined the central pillars of Saussure's linguistics – the sign and difference – such that 'after Derrida's analysis ... a certain number of [structuralist] concepts become inoperative as analytical tools'. In marking this breakdown, Donato labelled Derrida as one of the 'fanatics of the apocalypse ... one could hardly hope for more [a] appropriate [thinker] for the times we live in'.[46]

In a short space of time, then, Americans came to revise their understanding of Derrida; he went from being an unruly structuralist to being someone who marked the movement's end, a 'post-structuralist'. As such, his work contributed to the impression that French intellectual life was fast-paced and changing. In one of the first anthologies dedicated to the movement from 1979, *Textual Strategies: Perspectives in Post-Structuralist Criticism*, Josué Harari opens with this sense of disorientation and constant change: 'listening to the talk of Parisian intellectual circles often brings to mind Rica's unhappy refrain from Montesquieu's *Persian Letters*: "A woman who quits Paris to go and spend six months in the country comes back as antique as if she had sequestered herself there for thirty years."'[47] As the person who had compiled one of the earliest bibliographies of structuralism only eight years earlier, one might well imagine that Harari was talking about himself.[48]

Deconstruction, the 'New Criticism' and the problem of history

If in the American imagination Derrida had indeed broken through and out of structuralism, there was no consensus about how he had done it. The divergence can be attributed to the way in which Anglophone critics grafted structuralism onto their own intellectual history. One of the reasons that scholars had been so eager to predict structuralism's demise was that they associated it with a home-grown formalism that by the 1970s was widely considered to be on its way out. As we shall see, scholars in Britain and the United States embraced Derrida because they saw him as an ally in their struggle against the 'New Criticism'.

The New Criticism had developed in the 1930s in response to an older form of historically minded literary scholarship. Rather than placing literary works into their political and social contexts, the New Critics undertook an internal formal analysis to reveal the work's aesthetic aspects. The turn away from history as an explanatory device coincided with a turn towards poetry as a privileged object of study because, of all literary forms, poetry seemed the most untouched by external forces. The goals of the New Criticism were in part disciplinary, an attempt to assert the singularity and independence of literature as a scholarly field. But New Criticism also involved political gestures. It was democratic – one did not need specialist knowledge to read texts, only a book and some time – and it simultaneously fostered an elitist sensibility in the sense that it required analytic brilliance. The New Critics valued the virtuosic analysis of a poem, which by identifying tensions and contradictions could, with a theatrical flourish, reconcile them in a final organic unity.

The idea that structuralism was a European analogue of the New Criticism has a long history. The connection can be traced back to René Wellek and Austin Warren's *Theory of Literature* (1949), which was widely used as a university textbook in the 1950s and 1960s.[49] The parallel also crops up across the early discussions of structuralism.[50] It is telling that in Jonathan Culler's 1975 *Structuralist Poetics*, the fullest and most influential attempt to construct an Anglophone structuralism (at least in the humanities), he felt compelled to counter the association on the first page.[51] This is not to say that most scholars identified the two; it was widely agreed that structuralism did not attribute the same status to poetry, and that it had different disciplinary commitments. Nevertheless, on the whole American academics saw in structuralism the same flaws they saw in the New Criticism, and so they sought to overcome the former for the same reasons they had criticized the latter.

For one influential group of scholars, the New Criticism and structuralism alike needed to be supplemented with a greater sensitivity to history.

Take Jameson's main argument. He claimed that structuralism, like the New Criticism, had failed because it had emphasized the synchronic and thus had been insufficiently attentive to temporal phenomena.[52] Jameson's proposed alternative to structuralism would reconcile 'the twin, apparently incommensurable, demands of synchronic analysis and historical awareness, of structure and self-consciousness, language and history'.[53]

Jameson did not see Derrida as part of the solution, but, as Mark Currie has recently shown, history became one of the guiding if contested themes of Derrida's first reception in America.[54] In Alexander Gelley's review of *Of Grammatology* for *Diacritics* from 1972, he argued that Derrida's work seemed 'to clear a new path for the historical study of cultural and philosophical concepts', and claimed that 'in contrast to many contemporary structuralists … he views this "formal organization which in itself has no sense" as susceptible to historical delineation'.[55] Gelley made clear that Derrida's argument could also be turned against the New Critics, and he claimed that Derrida had contributed to the process of breaking down the distinction between literary and non-literary texts, which had been a central plank of the New Critics' rejection of history. Derrida's ideas would thus allow the 'historical' to 'recover a central role in literary studies' even if it meant that it would 'require a revision of traditional forms of literary history'.[56]

We can see a similar move in Frank Lentricchia's 1980 book, *After the New Criticism*. Derrida had introduced a 'play' into signifying structures, which, Lentricchia thought, necessitated an appeal to historical forces. The key questions that needed to be asked, Lentricchia declared, were 'what discharges of power, under what networks of guidance, to what ends, and in what temporal and cultural loci have semiological systems been produced?' Lentricchia nonetheless thought that Derrida's openness to history was ultimately insufficient, and at times came close to an all-encompassing argument, where 'the environments (intellectual, social, political, etc.) of Plato, Descartes, Rousseau, and Lévi-Strauss are reassuringly interchangeable'. For these reasons he found it 'difficult to see … why Derrida's and others' attacks on structuralism for its courting of formalism and historical aridity do not apply to Derrida as well'.[57]

Lentricchia's reluctance to embrace Derrida fully can be explained by the fact that in the late 1970s when he was completing the book, he felt compelled to confront another self-proclaimed successor to the New Criticism, which had also co-opted the French thinker, but which understood Derrida's relationship to history in a very different way: the Yale School.[58] The core of the 'Yale School' was a group of four professors who taught at the Ivy League university: Harold Bloom, Geoffrey Hartman, Paul de Man and J. Hillis Miller. Like Lentricchia, the Yale School also positioned their work in opposition to the New Criticism, but rather than articulating their difference in terms of history, they aimed their challenge at the New Critics' teleological goal of reconciliation.[59] Thus while the Yale School resembled the New Critics in their focus on internal and formalist readings of a text, they presented the tensions and aporias that such readings revealed not as an intermediary moment before their harmonization in an organic whole, but rather as the end point of the analysis, which revealed the polysemy of literary texts.

The person who did most to link the new Yale School to Derrida's deconstruction was Paul de Man. De Man had written one of the earliest accounts of Derrida's work in the 1972 volume *Blindness and Insight*. The overall thesis of de Man's book was that texts often cultivated meanings that clashed with their explicit aims and that it was the role of the critic to draw out the insight to which the author had been blind.[60] The argument was a retort to the New Critics because it sought to pull down the barriers that had separated literary language from everyday language, and that had allowed critics to consider the former as immune to 'duplicity ... confusion ... and untruth'.[61] And again, while de Man was attentive to the differences, his major criticism of the New Criticism coincided with his major criticism of structuralism: both tended to reify form as harmony and forget the 'temporal structure of the act of interpretation'.[62] As de Man argued in an essay that had originally appeared in the French journal *Critique* in 1956, structuralist criticism, especially the work of Barthes, approached a 'formalism that, appearances notwithstanding, is not that different from New Criticism'.[63] Again, as for Lentricchia, Derrida played a privileged role in this argument, and de Man introduced him as a philosopher who had brought disruptive close reading to self-consciousness. In Derrida's work, de Man assured the reader, 'the discrepancy implicitly present in the other critics ... becomes the explicit centre of the reflection'.[64]

While Lentricchia thought that Derrida had opened up a new path to historical analysis but had been unable to take it himself, de Man argued that Derrida's sensitivity to discrepancy had been dulled because he remained wedded to a particular conception of history. According to de Man, Derrida had 'narrated' the repression of written language 'as a consecutive, historical process'. But for de Man – and this was, he thought, the insight to which Derrida was blind – the 'historical scheme is merely a narrative convention'.[65] This argument was also picked up by de Man's colleague J. Hillis Miller in his 1974 article 'Narrative and History'.[66] When the veteran literary critic M. H. Abrams complained that according to 'deconstructionist principles ... any history which relies on written texts becomes an impossibility', Miller responded, 'so be it. That is not much of an argument'.[67]

The debates over Derrida's relationship to history were soon invested with political meaning. As we have seen Jameson had attacked Derrida for being caught in the structuralists' 'prison-house of language'. Terry Eagleton developed this argument in his 1984 book, *The Function of Criticism*, which argued that deconstruction had blunted the political edge of literary studies. Derrida's claim that there was nothing outside of the text quashed all hope of something fundamentally new, and so encouraged acquiescence to existing forms of domination. This complaint was not restricted to Marxists. Edward Said made a similar criticism in his preface to the 1985 re-edition of his *Beginnings*. It was also the central argument in Lentricchia's book. In cutting themselves off from history the Yale critics had also cut themselves off from politics.

It would be wrong, however, to see this as a debate between political Marxists concerned with real history and the apolitical Yale School who concentrated on textual aporia. Rather it is better understood as a clash of different versions of politics. Jameson, Lentricchia and Eagleton criticized Derrida from a Marxist or quasi-Marxist perspective. But the Yale critics they attacked saw their work as a response to the political questions of the time, especially around what might loosely be called identity politics.[68] They argued that the New Critics had cut off their work from the political ferment occurring in America in the 1960s. Thus, for them, the attentiveness to aporia and contradiction provided a means to invest their readings with the type of political meaning that they noted had engulfed American society. Deconstructive reading could challenge racial, gender and sexual hierarchies, and thus participate in the broader political activism of the age.[69] This political reading of Derrida (and post-structuralism more generally) as a deconstruction of ethnocentrism, sexism and patriarchy was developed more fully and consistently by a younger generation of scholars including Gayatri Chakravorty Spivak, Joan Wallach Scott and Judith Butler amongst others.

The ever-expanding post-structuralist movement

The short-lived, but consequential, reading of deconstruction as a historical corrective to structuralism allowed scholars to include other French thinkers in the movement. Though in the 1960s and early 1970s Foucault had been often cited as a structuralist,[70] now he was paired with Derrida as a 'post-structuralist', who sought to root the types of structures described by Lévi-Strauss and the early Barthes within a broader historical moment. As Lentricchia put it, Derrida's work was solidary with the 'poststructuralist writings of Michel Foucault'; both thinkers sought 'to uncover the nonontological reincarceration of the signifier within cultural matrices'.[71]

The emphasis on disruption, characteristic of the Yale School, also allowed Foucault's inclusion under the rubric of 'post-structuralism', but in a different way. Donato, for instance, saw a relationship between Derrida's emphasis on temporality and Nietzschean themes in Foucault's work, ones that troubled the archaeological metaphor that had structured the latter's book, *The Order of Things*.[72] This argument became easier to make after the publication of Foucault's 'genealogical' texts from the mid 1970s, especially *Discipline and Punish*, which some scholars figured as a response to Derrida's criticisms.[73] Similar arguments, starting with Derrida at the core and building out to include other French thinkers, allowed American scholars to grow the movement. In his 1979 anthology, Harari identified the later Roland Barthes, Gérard Genette, and Gilles Deleuze, amongst others as 'post-structuralists'. Harari was attacked for privileging an 'international "old boy" fraternity', and neglecting women like Kristeva and Irigaray, on the French side, and Spivak and Shoshana Felman on the American.[74] By the early 1980s all the above were regularly mentioned in overviews of the movement.

While some sought to use post-structuralism as a way of categorizing an upcoming generation in France, others expanded its reach further into the past. As we have seen, Derrida had emerged as a post-structuralist in the American reading, because the mechanics of transatlantic transfer recast his passing engagement with structuralist ideas as both identification and radical critique. The same could be said of Foucault, who considered himself *neither* a structuralist *nor* a post-structuralist. In the American imagination, however, he was *both and*. As Hayden White argued in a 1972 article on Foucault, 'what makes him a post-Structuralist, not to say anti-Structuralist, thinker is the fact that he turns this interpretative strategy upon the human sciences in general and on Structuralism itself in particular'.[75] From this point of view, then, structuralism had contained the seeds of its own destruction; there was *post*-structuralism from the beginning. In his 1981 *Post-Structuralist Reader*, Robert Young generalized this argument: 'Structuralism as an origin never existed in a pre-lapsarian purity or ontological fullness: post-structuralism traces the trace of structuralism's difference from itself.'[76] As late as 1986 John Sturrock could argue that 'post-structuralism is not "post" in the sense of having killed Structuralism off, it is "post" only in the sense of coming after and of seeking to extend Structuralism in its rightful direction'.[77] The result was that many of the figures previously associated with structuralism, including Althusser and Lacan, could be welcomed into the post-structuralist camp.

The difficulty of drawing a clean line between structuralism and post-structuralism, separating structuralists from post-structuralists, meant that many did not even try. In the 1970s, the two terms were often uttered in the same breath, as a shorthand for the intellectual activity in the French capital.[78] The multiple and mutual implications of structuralism and post-structuralism led the critic David Harland to coin the term 'superstructuralism' in his 1987 book of the same name, which covered both structuralism and its post-structuralist heirs.[79]

Some took this argument one step further, challenging not only the idea of a clear dividing line between structuralism and post-structuralism, but also the idea of a simple chronological relationship. As Harari wrote:

> Without blurring the issues, we could say that whatever came after structuralism and transformed it was also, and at the same time, *before* it (without any exaggeration, one can trace the tradition which questions logocentrism back to Nietzsche), *with* it (the example of the two Barthes), and as a *counterpoint* to it (Lévi-Strauss versus Derrida, for instance).[80]

The Derrida scholar Geoff Bennington concurred: '[I]t is already a historical simplification to assume that post-structuralism simply comes *after* structuralism.'[81]

The most concrete consequence of this disengagement from traditional temporal schemes is that Anglo-American scholars granted themselves licence to search for post-structuralists even further into the past and even further afield. Alongside Nietzsche, Martin Heidegger and Maurice Merleau-Ponty were added to the canon. Sturrock tied the history of post-structuralism back to the critics of Russian formalism in the interwar period: 'Without knowing it, and well ahead of time, Bakhtin and Medvedev here inaugurate the age of post-Structuralism.'[82] Gathering together a range of historically and geographically distant thinkers, post-structuralism started to cut its historical anchoring to structuralism, and it became easier to see it as an autonomous movement. In its heyday in the 1980s and 1990s, 'post-structuralism' was no longer necessarily defined by its relationship to structuralism. Indeed one could argue that the development of 'post-structuralism' as a 'method' (though that word was often taboo) applicable to a range of different fields was reliant on the fact that it had been detached from historicist narratives.

Conclusion

In France, structuralism was too robust and too diverse to be easily dispatched. Structuralism was a space in which debates took place, and a common set of sources that could be read in a variety of ways. It was possible to ignore structuralism, but it was difficult to overcome it, because it remained unclear what structuralism actually was. In order for structuralism to earn its post-prefix, the internal intellectual tensions that had animated it in France would need to be recast as decisive and revolutionary critique. This occurred in two ways: first by transporting structuralism to America, and second by associating it with an intellectual movement, the New Criticism, that many had already declared to be obsolete. In this way, Derrida's short-lived and contingent articulation of structuralism's fault lines in France was heard in America as the rallying cry for a new intellectual movement. And yet just because Americans felt able to treat structuralism as surpassed did not mean that it was now beyond debate, and how precisely post-structuralism had overcome its structuralist predecessor remained an object of intense discussion, a debate that powered a rapid inflation of the term to cover an ever-larger and more disparate groups of thinkers. For if history is not, as the Yale School argued, simply a fictitious narrative, neither is it, as their critics thought, a refuge from the interpretative dilemmas of literature. When we examine the reception of (post-)structuralism in America we realize that the post-prefix designates not a temporal relationship, but rather a historical problem.

Notes

1 Gérard Raulet, 'Structuralism and Post-Structuralism: An Interview with Michel Foucault', *Telos*, 55 (1983), 205.
2 Jacques Derrida, 'Marx and Sons', in Michael Sprinker (ed.), *Ghostly Demarcations: A Symposium on Jacques Derrida's Spectres of Marx* (London: Verso, 1999), p. 229.
3 Raulet, 'Structuralism and Post-Structuralism', 195.
4 For the difficulty of identifying 'post-structuralism' in France, see Johannes Angermüller, *Why There Is No Post-Structuralism in France* (London: Bloomsbury, 2015). Angermüller provides a helpful institutional analysis of the rise and fall of what he calls the 'structuralist generation'.
5 Vincent Descombes, 'Philosophy and Anthropology after Structuralism', *Paragraph*, 14 (1991), 217.
6 François Châtelet, 'Où en est le structuralisme?', *Quinzaine Littéraire* (1 July 1967).
7 Ibid.
8 François Wahl, 'Introduction', in *Qu'est-ce que le structuralisme?* (Paris: Éditions de Seuil, 1968), p. 8.
9 Michel Foucault, *Quinzaine Littéraire* (1 March 1968).
10 Ferdinand de Saussure, *Course on General Linguistics* (London: P. Owen, 1960), p. 116.
11 Ibid., pp. 87–8.

12 Ibid., p. 71.
13 François Dosse, *A History of Structuralism*, trans. Deborah Glassman, vol. 1. (Minneapolis, MN: University of Minnesota Press, 1997), p. 11.
14 See, for instance, Claude Lévi-Strauss, *La pensée sauvage* (Paris: Plon, 1962).
15 See, for instance, Lévi-Strauss, *Le totémisme aujourd'hui* (Paris: Presses Universitaires de France, 1962), p. 130.
16 See Jacques Lacan, *Ecrits: A Selection*, trans. Bruce Fink (New York: W. W. Norton, 2006), p. 205. See also, in the same volume, 'The Mirror Stage as Formative of the Function of the I as Revealed in Psychoanalytic Experience'.
17 See especially Roland Barthes, 'Myth Today', in Barthes, *Mythologies*, trans. Annette Lavres (New York: Hill and Wang, 1972), pp. 225–6.
18 Michel Foucault, *Madness and Civilization: A History of Insanity in the Age of Reason*, trans. Richard Howard (New York: Vintage Books, 1973).
19 Michel Foucault, *The Order of Things: An Archaeology of the Human Sciences*, trans. Alan Sheridan (New York: Pantheon Books, 1971).
20 See Dosse, *History of Structuralism*, vol. 1, p. 240.
21 See Louis Althusser et al., *Reading Capital* (New York: Verso, 1971).
22 See, for instance, Louis Althusser, 'On Lévi-Strauss', in Althusser, *The Humanist Controversy and Other Writings*, trans. G. M. Goghgarian (London: Verso, 2003).
23 See Louis Althusser, 'Séminaire 1962–3', in ALT 2 A40–02.02 in IMEC Archives, Caen.
24 See, for example, Jacques Derrida, *l'Écriture et la différence* (Paris: Editions de Seuil, 1967), pp. 48–9.
25 See Edward Baring, 'Derrida, Lévi-Strauss, and the Cercle d'Epistémologie; Or, how to be a good Structuralist', in Peter Hallward and Knox Peden (eds), *Concept and Form*, vol. 2. (London: Verso, 2012).
26 See Jacques Derrida, *Of Grammatology*, trans. Gayatri Chakravorty Spivak (Baltimore, MD: Johns Hopkins University Press, 1976), p. 114.
27 Ibid., p. 105.
28 Ibid., p. 158.
29 See George Cotkin, *Existential America* (Baltimore, MD: Johns Hopkins University Press, 2003).
30 See Mark Greif, *The Age of the Crisis of Man* (Princeton, NJ: Princeton University Press, 2015), p. 305.
31 Girard to Stephen Koch, 7 June 1965, in Author Correspondence: Macksey, 'The Structuralist Controversy, 1965–71', The Johns Hopkins University Archives.
32 Jacques Derrida, *Writing and Difference*, trans. Alan Bass (Chicago, IL: University of Chicago Press, 1978), pp. 283–6, 292.
33 Ibid., p. 293 (translation amended).
34 'The Languages of Criticism and the Sciences of Man 1966–7 Final Draft', Symposia, Dean of Arts and Sciences, The Johns Hopkins University Archives.
35 R. M. to J. G. Goellner, 31 January 1968. Author Correspondence: Richard Macksey 'Velocities of Change', The Johns Hopkins University Archives.

36 Edward Said, 'Abecedarium culturae: Structuralism, Absence, Writing', *TriQuarterly*, 20 (1971), 53.

37 Ibid., 65.

38 Gayatri Chakravorty Spivak, 'Translator's Preface', in Derrida, *Of Grammatology*, pp. lv–lix.

39 John Sturrock, *Structuralism and Since* (Oxford: Oxford University Press, 1979), pp. 3–4.

40 It was published four years later as Ehrmann, 'Introduction', *Yale French Studies*, 36 (1970), vii, x–xi.

41 Richard de George and Fernande de George, 'Introduction', in Richard de George and Fernande de George (eds), *The Structuralists: From Marx to Lévi-Strauss* (New York: Anchor Books, 1972), p. xxix.

42 Fredric Jameson, *The Prison-House of Language* (Princeton, NJ: Princeton University Press, 1972), pp. v–vii, 214–16.

43 Ibid., p. ix.

44 Ibid., p. 186.

45 Richard Macksey (ed.), *The Structuralist Controversy* (Baltimore, MD: Johns Hopkins University Press, 1972), p. ix.

46 Eugenio Donato, 'Structuralism: The Aftermath', *SubStance*, 3:7 (1973), 22–5.

47 Josué Harari (ed.), *Textual Strategies: Perspectives in Post-Structuralist Criticism* (Ithaca, NY: Cornell University Press, 1979), p. 9.

48 See Josué Harari, *Structuralists and Structuralism: A Selected Bibliography of French Contemporary Thought* (Ithaca, NY: Cornell University Press, 1971).

49 René Wellek and Austin Warren, *Theory of Literature* (New York: Harcourt, 1949). The same could be said of the work of Northrup Frye, who drew on Lévi-Strauss in his 1957 reformulation of New Criticism, *Anatomy of Criticism* (Princeton, NJ: Princeton University Press, 1957).

50 See Said, 'Abecedarium', 57 and Jameson, *Prison-House of Language*, pp. 45–7.

51 See Jonathan Culler, *Structuralist Poetics* (Ithaca, NY: Cornell University Press, 1975), pp. vii–viii.

52 Jameson, *Prison-House of Language,* pp. 45–7.

53 Ibid., p. 216.

54 See Mark Currie, *The Invention of Deconstruction* (New York: Palgrave Macmillan, 2013), pp. 28–63.

55 Alexander Gelley, 'Form as Force', *Diacritics,* 2 (1972), 10.

56 Ibid., 12.

57 Frank Lentricchia, *After the New Criticism* (Chicago, IL: University of Chicago Press, 1980), pp. 174–7.

58 Ibid., pp. 159–73, 177–88.

59 For Currie, de Man's argument should be seen as a different articulation of the relationship between language and history rather than the denial of history. Currie, *Invention of Deconstruction*, p. 93.

60 Paul de Man, *Blindness and Insight,* trans. Wlad Godzich, 2nd edn (Minneapolis, MN: University of Minnesota Press, 1983), p. 103.

61 Ibid., p. 9.

62 Ibid. For de Man, structuralism helps overcome the privileging of the literary in New Criticism. See, for example, ibid., p. 107.

63 Ibid., pp. 230–1. On the point of reconciliation see also p. 245.

64 Ibid., pp. 110–11.

65 Ibid., pp. 137–8.

66 J. Hillis Miller, 'Narrative and History', *English Literary History*, 41 (1974), 460–1.

67 J. Hillis Miller, 'The Critic as Host', *Critical Inquiry*, 3 (1977), 439.

68 See the lively account in François Cusset, *French Theory*, trans. Jeff Fort (Minneapolis, MN: University of Minnesota Press, 2008), chapter 6.

69 See Currie, *Invention of Deconstruction*, chapter 1.

70 See, for instance, Michel Pierssens, 'Introduction', *SubStance*, 3:7 (1973), 3.

71 Lentricchia, *After the New Criticism*, p. 174.

72 Donato, 'Structuralism: The Aftermath', 17–25.

73 Allan Megill, 'Foucault, Structuralism, and the Ends of History', *The Journal of Modern History*, 51:3 (1979), 491.

74 Steven Ungar, review of Gérard Genette, *Narrative Discourse*, and Josué Harari (ed.) *Textual Strategies*, in *SubStance* 9:3 (1980), 98. Harari does include Kristeva in the movement in his introduction. *Textual Strategies*, p. 20.

75 Hayden White, 'Foucault Decoded', *History and Theory*, 12 (1972), 24.

76 Robert Young (ed.), *Untying the Text: A Post-Structuralist Reader* (London: Routledge, 1981), p. 1.

77 John Sturrock (ed.), *Structuralism* (London: Paladin, 1986), p. 137.

78 See, for instance, Jeffrey Mehlman, 'Portnoy in Paris', *Diacritics*, 2 (1972), 21; and Jonathan Culler, 'Derrida', in Sturrock (ed.), *Structuralism*, p. 155.

79 David Harland, *Superstructuralism* (New York: Methuen, 1987), p. 1.

80 Harari, *Textual Strategies*, p. 30.

81 Geoff Bennington, 'Introduction', in Bennington (ed.), *Poststructuralism and the Question of History* (Cambridge: Cambridge University Press, 1987), p. 8.

82 Sturrock, *Structuralism*, p. 136.

7

The 'post' in literary postmodernism: A history

Hans Bertens

Introduction

Postmodernism as a literary-critical concept has followed a complicated trajectory that, now that the once heated debates no longer generate much interest, cannot be said to have led to much general agreement as to what exactly it stands for. We have a Wittgensteinian family of narrative strategies and poetic techniques that are indeed generally seen as postmodern, but that is as far as critical agreement goes. It might therefore be tempting to dismiss this particular incarnation of the 'post'-phenomenon, but there are excellent grounds to resist that temptation. Although the terms 'postmodern' and 'postmodernism' had occasionally been used – in rather diverse settings – before they entered the literary-critical vocabulary, it is in literary studies that they first were used systematically, initially in discussions of new modes of writing in American post-war poetry and fiction, but then also in analyses of far wider cultural developments and, finally, in ambitious attempts to understand the 'postmodern' world that we supposedly inhabit. And it is also in literary studies that the writings of the French so-called poststructuralists – Jacques Derrida, Roland Barthes, Michel Foucault and others – had their first impact outside France and gave rise to what soon came to be called postmodern theory, a mode of literary criticism that was – and still is – enormously influential and has forced disciplines within and without the humanities to reflect on their own practices.

This chapter will trace the history and development of the concept, with the important caveat that any such history will inevitably be incomplete and sketchy. The *International Bibliography* of the Modern Language Association of America, the most comprehensive and authoritative bibliography in literary studies, lists at the time of writing 8,932 publications under 'postmodernism', another 7,042 under 'postmodern', and again another 4,630 under 'postmodernist'. No doubt there will be a good deal of overlap between these lists, but clearly the number of articles and books on literary postmodernism is overwhelming. I shall therefore limit myself to what seem to me the most pertinent or interesting contributions to the discussion about postmodernism as it unfolded.

Postmodern poetry

When we think of literary postmodernism we tend to think first of all of fiction, since it is in fiction that postmodernism has easily had the largest impact, both because poetry is relatively marginal compared to fiction and because postmodernism's narrative innovations were better suited to fiction. However, long before it was first applied to fiction, the term 'postmodern' had already gained some currency in American poetry criticism. In 1947 the American poet-critic Randall Jarrell used it in a review and in 1948 another poet, John Berryman, picked up Jarrell's term in another review. More importantly, from the early 1950s onward American poet Charles Olson used 'postmodern' repeatedly to describe his own poetry and that of a number of like-minded poets. Olson's use of the term would for a long time echo in discussions of contemporary American poetry. For Olson postmodern poetry does not so much distance itself from modernist poetry as from the whole Western tradition, a tradition led astray by the rationalistic heritage of classical philosophy. That rationalism stands between us and authentic experience, as Olson's Heideggerian distinction between 'language as the act of the instant and language as the act of thought about the instant' (originally published in 1951)[1] makes clear. Olson's postmodernism is premodern, or, to adopt his terminology, pre-West, rather than postmodern (see, for a full discussion, George F. Butterick).[2] Olson's existentialist perspective makes an even more radical appearance in the postmodernism of William Spanos, one of literary postmodernism's most prominent early champions. For Spanos, co-founder (in 1972) of the highly influential journal *boundary 2: a journal of postmodern literature* – probably the first journal devoted to postmodernism –

> it was the recognition of the ultimately 'totalitarian' implications of the Western structure of consciousness – of the expanding analogy that encompasses art, politics, and metaphysics in the name of the security of the rational order – that compelled the postmodern imagination to undertake the deliberate and systematic subversion of plot – the beginning, middle, and end structure – which has enjoyed virtually unchallenged supremacy of the Western literary imagination ever since Aristotle.[3]

As Spanos makes clear, however, postmodernism's 'strategy of de-composition'[4] that must strip 'its audience of positivized fugitives of their protective garments of rational explanation'[5] is not new. As was the case with Olson, Spanos's postmodernism is, in fact, not post-anything but typological. He sees signs of the postmodern resistance to 'the Western structure of consciousness' in modernism and finds a fully developed postmodern impulse throughout the history of Western literature – in, for instance, Euripides' *Orestes*, Shakespeare's 'problem plays', Dostoyevsky's *Notes from Underground*, Jarry's *Ubu Roi*, and Sartre's *La Nausée*.

In one of the first attempts to distinguish postmodern poetry more sharply from its modernist predecessor, another influential critic, Charles Altieri, invoking the authority of Olson (next to that of Kierkegaard and Heidegger), argues that whereas modernist poetics were 'informed almost entirely by the symbolist tradition', postmodern poets seek 'to uncover the ways in which man and nature are unified'.[6] Echoing Olson, Altieri tells us that for postmodernists 'value is not mediated but stems directly from a direct engagement with the universal forces of being manifest in the particular'.[7] A prerequisite for such an engagement is the prior destruction of 'human forms', which is exactly what postmodernism seeks to do: '"[d]ecreation" ... is a basic process for the postmodern arts',[8] a process that enables '[i]nfinite modes of authenticity'.[9] For Altieri's postmoderns, as it was for Olson, language 'is directly linked with the experience of things'.[10] Still, although Altieri distinguishes postmodernism sharply from a symbolist modernism, it does not so much react against modernism as against a long poetic tradition. What we see in Olson, Spanos and Altieri is an argument that has accompanied all major literary transitions of the last 250 years, summed up in Altieri's 'authenticity'. Postmodern poetry's representation of reality is superior to that of all earlier literary modes. It gives us direct access to authentic reality, allowing us to participate in authentic being. As we will see, the question of representation is never far away in discussions of literary postmodernism and becomes especially important when, in the course of the 1970s, the (mostly American) participants in those discussions begin to embrace what they call poststructuralism.

Let us stay for a moment with Altieri because he presents an instructive case which illustrates the early instability of postmodernism. In 1979, in a contribution to an early symposium on postmodernism, Altieri has found a new postmodernism and, imagining an ideal practitioner, reflects wryly that 'my imaginary post-modern, who must be considered a 1979 post-modern [is] probably soon to be as obsolete as my 1972 post-moderns'.[11] This '1979 post-modern' produces 'the pure writerly text' as theorized by Roland Barthes, a text 'that refuses to stabilize meanings' and 'stresses the productive power of writing', thus 'free[ing] writing to disseminate multiple shifting codes that admit no clear synthesis or resolution'.[12] This postmodernism is clearly under the spell of poststructuralist thinking and is a far cry from Altieri's earlier postmodernism which worked to enable 'modes of authenticity'. But for Altieri, this poststructurally inflected postmodernism was not satisfactory either. By 1986 the poststructuralist siren song has become less persuasive and we find him telling us that 'the best critical account' of postmodernism is that of his fellow critic Marjorie Perloff, which he goes on to quote in full:

> Postmodernism in poetry, I would argue, begins in the urge to return the material so rigidly excluded – political, ethical, historical, philosophical – to the domain of poetry, which is to say that the Romantic lyric, the poem as expression of a moment of absolute insight, of emotion crystallized into a timeless pattern, gives way to a poetry that can, once again, accommodate narrative and didacticism, the serious and the comic, verse *and* prose.[13]

Perloff sees postmodern poetry as a contemporary revival of pre-romantic, rather than pre-modernist, poetic traditions, although not as a simple return to those traditions – we now have multiple voices or voice fragments and a collage mode that are wholly absent from pre-romantic poetics. To be fair to Altieri such conceptual readjustments were not at all uncommon as the debate on postmodernism kept developing. As Altieri said in 1979 of a conference he had recently attended, '[i]t turned out that often the participants simply did not know one another's example of post-modernism. And when they did, one man's post-modernism appeared to others as only slightly varied modernism, or nostalgic and mystified returns to the sixties, or mere fringe *avant garde* phenomena'.[14] Only the loosest, un-theoretical and unphilosophical formulation (which still emphasized postmodernism's superior representative qualities), such as the one offered in 1978 by Robert Kern, could capture what most of these postmodernisms had in common: 'Modernist poetics stresses the way in which the poem is a closed, self-sufficient object. [...] Postmodern writing, on the other hand, seeks a greater openness for the poem, an openness to the world and to experience.'[15]

Postmodern fiction

Even if there was not much agreement on what exactly it covered, American poetry criticism adopted the term postmodernism without serious resistance as a heuristic tool, catholically seeing it as a sort of umbrella term for various new departures in post-war poetry. Criticism of the novel, however, was more reluctant to adopt the new term. This was partly due to a false start. The first one to apply 'post-modern' to the novel was the influential socialist critic Irving Howe who in 1959 published an article titled 'Mass Society and Post-Modern Fiction'. Howe here sees postmodernism, represented for him by the fiction of such writers as Bernard Malamud,

Norman Mailer and Saul Bellow, as a phenomenon of the American 1950s. For Howe post-war American society is characterized by an erosion of traditional centres of authority and a loss of strong beliefs, of 'causes'. 'It was,' he tells us, 'as if the guidelines of both our social thought and literary conventions were being erased.'[16] Howe's postmodern novels reflect – and reflect upon – the 'malaise' of an 'increasingly shapeless' world: 'In their distance from fixed social categories and their concern with the metaphysical implications of the distance, these novels constitute what I would call "post-modern" fiction.'[17] No one would now consider Howe's authors postmodern, but his emphasis on representation – 'How can one represent malaise, which by its nature is vague and without shape?'[18] – and his linking of postmodernism with socio-economic causes (rather than with a changing of the literary guard) would much later find an echo in the enormously influential analyses of the Marxist critic Fredric Jameson.

Howe's negative view of the post-war breakdown of traditional values was rejected by another prominent critic, Leslie Fiedler, who in his 1965 essay 'The New Mutants' saw in the so-called counterculture of the 1960s a new dawn rather than the self-destructive endgame of Western civilization. What Fiedler sees is a celebration of 'disconnection' accompanied by an indifference to the social order and a refusal to accept existing religious, racial or sexual dividing lines. His 'post-modernists'[19] are not only post-modern, but their world is 'post-humanist, post-male, post-white, post-heroic'.[20] Fiedler is the first to connect postmodernism with the 1960s counterculture, claiming that this Pop-oriented countercultural postmodernism is a necessary and long overdue correction of the course of Western civilization (Fiedler, 'Cross the Border – Close the Gap').[21] As Gerald Graff pointed out, Fiedler's suggestion is 'that the entire artistic tradition of the West has been exposed as a kind of hyperrational imperialism akin to the aggression and lust for conquest of bourgeois capitalism'.[22] Like Howe's postmodern novels, Fiedler's examples of postmodern literature would now not be accepted as such. But their diametrically opposed and widely known views led to confusion rather than clarity. Moreover, such false leads – false in terms of how postmodernism would ultimately come to be seen – did not stop with Howe and Fiedler. Critics who adopted the term 'postmodernism' quite often applied it in idiosyncratic ways. As late as 1984 Charles Newman still saw the work of Saul Bellow as 'quintessentially Post-Modern'.[23]

On the other hand, many critics who did address what we now would call postmodern fiction avoided the term. In 1967 Robert Scholes, analysing the work of a number of contemporary writers, including such canonical postmodernists as Kurt Vonnegut and John Barth, calls them fabulators who practice a surrealist form of picaresque.[24] In 1968 Richard Poirier signals 'a newly developed ... literature of parody that makes fun of itself *as it goes along*',[25] but never mentions postmodernism. The prominent British critic Frank Kermode speaks of 'palaeo- and neo-modern' (and downplays the differences between them: 'There has been only one Modernist Revolution, and ... it happened a long time ago. So far as I can see there has been little radical change in modernist thinking since then').[26] Richard Wasson disagrees and discusses in detail the differences between 'moderns and contemporaries' (the latter including Alain Robbe-Grillet, John Barth and Thomas Pynchon), with the 'contemporaries' displaying a more sceptical attitude and coping with chaos where the 'moderns raged for order'.[27] In a pessimistically titled collection, *The Death of the Novel and Other Stories*, the writer Ronald Sukenick speaks of the 'post-realist novel'[28] while another writer, the English academic David Lodge, finds more realism than Sukenick in postmodern fiction and creates the category of the 'problematic novel'. For Lodge, one of whose examples is André Gide's *Les Faux-monnayeurs* of 1925, such a novel does not wholly abandon 'the reality principle' but makes the reader *'participate* in the aesthetic and philosophical problems the writing of fiction presents'.[29] Philip Stevick avoids the term 'postmodern' in his 1971 *Anti-Story: An Anthology of Experimental Fiction* (which includes stories by Borges, Barth and Robert Coover)[30] and prefers 'new fiction' to postmodern or postmodernist – 'an epithet that I, for one, find annoying and unhelpful'[31] – in a discussion of the differences between modernism and postmodernism (represented here by such canonically postmodern writers as Donald Barthelme, Richard Brautigan and Robert Coover). For Stevick, who lists seven major differences between this new fiction and modernism, the break between them is most clearly illustrated by the new fiction's 'implicit intention to let the surface be the meaning, let the possibility of a symbolistic level of reference be consistently undercut', and by the fact that it 'permits itself a degree of latitude from the illusionist tradition greater than in any body of fiction since the beginning of the novel',[32] while representing 'the act of writing as an act of play'.[33] Giving his own twist to the notion that fiction may present itself as surface, the writer Raymond Federman proposes the term 'surfiction' for a 'new fiction that will not attempt to be meaningful, truthful, or realistic; nor will it attempt to serve as the vehicle of a ready-made meaning'.[34] Albert J. Guerard speaks of 'anti-realist fiction',[35] Charles Russell of 'contemporary self- reflective literature'[36] and Jerome Klinkowitz comes up with the rather outlandish 'post-contemporary fiction'.[37] The list could easily be expanded. For some of these critics, Wasson, for instance, the postmodernism that they do not mention reacts against modernism, but for most of them the target is a much longer tradition of attempts at realistic representation of which modernism is only one practice out of many.

And then we have critics who accept the idea of 'postmodernism' in a general way, but single out a dominant mode that they then give a more personal label. An especially interesting example is Alan Wilde, who offers an attempt to distinguish the new fiction from its modernist predecessor. Whereas modernist irony is an 'equivocal irony' that secretly longs to transcend the ironic stance, the irony of Wilde's 'midfiction' is a 'suspensive irony', an irony of cautious assent, of tolerance – the 'tolerance ... of a fundamental uncertainty about the meanings and relations of things in the world and in the universe'.[38] Wilde's 'midfiction', the 'tertium quid' of contemporary fiction, neither realist nor experimental,[39] anticipates, as we will see, Linda Hutcheon's influential 'historiographic metafiction', which will be discussed below, while his observation, in an earlier discussion of modern and postmodern irony, that Donald Barthelme 'puts aside the central modernist preoccupation with epistemology' and that his 'concerns are, rather, ontological in their acceptance of the world'[40] anticipates Brian McHale's distinction between an epistemologically oriented modernism and an ontologically oriented postmodernism. Wilde's notion of a 'midfiction' also has much in common with the 'problematic fiction' of David Lodge, who in the later 1970s had adopted the term postmodernism. Lodge recognizes the continuities between modernism and postmodernism, but also sees a crucial difference in narrative strategies and formal properties: 'The difficulty, for the reader, of postmodernist writing is not so much a matter of obscurity (which might be cleared up) as of uncertainty, which is endemic, and manifests itself on the level of narrative rather than style.'[41] Like Wasson's contemporary writing, Stevick's new fiction and Wilde's midfiction, Lodge's postmodern writing faces up to its representational shortcomings and sees them as inevitable: given the chaotic and inscrutable nature of reality, representation can always be only partially successful. What I must emphasize here is that this inherent inadequacy of representation is not a matter of language, as it will be for many later critics who see postmodernism through a poststructuralist lens, but of the world – it is the chaotic nature of reality that effectively rules out adequate representation.

The avant-garde revisited?

Even Ihab Hassan, one of postmodernism's most indefatigable advocates, was fairly slow in adopting the term. In his *Paracriticisms: Seven Speculations of the Times* he refers to his 'The Dismemberment of Orpheus' of 1963 as '[p]ostmodern criticism'.[42] Perhaps the criticism was postmodern, but the term is never mentioned. Instead, Hassan discusses what he calls the 'literature of silence', a literature in which '[l]anguage aspires to silence and form moves toward anti-form',[43] and his examples of that literature are certainly not postmodern. Until he adopts the term postmodernism – 'The change in Modernism may be called Postmodernism'[44] – Hassan would seem to prefer 'the literature of silence'. And as late as 1980, he still considered postmodernism an 'uncouth' term.[45]

Like Charles Altieri, Hassan more than once changed his views on postmodernism. *The Dismemberment of Orpheus: Toward a Postmodern Literature* of 1971 presents the Marquess de Sade, Dada and Surrealism, Hemingway, Kafka, Existentialism, Genet and Beckett as belonging to a proto-postmodern tradition.[46] In *Paracriticisms* of 1975 'without a doubt the crucial text is [James Joyce's] *Finnegans Wake*'[47] while in 1982, in the second edition of *The Dismemberment of Orpheus*, 'the postmodernist attitude merges also with the poststructuralist stance'.[48] In Hassan's earlier writings the emphasis is on an anarchist sensibility (which he links with the avant-garde of the interbellum): 'whereas Modernism created its own forms of Authority, precisely because the center no longer held, Postmodernism has tended toward Anarchy, in deeper complicity with things falling apart'.[49] The 'Postmodernist Notes' in *Paracriticisms* list anarchy, antiauthorianism, Beat and Hip, the Hippie movement, the homosexual novel, the Counter Cultures, in short practically everything that we remember about 1960s cultural, political and sexual dissent.[50] As Matei Calinescu pointed out in an early discussion of Hassan's postmodernism, '[t]aking the term avant-garde in its continental acceptation we can argue that what Hassan calls postmodernism is mostly an extension and diversification of the Pre-World War II avant-garde. Historically speaking, many of the postmodernist notes defined by Hassan can easily be traced back to Dada and, not infrequently, to Surrealism'.[51] (In line with this, Calinescu, who makes an interesting distinction between an intellectual and theoretical Continental European avant-garde and a more spontaneous and an anarchistic British and American version, prefers 'new avant-garde' or 'contemporary avant-garde' to 'postmodernism'.) In a similar vein, the English writer and academic Christine Brooke-Rose, in a comment that calls to mind Robert Scholes's description of the new fiction as a surrealist form of picaresque, claimed that 'American "postmodernism" often seems a late and diluted imitation' of the 'basic philosophy of surrealism'.[52] In the meantime, Hassan's capacious postmodernism had come to include such undisputedly postmodern writers as John Barth, Thomas Pynchon and Robert Coover, while he had gone beyond anarchism in coming to see 'indetermanence', a combination of indeterminacy and immanence, as the defining element in postmodern fiction ('we cannot simply rest – as I have sometimes done – on the assumption that postmodernism is antiformal, anarchic, or decreative').[53]

Hassan could apply the term 'postmodern' to what he himself saw as a contemporary avant-garde because the 'modern' in his 'postmodern' refers to the rather narrowly defined modernism of the Anglo-American literary-critical tradition, which at the time did not include the avant-gardes of the interbellum. But because he kept adding on to his postmodernism he came to feel that postmodernism 'ought to be distinguished from the older avant-gardes',[54] a wish that was almost immediately gratified. In 1981 Andreas Huyssen published an important article in which he follows Calinescu in signalling 'the similarity and continuity between American postmodernism and certain segments of an earlier European avant-garde'[55] (and defines in passing as 'modernist' such features as self-reflexivity and indeterminacy that other critics, including Hassan, saw as typically postmodern). But there is also a significant difference. This 'American postmodernist avant-garde' has abandoned the avant-garde ideals of social change and the transformation of everyday life and 'is not only the endgame of avant-gardism. It also represents the fragmentation and decline of the avant-garde as a genuinely critical and adversary culture'.[56] Still, for Huyssen, as for his fellow European Calinescu, this American avant-garde is more modern than postmodern, although he is ready to grant that it may indeed seem postmodern in an environment with no history of avant-gardes comparable to Dada or Surrealism: 'Where Europeans might react with a sense of déjà-vu, Americans could legitimately sustain a sense of novelty, excitement, and breakthrough.'[57]

The linguistic turn: poststructuralist postmodernism

The avant-garde interpretation of literary postmodernism soon had to contest with a formidable rival. As early as 1974 Stanley Fogel had called attention to 'writers of metafiction'[58] who were as aware as Roland Barthes and Jacques Derrida of the deeply problematic status of language. In 1980, we see Craig Owens arguing that 'a deconstructive impulse is characteristic of postmodernist art in general' and that postmodernism 'works ... to problematize the activity of reference'.[59] For Huyssen, writing in 1981, it was clear that 'there are definite links between the ethos of postmodernism and the American appropriation of poststructuralism, especially Derrida',[60] and in 1982, as we have seen, Hassan noted a merging of the 'postmodernist attitude' with the 'poststructuralist stance'. In the course of the 1980s postmodernism and poststructuralism would indeed practically merge – under the banner of postmodernism – so that in 1991 John McGowan could declare that 'Derrida's work has been so crucially important to postmodernism'.[61] In the same year, Steven Best and Douglas Kellner's

Postmodern Theory: Critical Interrogations discussed the work of Foucault, Deleuze and Guattari, Baudrillard and Lyotard, with Derrida making frequent appearances.[62] Two years later, Joseph Natoli and Linda Hutcheon's *A Postmodern Reader* included articles and excerpts from Lyotard, Derrida, Foucault and Baudrillard,[63] and in 2003 Michael Drolet's *The Postmodern Reader: Foundational Texts* still presented the same cast.[64] For some twenty years literary critics routinely referred to 'postmodern thought' in their discussions of Barthes, Derrida, Deleuze, Foucault, Lyotard, Baudrillard and other less prominent so-called poststructuralists. 'Postmodernism' or 'postmodern theory' (as in Best and Kellner's title) now referred to an amalgam of poststructuralist ideas and assumptions. As a consequence of this identification of postmodernism with poststructuralism, postmodern fiction was increasingly seen as the creative counterpart of poststructuralist theory (see, for instance, Allen Thiher),[65] so that analyses of postmodern fiction came to focus on elements such as self-reflexivity that Huyssen still saw as modernist but that now were taken to present poststructuralist themes. In the course of the 1980s and 1990s, critics, inspired by what was now broadly seen as 'postmodern theory' (later simply called 'theory'), go with magnifying glasses through the (Western) literary tradition and find *différance*, aporias, ideologically constructed realities, linguistically constructed identities – in fact, the full gamut of poststructuralist themes – in an amazing range of texts, from the contemporary, via the modernist, to Chaucer's fourteenth-century *Canterbury Tales*. Here, representation – and not just postmodern representation – is forever out of reach. Reality is a construction and authenticity a mirage. But even the construction that we call reality cannot be represented. Given the premise that language is inherently subject to the play of difference and to an infinite deferral of meaning, no text will ever be able to plug all holes and to avoid aporias that will effectively forestall representation. From this perspective, all texts, whatever their pretensions, have always been postmodern. What distinguishes them from each other is their degree of blindness to that condition, with contemporary, 'postmodern', writing the most aware of its inadequacy. This poststructuralist mode of reading postmodern texts puts the most radical interpretation possible on every single feature that critics such as Stevick and Lodge had identified as 'new', as post-the-modern, and turns all postmodern texts into poststructuralist exhibits.

The growing importance of poststructuralism in the debate on postmodernism in the early 1980s is illustrated by a highly idiosyncratic, although influential, intervention by the one poststructuralist thinker who tried his hand at answering the question 'what is postmodern literature' (the title of his high-profile contribution). For Jean-François Lyotard the litmus test is not self-reflexivity or a combination of formal characteristics, but how the text positions itself vis-à-vis the sublime, 'the unpresentable' in his terms. The hallmark of 'modern aesthetics', which for Lyotard is an aesthetics of the sublime, is nostalgia. Modernism 'allows the unpresentable' – of which it is fully aware – 'to be put forward as the missing contents; but the form, because of its recognizable consistency, continues to offer to the reader or viewer matter for solace and pleasure'.[66] Postmodernism, however, refuses that solace and is wilfully disruptive in order to confront us with the 'unpresentable': 'The postmodern would be that which, in the modern, puts forward the unpresentable in presentation itself; that which denies the solace of good forms, the consensus of a taste ... that which searches for new presentations, not in order to enjoy them but in order to impart a stronger sense of the unpresentable.'[67] This postmodernism is definitely part of the modern, which Lyotard defines in historiographic terms, hence his suggestion that 'the essay (Montaigne) is postmodern'.[68] Lyotard implies an endless dialectic of modernist and postmodernist moments: the new anti-representational schemes offered by postmodern works of fiction (or art) will inevitably lose their shock value and their power to 'put forward the unrepresentable' and will themselves become 'pre-established'. Since for Lyotard, as for most poststructuralists, representation, because of its attempt to fixate reality, is inherently totalitarian, such pre-establishment will necessitate a new confrontation with the unpresentable. 'Let us wage a war on totality,' Lyotard urges, 'let us be witnesses to the unpresentable.'[69]

Against poststructuralism and beyond

In the course of the 1980s all the other terms that had been used to discuss postmodern literature gradually disappeared so that by the end of the decade 'postmodern' (without a hyphen) was the sole survivor. Terms such as metafiction (coined by the postmodern writer and philosopher William Gass) were still used, but only for a specific type of narrative that was itself seen as fitting within a larger postmodern framework. Primarily responsible for this apparent simplification of things was the identification of postmodernism with poststructuralism. Another reason was the publication, in 1983 and 1984, of two enormously influential articles in which the Marxist critic Fredric Jameson did not so much identify postmodernism with poststructuralism, but went one step further in defining poststructuralism as one of the manifestations of a much wider defined postmodernism. But the victory of the terms 'postmodern' and 'postmodernism' was pyrrhic in the sense that it never led to true consensus. In 1973, Philip Stevick had pointed out that, in the case of postmodern writing, 'what we have is not a movement, not a clique, not a group, not a school, not a unified assertion of anything nor a reaction against anything. [...] As for the manifestos, the polemical introductions, the defensive stance-taking so commonplace in the past, they are all virtually non-existent'.[70] Far more than earlier literary movements postmodernism was, and is, the product of academic theorizing, which, at least in literary studies, rarely leads to concurrence. Still, by the early 1980s a relatively clear pattern had emerged, with the discussion now dominated by only a few positions (and with existentialist, avant-garde, and other interpretations of literary postmodernism having either a marginal presence or having disappeared from view altogether).

One of the lasting ways of seeing literary postmodernism – as the creative version of poststructuralist theory – has been discussed above. For the advocates of this postmodernism, what Owens called its problematization of the activity of reference – in other words, of representation – was a political, emancipatory act. Another, diametrically opposed view of postmodernism was offered by Fredric Jameson. The impact of Jameson's Marxist approach is hard to overestimate. As Khachig Tölölyan observed in a 1990 article that reviewed a number of recent books on postmodernism: 'However heterogeneous the other concerns invoked during the debates that structure these books, the marxist ... and poststructuralist ... version of postmodernism remain formative.'[71] As we will see, Tölölyan overlooks another important, but at the time less prominent version, but apart from that he is absolutely right.

For Jameson, who opens the first of these articles with the, at that point, quite correct observation that '[t]he concept of postmodernism is not widely accepted ... today',[72] postmodernism is a periodizing concept so that his postmodernism is virtually omnipresent. It is the 'cultural dominant' of the contemporary period because it is the 'cultural logic', as he has it in the second article, of late capitalism (also referred to as multinational or consumer capitalism): '[P]ostmodernism expresses the inner truth of that newly emergent social order of late capitalism.' Jameson is prepared to concede that all the features of postmodernism that he lists 'can be detected, full-blown, in this or that preceding modernism' – with some of the avant-gardists already 'outright postmodernists, *avant la lettre*'[73] – but because of postmodernism's 'very different positioning in the economic system of late capital' and because of the 'transformation of the very sphere of culture in contemporary society' modernism and postmodernism are 'utterly distinct in their meaning and social function'.[74] Under the regime of late capital, culture has become completely commodified – 'aesthetic production today has become integrated into commodity production generally'[75] – while simultaneously we have witnessed 'a prodigious expansion of culture throughout the social realm'.[76] This 'expansion of capital into hitherto uncommodified areas' has eliminated the last 'enclaves of precapitalist organization',[77] and has had disastrous political consequences. Whereas modernism had been 'an oppositional art'[78] and still had the potential to offer political critique because of its relative autonomy – that is, its distance from capital – 'distance in general (including "critical distance" in particular) has very precisely been abolished in the new space of postmodernism'.[79] Postmodern literature is characterized by 'a new depthlessness' which Jameson also finds in poststructuralist theory – 'the very concept of "truth" itself is part of the metaphysical baggage which poststructuralism seeks to abandon'[80] – and by a 'weakening of historicity', apart from which modernism's alienation of the subject – which still allowed political critique – is now 'displaced by the fragmentation of the subject'.[81] Under the pressure of capital postmodern literature has given up on representation, which for Jameson is a prerequisite for political critique. This is not to say that all potential for political dissent has disappeared, but postmodern art and literature can offer no such vantage point. Whereas for Lyotard representation takes us on the road to totalitarianism, with only dissenting anti-representation offering emancipatory alternatives, for Jameson postmodernism's refusal to engage in representation – or its least its failure to do so – leads to political impotence.

A more Lyotardian way – minus the sublime – of looking at the postmodern/poststructuralist nexus is offered by Linda Hutcheon who developed her influential view of postmodernism in the course of the 1980s and in 1988 published her important *The Poetics of Postmodernism: History, Theory, Fiction*. Hutcheon does not claim that her 'historiographic metafiction' represents all of the ways in which literary postmodernism has expressed itself, but certainly presents it as the most important one.[82] Hucheon's dominant postmodern mode strikes a balance between representation and anti-representation. Her historiographic metafiction pits representational and anti-representational modes of writing against each other so that we have Lyotard's cycle of representation and anti-representation in every single text. Such a text offers elements that strongly suggest representation and create the illusion of reality, but it also offers elements that counteract that illusion and suggest that we are dealing with an autonomous linguistic construction. To see this in terms of reading instructions, we get elements that suggest depth and meaning and invite traditional interpretation, while practically simultaneously other elements will block and perhaps even ridicule attempts at interpretation. Such a text, then, sets up a dialogue that keeps the representational qualities of the fiction in question firmly in play while simultaneously casting doubt on its potential for representing the real. For Hutcheon, this dialogue enables political critique (because of the fiction's representational elements), while it prevents that critique from hardening into dogma (by countering the suggestion of representation). Hutcheon's model recognizes the force of poststructuralist arguments, but does not wholly want to give up on the traditional humanist view of language as a window on the world.

From the early 1980s onwards, poststructuralism was practically omnipresent in the debate on postmodernism – almost feverishly embraced, emphatically rejected or treated with optimistic caution. But there were exceptions, the most important one the formalist approach best exemplified by the work of Brian McHale who in 1982 (quite correctly) observed that '[m]ost writing about postmodern writing to date has been polemical or apologetic'.[83] But he also noted some contributions to the debate that had been 'more descriptive', among them those of David Lodge and Alan Wilde, and would go on to present the fullest descriptive account of postmodern literature to date. For McHale the difference between modernist and postmodernist fiction is to be found in a change of dominant – not the cultural dominant of Fredric Jameson, but the literary dominant of the literary theorist Roman Jakobson, who had defined it as 'the focusing component of a work of art' which 'rules, determines, and transforms the remaining components' (McHale's quotation).[84] Modernist fiction, McHale argues, is epistemological in the sense that it

> is designed to raise such questions as: what is there to be known? who knows it? how do they know it, and with what degree of certainty? how is knowledge transmitted from one knower to another, and with what degree of reliability? how does the object of knowledge change as it passes from knower to knower? what are the limits of knowledge? and so on.[85]

The dominant in postmodern fiction, however, is ontological. Postmodern fiction deploys strategies that foreground such questions as: 'what is a world? what kinds of worlds are there, how are they constituted, and how do they differ? what happens when different worlds are placed in confrontation, or when boundaries between worlds are violated ... how is a projected world structured? and so on.'[86] In this scheme of things, McHale points out, modernist fiction follows the epistemological structure of the detective novel while the postmodern novel prefers the ontological mode of science fiction – with both modes always sharing important elements with the other. To put this in other terms, McHale's modernism, with its focus on knowledge, is primarily concerned with the conditions that make representation possible (or, as the case may be, impossible), whereas his postmodernism, while certainly not uninterested in representation, allows itself a good deal of autonomy in the construction of its verbal worlds. McHale's *Postmodernist Fiction* of 1987, whose 'descriptive poetics' largely resists the lure of poststructuralism, offers the fullest catalogue of the various ways in which that autonomy is achieved.[87]

Conclusion

Postmodernism was by no means the natural, self-evident term for the 'new literature' of the 1960s and 1970s. On the contrary, in both poetry criticism and that of fiction it was initially applied to texts that would later disappear from the postmodern canon, while many critics who correctly identified what would later come to be called postmodern literature studiously avoided the term. And those who did use it, and took the full spectrum of modernism into account, felt uneasy about applying the term to what seemed a reshaping of the strategies of the continental avant-gardes, which had often involved anti-representational moves that were politically inspired. From their perspective, postmodernism looked more like avant-garde modernism than something that was genuinely post-modern. It took the extraordinary embrace of poststructuralism by American academe and its identification of postmodernism with poststructuralism to turn postmodernism into a generally accepted term and to create a definitive distinction between avant-garde modernism and postmodernism. While avant-garde anti-representation was interpreted as politically motivated, a form of protest against the bourgeois status quo, postmodern anti-representation was seen in poststructuralist terms as anti-essentialist, anti-metaphysical. This anti-essentialism had a political dimension, as argued by for instance Lyotard and Hutcheon, but its basis was philosophical.

Depending on how literary postmodernism's 'project' was interpreted, that postmodernism was pre-Socratic, pre-modern, avant-garde modern, self-consciously modern or indeed post-modern. It is not surprising, then, that the advent of postmodernism as a literary-critical concept affected but did not revolutionize our idea of modernism. As Astradur Eysteinsson pointed out a long time ago, attempts to redefine modernism in the light of postmodernism were 'frequently tied to narrow modernist canons ... that [we]re, moreover, restricted to a single language',[88] and he might have added that language was English. Those redefinitions of modernism construct a high modernism that is far less experimental and more conservative – in other words, more 'realistic' – than it actually was and tend to avoid writers such as André Gide, Gertrude Stein, Mikhail Bulgakov, Franz Kafka, Antonin Artaud and many others who would seriously compromise the picture. One solution to this dilemma is to lift such writers out of modernism altogether and make them honorary postmodernists – 'outright postmodernists, *avant-la-lettre*', as Jameson says of the avant-garde – but such sleights-of-hand too obviously serve definitional purposes to be convincing.

An important development connected with literary postmodernism, although not 'literary' in itself and applied far beyond the literary field, is the emergence and triumphal progress of postmodern criticism, also known as postmodern theory. Postmodern criticism adopted from poststructural-ism its central interest in problems of language and signification and radi-calized its questioning of Enlightenment humanism. It distrusted conceptual systems and saw universalism and its concomitant essentialism as ultimately totalitarian. It rejected the notion of the unique, self-determined and coher-ent subject and questioned notions of originality and authorship. In a later stage it developed an interest in how language was instrumental in establish-ing and perpetuating power relations and in processes of marginalization. It is this postmodernism that in the course of the 1980s and 1990s branched out in all directions, making itself felt in historiography, ethnography, musi-cology, religious studies, legal studies, cultural studies and other areas that experienced a postmodern moment or even a more lasting postmodern reor-ientation. And it is this postmodern criticism that widely came to be seen as radically relativist, fact-free, and anti-rational and that gave postmodernism its bad name. Let me offer some examples. In 1997 Alan Sokal, a physicist and mathematician at New York University, and his Belgian colleague Jean Bricmont published *Intellectual Impostors: Postmodern Philosophers' Abuse of Science*, reviewed by the biologist Richard Dawkins in an article called 'Postmodernism Disrobed' whose opening phrase left little to the imagination: 'Suppose you are an intellectual impostor with nothing to say, but with strong ambitions to succeed in academic life.'[89] In the same year another famous biologist, E. O. Wilson, exasperated by postmodern theo-ry's claims, told us that the 'postmodern hypothesis is blissfully free of exist-ing information on how the mind works'.[90] For Wilson postmodern theory was the unfortunate result of the 'pathetic reverence commonly given Gallic obscurantism by American academics'.[91] In the psycholinguist Steven Pinker's *The Blank Slate: The Modern Denial of Human Nature* of 2002 we find a similar indictment of postmodernism, which according to Pinker is 'based on a false theory of human psychology'[92] and 'a militant denial of human nature'.[93] For Pinker, the totalitarian regime that cynically keeps rewriting history in George Orwell's *1984* 'is thoroughly postmodernist'.[94] There is no dearth of prominent academics attacking what they saw as postmodernism's radical, irrational and irresponsible relativism. After 9/11 even newspapers turned against postmodernism. 'Attacks on U.S. Challenge the Perspectives of Postmodern True Believers' was the headline of a *New York Times* article two weeks after the destruction of New York's World Trade Center.[95] 'Postmodern Outlook Objectively Smashed' reported the *Washington Times*.[96] But here we have left the territory of literary post-modernism, even if this frontal assault did not leave postmodern literature's reputation unaffected. That is another story, for another time.

Notes

1 Charles Olson, *Human Universe and Other Essays* (New York: Grove Press, 1967), p. 4.
2 George F. Butterick, 'Charles Olson and the Postmodern Advance', *Iowa Review*, 11:4 (1980), 4–27.
3 William Spanos, 'The Detective and the Boundary: Some Notes on the Postmodern Literary Imagination', *boundary 2*, 1:1 (1972), 155.
4 Ibid.
5 Ibid., 157.
6 Charles Altieri, 'From Symbolist Thought to Immanence: The Ground of American Poetics', *boundary 2*, 1:3 (1973), 608.
7 Ibid., 612.
8 Ibid.
9 Ibid., 613.
10 Ibid., 629.
11 Charles Altieri, 'Postmodernism: A Question of Definition', *Par Rapport*, 2:2 (1979), 94.
12 Ibid.
13 Charles Altieri, 'The Postmodernism of David Antin's *Tuning*', *College English*, 48:1 (1986), 9; Marjorie Perloff, 'Postmodernism and the Impasse of Lyric', *Formations*, 1:2 (1984), 49.
14 Charles Altieri, 'Postmodernism', 89.
15 Robert Kern, 'Composition as Recognition: Robert Creeley and Postmodern Poetics', *boundary 2*, 6:3 and 7:1 (1978), 215.
16 Irving Howe, 'Mass Society and Post-Modern Fiction', *Partisan Review*, 26:3 (1959), 428.
17 Ibid., 433.
18 Ibid., 430.
19 Leslie Fiedler, 'The New Mutants', *Partisan Review*, 32:4 (1965), 515.
20 Ibid., 517.
21 Leslie Fiedler, 'Cross the Border – Close the Gap: Postmodernism', *Playboy*, 16:12 (1969).
22 Gerald Graff, *Literature Against Itself: Literary Ideas in Modern Society* (Chicago, IL: University of Chicago Press, 1979), p. 31.
23 Charles Newman, 'The Post-Modern Aura: The Act of Fiction in an Age of Inflation', *Salmagundi*, 63/64:3 (1984), 73.
24 Robert Scholes, *The Fabulators* (New York: Oxford University Press, 1967).
25 Richard Poirier, 'The Politics of Self-Parody', *Partisan Review*, 35:3 (1968), 339.
26 Frank Kermode, *Continuities* (London: Routledge and Kegan Paul, 1968), p. 24.
27 Richard Wasson, 'Notes on a New Sensibility', *Partisan Review*, 36:3 (1969), 476.
28 Ronald Sukenick, *The Death of the Novel and Other Stories* (New York: Dial Press, 1969), p. 47.

29 David Lodge, 'The Novelist at the Crossroads', *Critical Quarterly*, 11 (1969), 123.

30 Philip Stevick (ed.), *Anti-Story: An Anthology of Experimental Fiction* (New York: The Free Press, 1971).

31 Philip Stevick, 'Scheherazade Runs out of Plots, Goes on Talking; the King, Puzzled, Listens: An Essay on the New Fiction', *TriQuarterly*, 26 (1973), 338.

32 Ibid., 360.

33 Ibid., 361.

34 Raymond Federman, 'Surfiction: A Position', *Partisan Review*, 40:3 (1973), 431.

35 Albert J. Guerard, 'Notes on the Rhetoric of Anti-Realist Fiction', *TriQuarterly*, 30 (1974).

36 Charles Russell, 'The Vault of Language: Self-Reflective Artifice in Contemporary American Fiction', *Modern Fiction Studies*, 20:3 (1974), 350.

37 Jerome Klinkowitz, *Literary Disruptions: The Making of Post-Contemporary American Fiction* (Urbana, IL: University of Illinois Press, 1975).

38 Alan Wilde, 'Irony in the Postmodern Age: Toward a Map of Suspensiveness', *boundary 2*, 9:1 (1980), 9.

39 Alan Wilde, 'Strange Displacements of the Ordinary: Apple, Elkin, Barthelme, and the Problem of the Excluded Middle', *boundary 2*, 10:2 (1982), 182.

40 Alan Wilde, 'Barthelme Unfair to Kierkegaard: Some Thoughts on Modern and Postmodern Irony', *boundary 2*, 5:1 (1976), 54.

41 David Lodge, *The Modes of Modern Writing* (London: Arnold, 1977), p. 226.

42 Ihab Hassan, *Paracriticisms: Seven Speculations of the Times* (Urbana, IL: University of Illinois Press, 1975), p. 45.

43 Ihab Hassan, 'The Dismemberment of Orpheus: Reflections on Modern Culture, Language and Literature', *The American Scholar*, 32:3 (1963), 470.

44 Ihab Hassan, 'POSTmodernISM: A Paracritical Bibliography', *New Literary History*, 3:1 (1971), 11.

45 Ihab Hassan, 'The Question of Postmodernism', in Harry R. Garvin (ed.), *Romanticism, Modernism, Postmodernism* (Lewisburg, PA: Bucknell University Press, 1980), p. 123.

46 Ihab Hassan, *The Dismemberment of Orpheus: Toward a Postmodern Literature* (New York: Oxford University Press, 1971).

47 Hassan, *Paracriticisms*, p. 43.

48 Ihab Hassan, *The Dismemberment of Orpheus: Toward a Postmodern Literature*, 2nd edn (Madison, WI: University of Wisconsin Press, 1982), p. xiii.

49 Hassan, *Dismemberment of Orpheus* (1971 edition), p. 11.

50 Hassan, *Paracriticisms*, pp. 54–8.

51 Matei Calinescu, 'Avant-Garde, Neo-Avant-Garde, Postmodernism: The Culture of Crisis', *Clio*, 4:3 (1975), 332.

52 Christine Brooke-Rose, *A Rhetoric of the Unreal: Studies in Narrative and Structure, Especially of the Fantastic* (Cambridge: Cambridge University Press, 1981), p. 387.

53 Hassan, 'The Question of Postmodernism', p. 121.

54 Ibid., 124.
55 Andreas Huyssen, 'The Search for Tradition: Avant-Garde and Postmodernism in the 1970s', *New German Critique*, 35 (1981), 31.
56 Ibid., 34.
57 Ibid., 30.
58 Stanley Fogel, '"And All the Little Typtopies": Notes on Language Theory in the Contemporary Experimental Novel', *Modern Fiction Studies*, 20 (1974), 328.
59 Craig Owens, 'The Allegorical Impulse: Toward a Theory of Postmodernism. Part 2', *October*, 13 (1980), 79–80.
60 Andreas Huyssen, 'Search', 34.
61 John McGowan, *Postmodernism and Its Critics* (Ithaca, NY: Cornell University Press, 1991), p. 119.
62 Steven Best and Douglas Kellner, *Postmodern Theory: Critical Interrogations* (New York: Guilford, 1991).
63 Joseph Natoli and Linda Hutcheon (eds), *A Postmodern Reader* (Albany, NY: State University of New York Press, 1993).
64 Michael Drolet (ed.), *The Postmodern Reader: Foundational Texts* (New York: Routledge, 2003).
65 Allen Thiher, 'A Theory of Literature or Recent Literature as Theory', *Contemporary Literature*, 29:3 (1988), 337–50.
66 Jean-François Lyotard, 'Answering the Question: What Is Postmodernism?', in Ihab Hassan and Sally Hassan (eds), *Innovation/Renovation: New Perspectives in the Humanities* (Madison, WI: University of Wisconsin Press, 1983), p. 340.
67 Ibid.
68 Ibid., p. 341.
69 Ibid.
70 Stevick, 'Scheherazade', 335–6.
71 Khachig Tölölyan, 'The Second Time as Farce: Postmodernism without Consequences', *American Literary History*, 2:4 (1990), 759.
72 Fredric Jameson, 'Postmodernism and Consumer Society', in Hal Foster (ed.), *The Anti-Aesthetic: Essays in Postmodern Culture* (Port Townsend, WA: Bay Press, 1983), p. 111.
73 Fredric Jameson, 'Postmodernism, or the Cultural Logic of Late Capitalism', *New Left Review*, 146 (1984), 56.
74 Ibid., 57.
75 Ibid., 56.
76 Ibid., 87.
77 Ibid. 78.
78 Jameson, 'Postmodernism and Consumer Society', p. 123.
79 Jameson, 'Postmodernism, or the Cultural Logic', 87.
80 Ibid., 61.
81 Ibid., 65.
82 Linda Hutcheon, *The Poetics of Postmodernism: History, Theory, Fiction* (New York: Routledge, 1988).

83 Brian McHale, 'Writing about Postmodern Writing', *Poetics Today*, 3:3 (1982), 212.

84 Brian McHale, 'Change of Dominant from Modernist to Postmodernist Writing', in Douwe Fokkema and Hans Bertens (eds), *Approaching Postmodernism* (Amsterdam: Benjamins, 1986), p. 55.

85 Ibid., p. 84.

86 Ibid., p. 60.

87 Brian McHale, *Postmodernist Fiction* (London: Methuen, 1987).

88 Astradur Eysteinsson, *The Concept of Modernism* (Ithaca, NY: Cornell University Press, 1990), p. 130.

89 Richard Dawkins, 'Postmodernism Disrobed', in *A Devil's Chaplain: Selected Essays* (London: Weidenfeld and Nicholson, 2003), p. 55. Originally published in 1998.

90 Edward O. Wilson, *Consilience: The Unity of Knowledge* (New York: Knopf, 1998), p. 235.

91 Ibid., p. 234.

92 Steven Pinker, *The Blank Slate: The Modern Denial of Human Nature* (New York: Viking, 2002), p. 412.

93 Ibid., p. 416.

94 Ibid., p. 428.

95 Edward Rothstein, 'Attack in U.S. Challenges the Perspectives of Postmodern True Believers', *New York Times* (22 September 2001).

96 Herbert I. London, 'Postmodern Outlook Objectively Smashed', *Washington Times* (5 November 2001).

8

From political reference to self-narration: 'Postcolonial' as periodizer

Andrew Sartori

Introduction

The term 'post-colonial' proliferated rapidly in English and French start-ing in the 1950s, mirroring the acceleration of processes of decolonization. Down through the 1970s and 1980s, 'post-colonial' remained for the most part a relatively straightforward political periodizer. It named whatever institutional order followed the end of formal colonial rule – and by exten-sion, the social and cultural forms that accompanied that institutional order. But starting in the 1980s, a second usage of the term 'postcolonial' (increasingly in its unhyphenated form) began to bifurcate from its former meaning as a periodizer of political order, so that it began to function also as a periodizer of scholarly dispositions. As the term 'postcolonial' assumed significance in reference to a smaller world of scholarly interpretation, rather than in reference to a larger world of political and social order, the object of postcolonial scholarship was increasingly released from chrono-logical and geographical limits.

This chapter attempts no critical engagement with the substance of the various claims most often characterized as 'postcolonialist'. It rather offers a more modest attempt to characterize the main trajectories of the term's usage and of the field of scholarship that has ridden under its banner. In the first section, I draw on a combination of JSTOR and Ngram data to offer a descriptive analysis of the major trajectories in the frequency and usage of the term 'postcolonial'. In the second section, I take a closer look at the evolving significance of the term in the theoretical texts most closely associated with the development of the field of 'postcolonial studies'.

The rise of the 'post-colonial'

'Post-colonial' is not a new term. A search of the JSTOR archive dem-onstrates that it was already a not uncommon, if somewhat scholarly, term in the first half of the twentieth century. Its primary reference in this period seems to have been the United States, with secondary reference to Latin America; and its primary function was the periodization of political institutions based on an implicit tripartite schema of pre-colonial/colonial/ post-colonial, without any further specification of the meaning of the key intervening concept, 'colonial'. Hyphenation was the standard form, but dropping the hyphen was a recognizable occasional alternative throughout this period.

The late 1950s saw the first inklings of a new rise in the frequency with which the hyphenated form, 'post-colonial', was used. That upward trajectory would persist and accelerate all the way to the end of the millennium, when it peaked. (Parallel and contemporary developments were evident in both French and German.) It would be remarkable if that increase were not to be found, obviously, given the large-scale political transformations in global order occurring at that time.

Looking at JSTOR, it seems that of the 47,161 items that used the term between 1955 and 1980, 10 per cent were still tagged to American Studies – but this was down from 15 per cent in the period 1900–55. Meanwhile, 8.5 per cent were tagged to African Studies (up from 2 per cent in 1900–55), 7 per cent to Asian Studies (up from 3 per cent in 1900–55), and just under 5 per cent to Latin American Studies (around 2.5 per cent in 1900–55). Meanwhile, 31 per cent were tagged to History (28 per cent in 1900–55), just under 16 per cent to Political Science (13 per cent in 1900–55), 7.5 per cent to Economics (also 7.5 per cent in 1900–55), 7.5 per cent to Sociology (around 3.5 per cent in 1900–55), and only around 7 per cent to Language and Literature (6 per cent in 1900–55).[1] Taking these figures together – especially the relatively minor role of literary studies – it seems clear that the major shifts in usage turned: (1) on the increasing relevance of the term to the social sciences and to historical analysis, and (2) on the increasing relevance of the term to non-American referents, especially in Africa and Asia (hardly surprising in the era of decolonization). For the most part, 'post-colonial' remained until very late in the twentieth century a straightforward periodizing term primarily concerned with political institutions and their social correlates. Ngram analysis confirms this: in the period 1955–80, the most common words to follow the adjective 'post-colonial' were 'period', 'state' and 'era', followed at some distance by 'society', 'Africa', 'situation' and 'world'. (In fact, what followed the word 'post-colonial' as commonly as anything else, an impressionistic survey suggests, were specific place names, especially the names of nation states.) All of these phrases saw a significant upward trend throughout the period, but especially pronounced from around the mid 1960s.

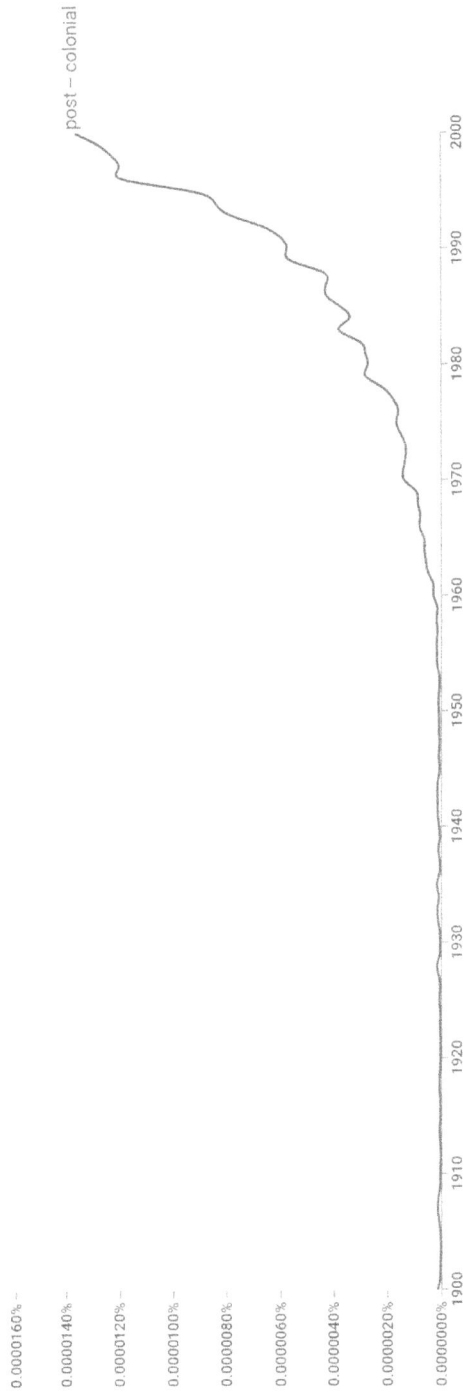

Figure 8.1 Uses of the term 'post-colonial', 1900–2008.

'Post-colonial' seemed to have named a set of circumstances that followed the withdrawal of (European) colonial rule. It remained unspecific in its assumptions about the character of the 'colonial' whose antecedence defined it, however, and correlatively did not seem to be seen as a concept carrying any specific heuristic burden. For example, in a 1985 reflection on the enduring legacies of colonialism in Latin America, Steve J. Stern suggested that it was the 'resilient grip of the past that has made terms such as "neocolonial" so appealing in discussions of post colonial history'.[2] Assumed in this formulation is that 'neocolonial' is a term of analysis whereas 'post colonial' is merely a periodization.

The unhyphenated form, 'postcolonial', largely tracked the fortunes of the hyphenated form in the period 1900–85. But starting around 1990, it began its own remarkable acceleration, so that whereas the two terms had enjoyed roughly equivalent usage frequency until the mid 1980s, by the year 2000 'postcolonial' had become the vastly more common usage. This is also more or less true in French and German at the same time, even though – due in no small part to the structure of the French and German academies – what would gradually emerge as the field of 'postcolonial studies' in the final decades of the twentieth century remained a predominantly Anglophone pursuit throughout this period.

In part this reversal may be explicable in terms of the changing aesthetic and economic concerns of (especially US-based) publishers, who began a war on hyphens more generally. But it also loosely correlated with a shift in the fields of discourse in which the term operated. This shift was marked by the rise of several newly frequent phrases that were still extremely rare in 1990 and that were most strongly associated with the unhyphenated version of the term. 'Postcolonial theory' overtook 'post-colonial state' in the mid 1990s to become the most common combination of terms involving either 'postcolonial' or 'post-colonial'. 'Postcolonial studies' overtook 'post-colonial state' at around the same time to become the second most common combination. Similarly, the usage frequency of 'postcolonial criticism' and 'postcolonial discourse' increased dramatically between 1990 and 2000 to become among the most common combinations. Associated terms, such as 'subaltern', also saw increased usage frequency starting around 1990. This increase was presumably directly linked to the new associations and expanded analytical relevance given the term by the rise of the Subaltern School of historians.

For the period 1990 to 2000, a JSTOR search for the hyphenated form 'post-colonial' returned 62,914 items, while a search for the unhyphenated form, 'postcolonial' only returned 16,257 items.[3] Suggestively, however, less than 16 per cent of the items containing the term 'post-colonial' are tagged to Language and Literature (as against almost 28 per cent to history); whereas almost 37 per cent of the items containing the term

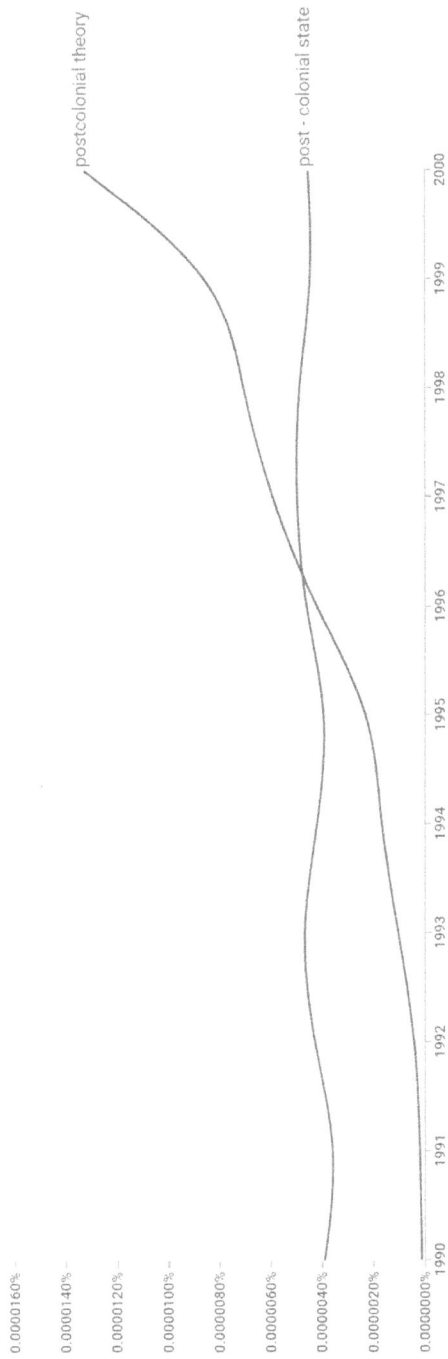

Figure 8.2 Uses of the terms 'postcolonial theory' and 'post-colonial state', 1990–2000.

'postcolonial' are tagged to Language and Literature (as against around 16 per cent to history). This may correlate with a distribution of scholarly focus between the more hyphen-averse USA and the more hyphen-friendly Commonwealth. Nonetheless, that the hyphen/no-hyphen distinction was at least partly coming to be mapped onto this larger discursive shift is further suggested by the fact that, even after the rise of 'postcolonial' as the more frequent form of the term in general (and the combinations 'post-colonial theory' and 'postcolonial studies' along with it), 'post-colonial' remained most commonly followed by the terms 'state', 'period' and 'era'. The new field of 'postcolonialism' was disproportionately associated with the unhyphenated form of the term.

The formation of postcolonial studies

As late as 1990, Robert Young's widely cited book, *White Mythologies*, could situate the writings of Edward Said, Homi K. Bhabha and Gayatri Chakravorty Spivak within a lineage stretching back to Sartre and Althusser without (so far as I can see) invoking the term 'postcolonial' at all.[4] The commitment to 'postcolonial criticism' first emerged into stuttering self-consciousness out of the vibrant field of colonial studies in the second half of the 1980s. In the wake of both deepening disillusionment with the regimes that had followed colonial rule, and the movement into Western universities of intellectuals who had emerged out of the milieu of twentieth-century left nationalism, dissatisfactions with existing national and developmental narratives intersected with a whole set of intellectual repudiations in the United States and Western Europe that travelled under the loose banners of postmodernism and poststructuralism.

Edward Said identified himself as an anti-colonial activist, and he understood the contemporary object of his writings as still an essentially colonial situation. He correlatively seems to have had little use for the term 'postcolonial' until later in his career. It wasn't really until 1989 that he was invoking the 'postcolonial effort to reclaim traditions, histories and cultures from imperialism', and even then he clearly understood such 'postcolonial efforts' as a direct continuation of anti-colonialism and anti-racism.[5] In his three most famous essays from the 1980s, meanwhile, Homi K. Bhabha seems to have used the term 'postcolonial' only once, and then in a slighting reference to 'the despair of postcolonial history'.[6] In 1986, Rajeswari Sunder Rajan used a discussion of the impact of Said's *Orientalism* as the occasion 'to reflect upon the English literature academic in India as post-colonial intellectual'.[7] As late as 1989, even when the subtitle of Trinh T. Minh-ha's *Woman, Native, Other* identified as its conceptual burden the task of *Writing Postcoloniality and Feminism*, the term 'postcolonial' seems to have been entirely absent from the text itself. When she published *When the Moon Waxes Red* two years later, there was still only one reference to 'the postcolonial other' in the text.[8]

From the mid 1980s, Gayatri Chakravorty Spivak was beginning to identify the standpoint of the 'postcolonial critic' as generative of the readings she proposed. It was 'the postcolonial reader' who found 'satisfying' the ways in which Mary Shelley's *Frankenstein* subtly exceeded imperialist frames;[9] and it was the 'situation of the post-colonial critic of imperialism' that rendered visible the limitations of Dominick LaCapra's approach to historical reading.[10] It is nonetheless striking that, in her 1988 introduction to *Selected Subaltern Studies* (a text that would ultimately play no small part in consolidating the relationship between the subaltern and the postcolonial, and in establishing the Subalternists as key figures in postcolonial studies), the term 'post-colonial' had little role to play in her exposition of the theoretical problem. In the essays themselves we find references to 'a post-colonial state' (in an essay by Gautam Bhadra) and the more ambiguous 'colonial (and post-colonial) societies' (in an essay by Partha Chatterjee); while Spivak's own reference to the '(post)colonial intellectual' could be taken to imply that the 'post' in this formulation was for the most part conceptually redundant.[11]

In 1987, Simon During was questioning whether 'the concept postmodernity' (already without hyphen) stood in irresolvable tension with the 'possibility of post-colonial identity' (still with hyphen). 'Post-colonialism' could look to postmodernism for affiliation and support in its aspiration to affirm the possibility of an Otherness 'uncontaminated by universalist or Eurocentric concepts and images'. Yet it would nonetheless find itself confounded by postmodernism's concurrent insistence that 'the Other can never speak for itself *as* the Other'.[12] It is striking, three decades later, to see how immediately During still identified the problematic of 'postcolonialism' with the problematic of nationalism, which had been at the core of the rising frequency of the term 'post-colonial' in the post-World War II period of decolonization.[13] The same was still largely the case in 1989, when Laura Kipnis argued that the 'emergence in feminist theory of the periphery, the absence, and the margin implies a theory of women not as class or caste, but as colony'. This implied that 'the theoretical emergence of these political spaces now being described by continental feminists parallels the narrative of the decline of the European empires and the postcolonial rearrangements of the traditional centers on a world scale', rendering feminism into a kind of 'decolonizing movement'.[14] Here postcolonialism was being construed as one dimension of the ongoing conceptual sequelae of the formal dismantling of European empire.

It seems that 1989/1990 was the axial moment around which 'post-colonialism' was solidified as a new field of (especially literary-critical) scholarly discourse that had inherited (1) the concerns of anti-colonial and anti-racist intellectuals like W. E. B. Du Bois, Aimé Césaire, Frantz Fanon, Albert Memmi, C. L. R. James, Chinua Achebe, and Ngũgĩ wa Thiong'o; (2) the critique of elite nationalism in *Subaltern Studies*; and (3) the critique of colonial knowledge and colonial discourse pioneered in the work of Abdallah Laroui, Anouar Abdel-Malek, Edward Said, Bernard Cohn, Abdul JanMohamed, Chandra Talpade Mohanty, Lata Mani, and others. Crucially, the problematic of 'the postcolonial' was increasingly distanced from the problematic of anti-colonial nationalism.

One text that served as a common point of reference for discussion and debate, whether appreciative or sceptical, was Bill Ashcroft, Gareth Griffiths and Helen Tiffin's *The Empire Writes Back: Theory and Practice in Post-Colonial Literatures*, which emerged out of Australia in 1989. It sought, probably for the first time, to introduce postcolonial studies as a coherent field of literary study. It announced an expansive vision of postcolonialism's appropriate object of study: 'We use the term "post-colonial", however, to cover all the culture affected by the imperial process from the moment of colonization to the present day ... because there is a continuity of preoccupations throughout the historical process initiated by European imperial aggression.' The volume treated 'post-colonial literatures' as defined by their emergence out of a common 'experience of colonization' and by a common emphasis on 'their differences from the assumptions of the imperial centre'.[15] The volume defended the idea of a 'post-colonial literary theory' as a response to the 'inability of European theory to deal adequately with the complexities and varied cultural provenance of post-colonial writing'.[16]

On the one hand, Ashcroft, Griffiths and Tiffin thus proposed a conception of the postcolonial as an epochal totality that defined the condition of the literary: '[T]his book is concerned with the world as it exists during and after the period of European imperial domination and the effects of this on contemporary literatures.'[17] On the other hand, working with this expansive definition of the 'post-colonial', *The Empire Writes Back* was effectively displacing the conventional periodizing function of the term in favour of an emphasis on positionality. The 'post' marked a subjective distance, dissonance and/or difference from the norms of colonial discourse generated as a direct result of the experience of European colonialism. From the end of the fifteenth century, they suggested, the conceptual vocabulary of colonial discourse – the discourse of the metropole – was incapable of adequately expressing the experience of the colonized, or of recognizing the ways in which, read carefully, cultural artefacts emerging from the colonized margins effectively performed or instantiated that impossibility. This impasse generated an inescapable condition secondary to (hence 'post') the experience of colonialism. The 'postcolonial' that the postcolonial literary critic inhabited was thus fundamentally continuous with the postcolonial that had emerged contemporaneously with the projection of European power on the rest of the world – even as the successes of anti-colonialism in the twentieth century had created new possibilities for the self-conscious critique of 'neo-colonialism'.

It was also in 1989–90 that Spivak first began to identify the domain of subalternity that lay beyond the limits of the colonial text (in her expansive sense of that term) as 'a representation of decolonization *as such*', and thus the limit that defined the problematic of 'postcoloniality'.[18] Here the problematic of the postcolonial and the problematic of nationalism were definitively coming apart; and subalternity (which in the initial vision of Ranajit Guha was very much a self-conscious contribution to left nationalism) was being conceptualized as distinct from and even incommensurable with the nation-state project.[19] By 1990, a volume of interviews unequivocally identified Spivak as *The Post-Colonial Critic*.[20] It was also in 1990, with the publication of *Nation and Narration*, that Homi K. Bhabha began to embrace the term 'post-colonial'.[21]

In 1991, Kwame Anthony Appiah published his influential essay, 'Is the Post- in Postmodernism the Post- in Postcolonial?' Like the earlier text by During, Appiah emphasized the asymmetries between the 'postcolonial' and the 'postmodern'. And like During, he emphasized that the postcolonial gesture differed from the postmodern gesture in no small part by the fact that postmodernism looked to the non-Western intellectual to be an 'otherness machine' whereas postcolonialism critiqued the appeal to otherness in the name of an 'ethical universal'. Appiah identified the nationalist problematic that was the core of During's conception of postcoloniality, however, as bound to colonialism; whereas the 'space clearing gesture' of postcolonialism increasingly represented the 'postnativist' and 'postnationalist' 'pessimism' of a '*comprador* intelligentsia' disillusioned by the experience of the postcolonial state yet bound nonetheless to the university and the Euro-American publisher for its existence. The post- of postcolonialism is thus the 'after' of disillusionment with everything that colonialism and nationalism had promised, but it was an 'after' that nonetheless refused the celebration of the proliferation of differences that was central to postmodernism.[22] As with Spivak, postcolonialism here was coming apart from the history of the nation state, the history that had been the primary engine of the proliferation of its usage through the second half of the twentieth century.

In 1992, the disjuncture between the analytical work intended by the concept of the postcolonial and the history of anti-colonial nationalism was further cemented by the publication of Dipesh Chakrabarty's essay, 'Postcoloniality and the Artifice of History'. A hyperreal figure of 'Europe', he argued, remained the 'sovereign, theoretical subject of all histories, including the ones we call "Chinese", "Indian", "Kenyan", and so on ... In this sense, "Indian" history itself is in a position of subalternity'. To find a way to articulate what could not be articulated within the discursive protocols of academic history implicitly meant that such a historical account would have to be rendered incommensurate with the constitutive assumptions underlying 'third-world nationalisms, as modernizing ideologies *par excellence*'.[23] The object of Chakrabarty's postcolonial critique was thus precisely what could not be recuperated to the project of post-colonial state formation. That this excess cannot be further specified turns on the radically colonial constitution of the epistemological status of history itself.

The year Chakrabarty's essay was published saw the definitive fruition of the self-consciousness of the scholarly formation of 'postcolonial studies' with the publication of a large cluster of writings problematizing the increasing analytical weight being ascribed to 'postcolonial' as a field-defining and field-unifying term. The debate surrounding these concerns in 1992 was at least as important as the forceful innovations connected with the affirmatively elaborative literature of two or three years earlier, sharpening the contours of argument and defining the limits of the field more clearly.

It was in 1992 that Sara Suleri expressed deep scepticism about the ethical elevation of 'postcolonial feminism' and its celebration of the 'racially female voice'. Whereas 'postcolonial' had previously referred to 'the discursive practices produced by the historical fact of prior colonization in certain geographically specific segments of the world', it was coming to function more as 'an abstraction available for figurative deployment in any strategic redefinition of marginality'. On the one hand, that displacement 'helpfully derails the postcolonial condition from the strictures of national histories'. On the other hand, it threatened to render the concept 'so amorphous as to repudiate any locality for cultural thickness'.[24]

It was also in 1992 that Anne McClintock complained in the pages of *Social Text* that, while '"post-colonial studies" has set itself against the imperial idea of linear time ... the *term* "post-colonial" ... is haunted by the very figure of linear "development" that it sets out to dismantle. Metaphorically, the term "post-colonial" marks history as a series of stages along an epochal road from "the pre-colonial", to "the colonial", to "the post-colonial"', effecting a 're-centering of global history around the single rubric of European time' by conferring on 'colonialism the prestige of history proper'. In effect, she suggested, not only did postcolonialism fail to overcome the colonial stadialisms and Eurocentrisms it set out to uproot, but it also threatened to erase the substantial differences between cultures subjected to colonialism and the forms of colonialism to which they were subjected, even as it could too quickly lapse into a 'prematurely celebratory' characterization of the existing world.[25]

In the same 1992 issue of *Social Text*, Ella Shohat echoed many of the same concerns about homogenization, premature celebration and the ascendance of colonialism as the master-sign of history. She acknowledged the 'rising institutional endorsement of the term "post-colonial" and of post-colonial studies as an emergent discipline', but was critical of the 'depoliticizing implications' of the transition from the 'anti-colonial' and 'activist' to the 'professional' and 'theoretical' concerns that its ascendancy marked. The usage of 'post-colonial' systematically confounded two distinct periodizations: on the one hand, that of 'going beyond anti-colonial nationalist theory' through a series of 'disciplinary advances characteristic of intellectual history', and on the other hand, 'a movement beyond a specific point in history, that of colonialism and Third World nationalist struggles' as a movement taking place within 'the strict chronologies of history *tout court*'. The primacy of the former periodization over the latter in postcolonial criticism threatened to obscure the 'broad political-economic' dimensions of the 'imperialized formations' that perdured across the caesura of formal decolonization.[26]

Most impactfully of all, perhaps, 1992 also saw the appearance of Aijaz Ahmad's searing 350-page diatribe against the broadly poststructuralist tendencies of colonial and postcolonial criticism in his controversial book, *In Theory*. Ahmad's primary complaint was that the discourse-focused approach of postcolonial studies failed to engage with the broader social realities of global political economy, resulting in a critical practice whose self-indulgently inflated claims to oppositional politics were substantively empty. Its 'mystique of theoretical professionalism' served to depoliticize and domesticate the impulses of an older leftist activism, even as its narrowly rhetorical radicalism belied the comprador class origins and elite Western institutional affiliations of its key advocates.[27] Ahmad's book was arguably not lastingly significant as a theoretical intervention in itself. Even many of those most inclined to sympathize with the broadly Marxist thrust of his critique found the argumentation unconvincing and its tendency to 'polemical assassination' reprehensible.[28] But in capping 1992's attempts to push back at the ascendance of the postcolonial as a field-defining concept, it provided the occasion for precisely the kind of defensive gesture that fully demarcated the field. By the time *Public Culture* issued its special issue dedicated to 'Debating In Theory' in 1993, the wagons had been sufficiently circled that its essays could be read as sophisticated explorations of the proper boundaries of permissibility and impermissibility defining an interdisciplinary field of 'postcolonial studies'.

Back in 1987, Simon During had characterized postmodernism as internally fissured by its simultaneous refusal 'to turn the Other into the Same' and its recognition that 'the Other can never speak for itself *as* the Other'. But he had also characterized the postcolonial impulse as similarly fissured between what he called 'the post-colonized', who 'identify with the culture destroyed by imperialism and its tongue', and the 'post-colonizer', who 'cannot jettison the culture and tongues of the imperialist nations' even if they did not identify with them. That tension between the appeal of transcendence and the inescapability of immanence was on full display in Chakrabarty's famous essay, where 'Europe' represented the inescapable limit of historical discourse even as it represented a limit that had to be overcome. But the field that flourished in the subsequent two decades was also riven by a different tension that many of the critiques of 1992 were pointing towards. On the one hand, a politicizing impulse located postcolonialism within a long pedigree reaching back to the anti-colonial struggles of the twentieth century. This impulse remained central to the constitution of a genealogy for the field in both *The Post-Colonial Reader* of 1995, and even more powerfully in Robert Young's historical introduction to the field in 2001, where postcolonialism was directly identified with the 'tricontinentalist' anti-colonial tradition.[29] On the other hand, a metaphorizing impulse displaced postcolonialism from that pedigree through an emphasis on the colonial foundations of the anti-colonial commitment to national liberation. In During's terms, the conception of the 'post-colonized' turned out to be at profound odds with the political aspirations of anti-colonialism, in so far as anti-colonialism was pervasively nationalist and developmentalist, and thus simultaneously expressive of a 'post-colonizer' vision.

The result was, as Shohat had in some sense already anticipated, a tendency to shift the burden of postcolonial analysis from a specific *object of study* – the colonial situation and its sequelae – to a particular *mode of analysis* – a practice of reading committed to recognizing the colonial roots of its own epistemological assumptions and to overcoming the resulting limitations to whatever extent possible. The tradition of interrogating forms of subjectivity under colonial conditions – a thriving literature from Frantz Fanon to Ashis Nandy – no doubt played a crucial role in mediating the relationship between these two distinct problematics.

So if the 'post-colonial' had begun in the 1960s as a concept bound to the historical era of decolonization for its vibrancy, the 'postcolonial' became increasingly by the 1990s a concept contiguous and contemporary with the colonial, bound to an internal narrative about the colonial foundations of the protocols of disciplinary knowledge. Postcolonialism named an approach to reading texts that could be applied to almost any object.

The tension was sharp enough that by 1997, Edward Said was distancing himself from 'postcolonial studies' on the grounds that he cared more 'about the structures of dependency and impoverishment that exist' in the global South;[30] while Spivak declared herself a critic of 'metropolitan postcolonialism' in 1999.[31]

Four broad and instructive tendencies became evident in the proliferation of the postcolonial in the 1990s.

First, forms of scholarship that had previously travelled under the rubric of colonial studies came to be retrospectively identified under the rubric of 'postcolonial studies'. Works by Edward Said, Bernard Cohn, Talal Asad, Jean Comaroff and John Comaroff could all be grouped within the larger framework of postcolonial studies, despite not having been conceptualized under that rubric. By 1993, the literary scholar Ambreen Hai could complain of Ralph Crane's *Inventing India* (published the previous year) that it had neglected 'the last twenty years of British and American scholarship in postcolonial theory and cultural criticism'.[32]

Second, the invocation of postcoloniality began to spread beyond its early development in literary studies into other disciplines in the human sciences. This proliferation tended to track the relative proximity of diverse disciplines to literary studies. As early as 1990, Henry Giroux had embraced the analytical power of the postcolonial, as part of a package of intellectual practices that included postmodernism and feminism, for educational studies.[33] In 1991, Donna Haraway was imagining a practice of science studies that engaged 'with postcolonial, antiracist, and feminist cultural politics', and by 1992 Sandra Harding was outlining programmatic possibilities for 'postcolonial science studies'.[34] History's engagement with the concept also happened early, in a period when the discipline enjoyed strong connections with literary studies, thanks to the ascendance of the new historicism – a conjuncture that was reinforced by the specific role Spivak played in brokering a relationship between the Subaltern Studies project and postcolonial theory, as well as by the broad reception in 1992 of Chakrabarty's essay, 'Postcoloniality and the Artifice of History', and Gyan Prakash's response to Rosalind O'Hanlon and David Washbrook, 'Can the Subaltern Ride?'[35] Similarly, the centrality of literary scholarship to the American model of area studies meant that the postcolonial was recognized as a periodizer of scholarly dispositions by the early 1990s (especially but by no means exclusively in South Asian studies). In contrast, whereas anthropology was an important incubator of critical analysis of colonialism's significance to the developments of modern epistemological norms, it was slower to embrace the rubric of postcolonialism as a descriptor of these concerns. While the introduction to a 1992 special forum on 'Contested Pasts and the Practice of Anthropology' in *American Anthropologist* advocated that anthropologists engage more actively 'in the multidisciplinary debates over colonial discourse and postcolonialism', and a critical response the following year expressed 'misgivings about the discourse on postcolonialism' in 'American anthropology', the actual contributors to the forum reflected a more general indifference towards the postcolonial as a rubric for locating their own contributions (except in the older sense of political periodization).[36] In political science and economics, the reach of postcolonialism was felt least. By the late 1990s, however, a postcolonial heterodoxy was being elaborated even in a discipline as far from literary studies as international relations.[37]

Third, the geographical reach of the theoretical applicability of postcolonial criticism extended centripetally to include the European metropole within its analytical ambitions. Of course, from the very beginning of its emergence in literary studies, the concept of the postcolonial had been framed expansively from the beginning to encompass 'all the culture affected by the imperial process from the moment of colonization to the present day'.[38] That definitely included Europe within its scope, as the frequent focus on metropolitan and canonical texts in the practice of postcolonial criticism. But in more recent years, self-identifiedly postcolonial analysis of European contexts has turned not only on the post-imperial condition of Europe: Southern Europeanists have begun, as Roberto Dainotto observes, to draw 'a new lexicon to discuss the old facts of Europe's internal colonialism' from the repertoire of 'postcolonial and subaltern studies'.[39] Here, the experience of marginalization in Southern Europe becomes its own form of colonization, which in turn opens the space for the reconceptualization of the region's experience through the theoretical lens of postcolonial theory.

Fourth, the postcolonial expanded its temporal reach to include the study of historical periods before the era of the early modern European expansion. Both the tendencies towards geographical and temporal extension were emblematic of an increasingly metaphorizing tendency in the construal of the epistemic object that the rubric of the postcolonial invoked. Perhaps most emblematic of the metaphorizing tendency has been the thriving field of (self-identified) 'postcolonial studies' of the European Middle Ages.[40] Because the 'medieval past can be colonized, like a distant continent', medievalists 'cannot be blamed for trying (like a third world country) to catch up' to the modernists who dominate the academy.[41] Postcolonial medievalists are eager to show that the 'ideological groundwork for colonialism was being laid well before 1492', but they are much more fundamentally concerned with how an engagement with postcolonial theory can produce a rethinking of inherited spatial frames, periodizations and normative assumptions through the confounding of conventional assumptions about the modern/premodern binary.[42] For a 'criticism that has detailed the imperialistic colonization of space surely must now turn to an examination of the epistemological colonizations of time'.[43] The violent incursion on the rights of the dead is clearly first and foremost a problem of the scholarly subject and the protocols of knowledge production that frame it. Decolonizing the past then functions as a metaphorical reflex of decolonizing our own contemporary forms of knowledge.

Does such a development represent a provocative extension of postcolonial inquiry, and or does it represent a 'supernova' tendency that threatens the dissolution of postcolonial studies as an interdisciplinary field? Postcolonial studies arguably peaked in the early 2000s – not much more than a decade after its fruition to epistemological self-consciousness – and since then the question of its exhaustion or even 'end' as a field has been voiced many times.[44] The significance of these concerns, however, is inevitably obscured by the confounding anxieties produced by the simultaneous crisis in the reproduction of literary studies (still the core of postcolonial studies) within the post-2008 US academy.[45] The institutional successes of postcolonial thought have certainly blunted some of the boundaries that helped define it as a discrete field of inquiry. For the moment, its most prominent exponents occupy some of the most desirable and powerful institutional positions in the Anglophone academy – so there seems little reason to anticipate an imminent demise in its fortunes more precipitous than the general crisis in humanities education.

Notes

1 Accessed 7 August 2020.
2 See Steve J. Stern, 'Latin America's Colonial History: Invitation to an Agenda', *Latin American Perspectives*, 12:1 (1985), 3–16.
3 Accessed 7 August 2020.
4 Robert Young, *White Mythologies: Writing History and the West* (London: Routledge, 1990).
5 Edward W. Said, 'Representing the Colonized: Anthropology's Interlocutors', *Critical Inquiry*, 15:2 (1989), 205–25, 219.
6 Homi K. Bhabha, 'Signs Taken for Wonders', *Critical Inquiry*, 12:1 (1985), 144–65, 149. The other two essays on which his reputation was built are 'Of Mimicry and Man: The Ambivalence of Colonial Discourse', *October*, 28 (1984), 125–33, and 'Sly Civility', *October*, 34 (1985), 71–80.
7 Rajeswari Sunder Rajan, 'After 'Orientalism': Colonialism and English Literary Studies in India', *Social Scientist*, 14:7 (1986), 24.
8 Trinh T. Minh-ha, *Woman, Native, Other: Writing Postcoloniality and Feminism* (Bloomington, IN: Indiana University Press, 1989); *When the Moon Waxes Red:*

Representation, Gender and Cultural Politics (New York: Routledge, 1991), p. 186.

9 Gayatri Chakravorty Spivak, 'Three Women's Texts and a Critique of Imperialism', Critical Inquiry, 12:1 (1985), 259.

10 Gayatri Chakravorty Spivak, 'The Rani of Sirmur: An Essay in Reading the Archives', History and Theory, 24:3 (1985), 251.

11 Ranajit Guha and Gayatri Chakravorty Spivak (eds), Selected Subaltern Studies (New York: Oxford University Press, 1988), pp. 10, 175, 389.

12 Simon During, 'Postmodernism or Post-Colonialism Today', Textual Practice, 1:1 (1987), 33.

13 Ibid., 43–6.

14 Laura Kipnis, 'Feminism: The Political Unconscious of Postmodernism?', Social Text, 21 (1989), 149–66, 161, 163.

15 Bill Ashcroft, Gareth Griffiths and Helen Tiffin, The Empire Writes Back: Theory and Practice in Post-Colonial Literatures (London: Routledge, 1989), p. 2.

16 Ibid., p. 11.

17 Ibid., p. 2.

18 Gayatri Chakravorty Spivak, 'Woman in Difference: Mahasweta Devi's "Douloti the Bountiful"', Cultural Critique, 14 (1989–90), 105–28, 106.

19 See Ranajit Guha, 'On Some Aspects of the Historiography of Colonial India', in Ranajit Guha and Gayatri Chakravorty Spivak (eds), Selected Subaltern Studies (New York: Oxford University Press, 1988), pp. 37–44.

20 Gayatri Chakravorty Spivak, The Post-Colonial Critic: Interviews, Strategies, Dialogues (New York: Routledge, 1990).

21 See Homi K. Bhabha, 'DissemiNation: Time, Narrative, and the Margins of the Modern Nation', in Bhabha (ed.), Nation and Narration (London: Routledge, 1990), pp. 291–322.

22 Kwame Anthony Appiah, 'Is the Post- in Postmodernism the Post- in Postcolonial?', Critical Inquiry, 17:2 (1991), 336–57.

23 Dipesh Chakrabarty, 'Postcoloniality and the Artifice of History: Who Speaks for Indian Pasts?', Representations, 37 (1992), 1, 21.

24 Sara Suleri, 'Woman Skin Deep: Feminism and the Postcolonial Condition', Critical Inquiry, 18:4 (1992), 756–69, 759.

25 Anne McClintock, 'The Angel of Progress: Pitfalls of the Term "Post-Colonialism"', Social Text, 31/32 (1992), 84–98, 85–7.

26 Ella Shohat, 'Notes on the "Post-Colonial"', Social Text, 31/32 (1992), 99–113.

27 Aijaz Ahmad, In Theory: Classes, Nations, Literatures (London: Verso, 1992), quotation from p. 1.

28 See Benita Parry's review in History Workshop Journal, 36 (1993), 232–42, 232.

29 Bill Ashcroft, Gareth Griffiths and Helen Tiffin (eds), The Post-Colonial Studies Reader (London: Routledge, 1995); Robert Young, Postcolonialism: An Historical Introduction (Oxford: Blackwell, 2001).

30 Ania Loomba, 'Remembering Said', Comparative Studies of South Asia, Africa and the Middle East, 23:1/2 (2003), 12–14, 12.

31 Gayatri Chakravorty Spivak, *Critique of Postcolonial Reason: Toward a History of the Vanishing Present* (Cambridge, MA: Harvard University Press, 1999), p. xii.

32 Ambreen Hai, review of Ralph J. Crane, *Inventing India: A History of India in English-Language Fiction*, *Journal of Asian Studies*, 52:1 (1993), 183.

33 Henry A. Giroux, 'Rethinking the Boundaries of Educational Discourse: Modernism, Postmodernism, and Feminism', *College Literature*, 17:2/3 (1990), 18, 20, 21.

34 Donna Haraway, 'The Actors Are Cyborg, Nature is Coyote, and the Geography is Elsewhere: Postscript to "Cyborgs at Large"', in Constance Penley and Andrew Ross (eds), *Technoculture* (Minneapolis, MN: University of Minnesota Press, 1991), p. 24; Sandra Harding, 'After Eurocentrism: Challenges for the Philosophy of Science', *PSA: Proceedings of the Biennial Meeting of the Philosophy of Science Association*, 1992, vol. 2, 311–19.

35 Gyan Prakash, 'Can the "Subaltern" Ride? A Reply to O'Hanlon and Washbrook', *Comparative Studies in Society and History*, 34:1 (1992), 184.

36 Jonathan D. Hill, 'Overview', *American Anthropologist*, 94:4 (1992), 814; Takami Kuwayama, 'A Japanese Anthropologist's Response to "Contested Pasts and the Practice of Anthropology"', *American Anthropologist*, 95:3 (1993), 704.

37 Albert J. Paolini, *Navigating Modernity: Postcolonialism, Identity, and International Relations* (Boulder, CO: Lynne Rienner, 1999).

38 Ashcroft, Griffiths and Tiffin, *The Empire Writes Back*, p. 2.

39 Roberto M. Dainotto, *Europe (In Theory)* (Durham, NC: Duke University Press, 2007), p. 172.

40 The impulse has been strong enough that a recent introduction to postcolonial historical studies gives an entire chapter to the field: Rochona Majumdar, *Writing Postcolonial History* (London: Bloomsbury, 2010), chapter 4.

41 Ananya Jahanara Kabir and Deanne Williams, 'Introduction: A Return to Wonder', in Ananya Jahanara Kabir and Deanne Williams (eds), *Postcolonial Approaches to the European Middle Ages: Translating Cultures* (Cambridge: Cambridge University Press, 2005), p. 1; Margreta de Grazia, 'The Modern Divide: From Either Side', *Journal of Medieval and Early Modern Studies*, 37:3 (2007), 453–67, 457.

42 Lisa Lampert-Weissig, *Medieval Literature and Postcolonial Studies* (Edinburgh: Edinburgh University Press, 2010), pp. 2, 4.

43 Jeffrey Jerome Cohen, 'Introduction: Midcolonial', in Jeffrey Jerome Cohen (ed.), *The Postcolonial Middle Ages* (New York: Palgrave, 2001), p. 5.

44 See, for example, the special forum on 'The End of Postcolonial Theory?', *PMLA*, 122:2 (2007), 633–51.

45 *The Chronicle Review: Endgame: Can Literary Studies Survive?* (2020), http://connect.chronicle.com/rs/931-EKA-218/images/ChronicleReview_Endgame.pdf (accessed 7 August 2020).

9

The tradition of post-tradition

Stephen Turner

Introduction

According to its Google Ngram, the term 'post-traditional' arrives at the turn of the twentieth century, but only begins to be widely used after 1960, probably as a result of its appearance in a subtitle of a book by Robert Bellah,[1] after which its use has continued to increase geometrically, up to the present. There is a core problem with the term which is signalled by this citation pattern. It can be understood as a novel theoretical concept which applies to the last half of the twentieth century, telling us something about the meaning of our own time. The term, however, has a problematic relation to a much deeper, older and more pervasive set of distinctions, involving modernity and the larger trajectory of European society from the medieval period on, the Enlightenment, democratization, capitalism and industrialization, urbanism, and 'rationalization' and differentiation. It also followed, and resembled, a long-running discussion of the prospects for a new kind of society, based on a new or revised spiritual order or new values, that paralleled this discussion. Although there is a vague connection to the classical sociological literature, there is a sharp break between the 'post-traditional' literature and the 'spiritual order' and new values literature. The new literature neither engages nor cites it. Yet these literatures closely resemble one another, and share the same themes and much of the same anti-liberal, anti-individualist normative orientation.

This poses a problem for writing an intellectual history. Why was there so little textual continuity or engagement with the earlier literature in the discussion of these topics? Did they identify something genuinely novel with the term, as they claimed? Or did they unwittingly reproduce the distinctions made in the past? These turn out to be less questions of intellectual history – though there is an important historical fact that bears on them – than questions about the concept itself. Does it capture something new? The question can't be answered without getting a clear understanding of the concept itself. In what follows, I will focus on explication, and particularly on the problem of novelty as it appears within the texts themselves, which struggle, largely unsuccessfully, with the question of how post-traditionalism differs from modernity, which is at the core of the claim to novelty. But to see why the claim of novelty is problematic also requires some intellectual history and biography.

The original problem

It is not too much to say that characterizing the transition to modernity was the core problem of the modern social sciences, and certainly of sociology. The Enlightenment thinkers problematized tradition in contrast to reason, Burke problematized their notion of tradition, the Saint-Simonians problematized and historicized the Enlightenment thinkers themselves as products of the decay of the previous 'organic' epoch. The revisions of Saint-Simon's account, in the hands of Comte and Marx, who introduced their own periodizations, dominated early sociology and much of the social thinking of the mid nineteenth century. Their successors offered multiple versions of the distinction between the two kinds of society: Howard P. Becker's sacred and secular; Durkheim's mechanical and organic solidarities; Henry Sumner Maine's status and contract; Robert Redfield's folk and urban; Herbert Spencer's military and industrial; Tönnies' *Gemeinschaft* and *Gesellschaft*; and the one to which the users of term 'post-traditional' most typically refer, Max Weber's distinction between traditional and rational authority. These were synthesized in an influential way for professional sociology in Talcott Parsons' pattern-variables, which divided the basic tendencies of societies, which themselves clustered into modern and pre-modern.

A good baseline for understanding this literature is the account given by Herbert Spencer, the most influential source in the nineteenth century and the one to whom most of these alternative accounts were addressed. Spencer was a resolute defender of the rise of the autonomous individual,[2] a notable optimist about the changes, and rejected the idea that liberalism was an interregnum. He believed that the decline of religion meant that mutual tolerance, the 'daily habit of insisting on self-claims while respecting the claims of others, which the system of contract involves', would be characteristic of 'a life carried on under voluntary co-operation' rather than the traditional 'life carried on under compulsory co-operation'[3] of the past. But for many of these thinkers, the evaluation was reversed: the corrosive effects of Protestant individualism are the central fact of modernity, the product of which was political and moral individualism. At the core of the critiques on both sides – the moral regeneration and the new values sides – is nostalgia for the integrated and ordered societies of pre-modern Europe. Modernity, accordingly, was the destruction of this order.

This was, so to speak, a professional literature, or a proto-professional one: these texts became the core of 'classical social theory' and early sociology. But there was a public, non-professional discourse on these issues that was 'public', and was bound up with the problem of religion. This was a discussion that began with the challenge of Saint-Simon, which was taken up, loudly, in England, initially by Anglican thinkers.[4] The Saint-Simonians not only looked back to the organic periods of the past, but to the organic period to come, which for them meant a completely new system of morality and, not incidentally, relations between the sexes. For them, and for many of the thinkers listed above, such as Comte, the period of liberalism was an interregnum: an unsustainable anarchy of opinions. This was an idea with special resonance in religious circles throughout the nineteenth century. Their reaction to Saint-Simonianism took two basic forms: the first was to accept it and to begin to construct a replacement religion or religious object, appropriate for the next organic period, as Comte did; the second was to reconstruct Christianity in such a way, for example as a kind of socialism, to make the new model Christianity into the replacement religion. Prominent public intellectuals such as Balfour actively engaged in this discussion in the late nineteenth century.[5] And there were many variations on these ideas, and reactions to them, such as the writings of Karl Pearson, who blamed Protestantism for the ills of modernity and spent his time in Germany as a student seeking out Passion Plays (even writing one of his own, which, as Ted Porter puts it was 'also about applying lessons from the study of medieval culture to the needs of the present'),[6] wished to substitute the worship of the state for religion and have scientists revered as priests.[7] The fundamental options that remained after a discussion that spanned a century were the same as those with which the discussion began: spiritual regeneration or new values that would produce the solidarity and authority that older doctrines were failing to produce.

In the interwar period, this long-running discussion took a darker and more radical turn. The Great War led to disillusionment with the idea of progress. The Bishop of Ripon made a much-publicized plea to suspend science until the culture could catch up.[8] And culture was trying to: new ideas about women's roles, marriage and sex were widely discussed, reaching a peak in Bertrand Russell's *Marriage and Morals*,[9] and the response to Russell included a reaffirmation, along with a rethinking, of Christian doctrine.[10] There was a parallel discussion in the United States, in terms of the idea of companionate marriage, and its model of personal development and individual satisfaction for both sexes.[11] There were parallel discussions of religion as well. Charles Ellwood, in an influential book, called for the reconstruction of religion, a variation on the earlier themes of spiritual regeneration in a 'social' direction, going beyond the Social Gospel of the pre-war period.[12] Reinhold Niebuhr provided an even more successful, but darker, alternative to this, rejecting social optimism, in such books as *Moral Man and Immoral Society*.[13]

By the time of the economic crisis of the 1930s, the British side of this literature had turned into a rich mix of nostalgia for the orderly societies of the Middle Ages combined with Christian socialism, for example in the writings and activism of R. H. Tawney,[14] as well as to curiosity about the apparent successes of the Bolshevik regime and both Nazi and fascist 'planning', which contrasted both to liberal politics and liberal economics, both of which were seen as failing to meet the demands of the day. But the crisis in question was framed in moral terms. The Moral Rearmament movement, which had an international reach and agenda, was launched in 1938 in response to the spiritual crisis of the time, and explicitly conceived in response to Nazism.

The arrival of the war focused the discussion of the moral crisis. One theme was the question of what the war was being fought for: Robert Maynard Hutchins and John Dewey debated the question in the pages of *Fortune*.[15] The famous London discussion group The Moot debated the possibility of reviving Anglicanism or alternatively of creating a new social doctrine with the force of religion,[16] in contiguity with the writings of T. S. Eliot, such as his tract *Christianity and Culture*.[17] The Moot's participants were concerned with the biggest of pictures, the problem of how the lessons of past societies and social change could inform the creation of future societies. They tended to think of the present as an unsatisfactory interregnum between coherent orders. And they were not alone in having difficulty coming to agreement. In *The Year of Our Lord 1943* Allan Jacobs shows the idea of the war as a contest of values with Nazism was widely accepted, but the many intellectuals who contributed to this discussion had trouble agreeing on what these values were.[18]

Then it all stopped. The end of the war meant the end of this self-searching dialogue, and a turn to the conflicts of the Cold War and to the celebration of the victory of liberal democracy and the expanded place of Communism in the world. Tawney's Christian socialism was institutionalized into the bureaucracy of the welfare state and lost its spiritual character.[19] Mannheim's ideas on planning a social order complete with planned values had the same fate.[20] In Britain, the kind of non-professional public sociology that had provided a home for this kind of work was replaced by a newly professionalized British Sociological Association that lacked interest in these civilizational concerns, and disdained their predecessors.[21] In the United States, a new historiography and social theory of consensus was created in such works as Richard Hofstader's *The American Political Tradition*.[22] The sense of living in an interregnum evaporated, as did the urgency of the concerns of the earlier discussion.

The fresh start

Alasdair MacIntyre, Robert Bellah and Anthony Giddens are the three most prominent thinkers associated with the concept of post-traditionalism. None of them ever engaged this earlier literature, and apparently were unaware of it though much of their thinking repeats its core ideas, and ultimately came to the same options: spiritual regeneration or new solidaristic values, together with opposition to liberal values such as the ideal of the autonomous individual. Their path was, however, through a different route: Marxism, and a dissatisfaction with Marxism. The ten years between the older members of the group, born in 1928, and Giddens, born in 1938, turned out to be decisive. When the Hungarian revolution and the death of Stalin split the left, and drove many intellectuals out of the Communist party, Bellah and MacIntyre were adults for whom the party had been a primary source of identity. MacIntyre had an established reputation as a Marxist writer, writing dozens of articles for journals on the left, and had been a party member. Bellah, as a Harvard undergraduate, had been a leader of the John Reed Club and was a party member until 1949. In 1956, he was still at Harvard, refusing to testify against his former comrades.[23] Both of them had a developed distaste for modern liberal society. Giddens was just eighteen, three years from graduation from Hull. But Marx was the dominant social thinker in Giddens' own academic preparation. Giddens' first book, *Capitalism and Modern Social Theory*, reiterated the thesis that capitalism was the fundamental structuring fact of modern society. For him, the 1960s were the break with the past that needed to be theorized in a new way: post-traditionalism supplied him with terminology to do so.

For these three thinkers the Marxist background, and their different attempts to go beyond it, were decisive for their development. MacIntyre's Marxist writings of the late 1950s reveal precisely what was at stake: the desire for a new moral order, 'an alternative to the barren opposition of moral individualism and amoral Stalinism'.[24] This was a commitment he never abandoned. Liberalism was never an option: Marxism had revealed that liberalism was 'a deceiving and self-deceiving mask for certain social interests' which 'tends to dissolve traditional human ties and to impoverish social and cultural relationships'.[25] Bellah shared MacIntyre's horror of moral individualism. He later cited as an early motivation his 'Ambivalence toward the Southern California culture in which I grew up', and 'the apparently chaotic society in which I lived'.[26] He was to become famous for his leadership of the team that wrote the bestselling *Habits of the Heart*, a condemnation of American individualism. For Giddens, the problem was more academic: he came to believe that the tradition of social theory, dominated by Marx, was no longer informative and needed to be replaced. His later, political, phase, reflected his rejection of the traditions of the Labour Party; without embracing liberalism: he sought a 'third way'.

The disconnect between the literature deriving from the reaction to Saint-Simon and the post-Marxist, or more precisely post-Stalinist literature, was a result of this different starting point. The former Marxists who faced an existential moral crisis after the death of Stalin and the Hungarian revolution were not searching for a new moral order to solve the problems of civilization, nor for moral regeneration as the older discussion did. They were searching for a replacement for the moral orthodoxy and vision of the future they had derived from Communism and the Soviet model. They only came to solutions to this problem that resembled the other tradition long after the moment of crisis had passed. Post-traditional, in this intellectual context, means post-bourgeois. But Marxism did not have a category for a society that was post-bourgeois in its morality and other than proletarian-revolutionary. This was the gap that the concept served to fill for them. The concept suffered from fundamental problems, most of which were the indirect result of the Marxist origin of the problematic itself. It lacked a coherent account of tradition to be 'post', and faltered in distinguishing the post-traditional from the modern, a concept that came, confusingly, to replace 'bourgeois society', and in characterizing tradition itself.

Because these three thinkers, with the partial exception of Giddens, did not proceed from a critique of their predecessors either in the proto-professional 'modernity' tradition or the long tradition of arguing over the reinvention of the medieval social order or new values, we are left with a lacuna. Their characterizations of post-tradition use concepts that resemble the concepts in these literatures. But we do not have a developed account in their own voice of the differences between 'post-traditionalism' and this myriad of past voices. So what was novel? There seems to be a simple answer to the question. Tradition and traditional societies suppressed the 'self' in a prison of duties, ascriptive demands and restrictions, typically with religious justifications. This was never fully effaced by modernization. The concept of 'post-traditional' appears to be a radicalization in the face of such issues: it implies, in the term itself, to be about a break not only with particular traditions, which even theorists of modernity acknowledge persist into the modern world, but with tradition as such, or at least with tradition in the normal understanding of tradition. In the later incarnations of the concept, for example with Giddens and Scott Lash, post-traditionalism means the end of traditional social roles and the possibility – or burden – of self-invention, a change whose full force has only recently been felt.[27] But how novel was this, as a concept to be applied to historical change or as a historical phenomenon itself?

We can give a brief account of this problem by starting with the thinker who provides the most complete attempt to distinguish modernity and post-traditionalism: Anthony Giddens. Writing on modernity, Giddens provides the following rough definition: 'As a first approximation, let us simply say the following: "modernity" refers to modes of social life or organization which emerged in Europe from about the seventeenth century onwards and which subsequently became more or less worldwide in their influence.'[28]

The goal of Giddens' own analysis is to identify the features that make modernity unique as a form of social life:

> The views I shall develop have their point of origin in what I have elsewhere called a 'discontinuist' interpretation of modern social development. By this I mean that modern social institutions are in some respects unique – distinct in form from all types of traditional order. Capturing the nature of the discontinuities involved, I shall argue, is a necessary preliminary to analysing what modernity actually is, as well as diagnosing its consequences for us in the present day.[29]

The term 'some respects' is telling. Giddens identifies multiple discontinuities: 'the sheer pace of change', the global 'scope of change'; the fact that at least some 'modern social forms are simply not found in prior historical periods – such as the political system of the nation-state, the wholesale dependence of production upon inanimate power sources, or the thoroughgoing commodification of products and wage labour'[30]; and the fact that even sites of apparent continuity, such as cities, are ordered according to quite different principles from those which set off the pre-modern city from the countryside in prior periods.

These are largely changes external to the individual and the individual mind. In contrast, post-traditional society, or late modernity, is characterized by an internal change, the rise of a new kind of self: a reflexive self, which does not merely occupy social roles, even chosen roles, but which creates for itself, through its beliefs about the self, a new kind of self, based on 'a person's own reflexive understanding of their biography',[31] a kind of therapeutic self in which a person's self-conception depends on monitoring and revising their self-understanding. This gives us a reasonably clear distinction: modernity is characterized by a mixture of traditional and novel forms; late modernity or post-traditional society is characterized by a particular novelty, the reflexive self.

But with Bellah we can see the difficulties with this claim of novelty as a historical thesis. The notion of the self appears to be novel, but it too has a long history. Bellah, in the essay on secularization he included in the book in which the term post-traditional was introduced, employs a periodization of religious types based on the self: 'The historic religions discovered the self; the early modern religion found a doctrinal basis on which to accept the self in all its empirical ambiguity; modern religion is beginning to understand the laws of the self's own existence and so to help man take responsibility for his own fate.'[32] This raises the question of the dating of the reflexive self, and the modern self, and whether it is the product of an internal or an external change.

The concept of traditional *societies* appears in connection with the 'modernization theory' that flourished in the 1950s. Here we get a puzzling answer to this question of dating, and a different answer to the question of what is internal and what is external. 'Traditional societies' were undergoing 'development' and decolonization, driven by external changes, but also motivated by internal issues: a case of the explanation of the new based on elements of the old. As Bellah noted:

> The pressures of modernization, then, do not undermine idyllic societies of happy farmers whose lives would be perfectly happy if they were only left alone. It provides the concepts to express doubts and demands that were already just below the surface of consciousness. It provides an atmosphere of hope, often unrealistic, that things will soon be better.[33]

This is a less than nostalgic view of traditional societies, and presents modernization as a good – a highly desired, but not unalloyed, good. And there is another side to modernization theory and the theory of 'traditional' societies that emphasizes quasi-rational resistance to change and also the quasi-rational motives for modernization such as the imitation of 'modern' forms for the purpose of prestige. These reflect the idea of a kind of self-creation based on motives that were already just below the surface of consciousness – supposedly a feature of the post-traditional, but in classically peasant societies.

Like Giddens, Bellah is concerned with the co-existence of modern and traditional elements. He presents an account of the good kind of modernization, one that tempers liberalism and individualism with modern versions of traditional collectivizing institutions that are functional substitutes for them, but which support the autonomous individual without oppressing. It is worth quoting a passage at length.

> Modernization carries with it a conception of a relatively autonomous individual with a considerable capacity for adaptation to new situations and for innovation. Such an individual has a relatively high degree of self-consciousness

and requires a family structure in which his independence and personal dignity will be recognized and where he can relate to others not so much in terms of authority and obedience as in terms of companionship and emotional participation. Such an individual also requires a society in which he feels like a full participating member, whose goals he shares and can meaningfully contribute to. Finally he requires a worldview that is open to the future, gives a positive value to amelioration of conditions in this world, and can help to make sense of the disruptions and disturbances of the historical process.[34]

This vision of modernization echoes Spencer with respect to the demise of priestly authority and rise of the autonomous, contract-making individual. It also provides a normative standard of feeling like a member of a society with goals and having a progressive social vision: solidaristic values. And in Bellah's later writing he uses this same image as a counterpoint to the excessive individualism he ascribes to contemporary America.[35]

It raises a question. The degree of autonomy allowed to what was called in the 1930s and 1940s 'the new socialist man' was a problem: the new socialist man was a man of the left, with a collective orientation, but whose orientation was a product of his maturity and autonomous choice – distinct from 'economic man', enslaved to acquisition. This 'autonomy' was always problematic, and became more so after Stalin's death, when the moral confusion noted by MacIntyre set in. The new normative standard allowed for more autonomy and recoiled from Stalinist submission. But the relatively autonomous individual of Bellah, with his new-found self-consciousness, seems indistinguishable not only from the reflexive self of Giddens but also from the optimistic autonomous self of Spencer, who, on Spencer's own account, as part of his moral development, becomes averse to harming others.

> [T]he thief takes another man's property; his act is determined by certain imagined proximate pleasures of relatively simple kinds, rather than by less clearly imagined possible pains that are more remote and of relatively involved kinds. But in the conscientious man, there is an adequate restraining motive, still more re-representative in its nature, including not only ideas of punishment, and not only ideas of lost reputation and ruin, but including ideas of the claims of the person owning the property, and of the pains which loss of it will entail on him: all joined with a general aversion to acts injurious to others, which arises from the inherited effects of experience.[36]

This seems to accommodate Bellah's vision, and even imply its soldaristic elements, which would follow from the aversion to harming others. But at the same time this is a picture of tradition: that is what Spencer means by 'the inherited effects of experience', which he took to be the product of 'mass of individual inductions [which becomes transformed] into a public and traditional induction impressed on each generation as it grows up'.[37]

We seem to be faced with a conundrum. Is Bellah's post-traditional autonomous individual actually different from the liberal autonomous one? Or is the difference this: that Spencer thinks that this individual has morally desirable qualities resulting from experience and from experience congealed into tradition, while Bellah does not? Or is it that Bellah, as his rejection of the 'chaotic' society of southern California from which he came suggests, does not think that people raised under the influence of individualism have these qualities? Or that, unlike southern California, it is 'a society in which he feels like a full participating member, whose goals he shares and can meaningfully contribute to'?

The most plausible answer to this question is that Bellah does not think his subjects live in such a society, but that they secretly crave one, or would be better off if they were in one. But this is no longer a historical question alone: it is a morally freighted normative judgement derived from his Marxist past, which is no longer an empirical claim but a definitional one, in which the definition of such terms as 'meaningfully contribute to' carry the burden of the definition rather than the subjective experience of participation. The same can be said for MacIntyre, and perhaps for Giddens. To point this out is to ask whether the concept of post-traditionalism can be separated from the grand narratives of anti-liberalism and its philosophical anthropology, and from its normative ideals of solidarity and equality.

The normative dimension

When we trace the history of ideas about modernity, we can see the different normative attitudes toward it through the litmus test of the vision each of them has toward what they take to be the modern self. Spencer embraced it, and did not regard liberalism as an interregnum, as a chaos to be overcome; the post-traditionalists differed. The normative stance we can associate with the idea of post-traditionalism contains elements of Bellah's positive vision of the right kind of modernity. Bellah's model, decoded, is traditional Left modernism, a kind of socialism minus the idea of the public ownership of the means of production. The idea of participation and sharing goals of amelioration do the work that traditional socialist programmatics did. But the focus is now different, and the difference is key to understanding the normative force of the idea of post-traditionalism, one aspect of which is the recognition of the end of ideology and the turn from ideological orthodoxies to ideas of process and participation.

Alasdair MacIntyre, in his early writings, makes a sociological distinction, in terms of what he describes as 'two quite different sets of phenomena, which do as a matter of fact coexist within our society'.

There are on the one hand the language and the concepts of those people who have continued to live within a tolerably well-established moral framework with a tolerably well-established moral vocabulary. [...] Members of this type of social group possess a list of what they take to be the virtues and vices; moreover they possess a concept of the virtues such that the authority which requires their practice is not conferred by the agent's choice. [...] Indeed choices of moral standards are judged correct or incorrect in the light of their understanding of the virtues and vices.[38]

On the other hand,

There are ... individuals who have a different kind of moral vocabulary. They do not belong to a single homogeneous moral community with a shared language and shared concepts. Instead they find themselves solicited from different standpoints. They cannot avoid choice, and what moral standards they adopt depends upon their own choices. So choice is the fundamental moral concept and there are no objective impersonal standards in the light of which ultimate choices can be criticized.[39]

MacIntyre is decidedly hostile to the latter type, which looks like the reflexive self of Giddens, and comments that '[t]he greatest contemporary moral achievement is the creation of the type of community where shared ends and needs make possible the growth of a common life and a common commitment, which can be expressed in a common language'.[40]

The fact that there is no such moral achievement on the horizon is, so to speak, the post-traditional condition: in this respect the three are in agreement. The distance between this vision and Bellah's at this point is small: perhaps it is no more than the space marked by the 'relatively' that appears in Bellah's account, which tries to preserve the modern autonomous self in a new moral community.[41] But MacIntyre's version introduces an element that threatens the possibility of any such community: individuals who are autonomous are forced to choose between 'standpoints' which provide them with moral standards, but these are standards that conflict with the standards of others. And this points to a crucial feature of the present: the problem of the actual existence of different moral standpoints, mostly deriving from 'traditional' subcultures, co-existing within the same community, and faced with the problem of accommodating one another.

This gives us a new problem: multiculturalism. But we are thrown back to the old trilemma. Either we accept something like a liberal framework, of shared rules but few shared ends, and treat individuals as autonomous bearers of culture who get along with one another under these rules, or we can hope for spiritual regeneration that overcomes difference, or we can seek new values that allow for a positive relation between cultures.

Giddens formulates this problematic most clearly, as a normative, or one might say 'performative', idea. Tradition once supplied a basis for community, but it was a rigid and oppressive basis that 'crushed individual autonomy'.[42] It was also based on exclusion and 'traditions of family and gender'[43] that are themselves oppressive. The existence of a variety of cultures in modern societies makes a return to this kind of community impossible. What is needed is something different, and cosmopolitan in character, meaning accepting of the existence of this variety and seeking a peaceful way of accommodating it. But to appeal to cosmopolitanism as a solution is to concede that non-cosmopolitanism, meaning mutual intolerance between traditions, is the problem. This is thus a somewhat paradoxical argument: it concedes the persistence of traditions in the different cultural communities, without which there would be no multiplicity of cultures. Tradition, for Giddens, is thus normatively bad – oppressive – but still powerful and in need of more than mere accommodation, namely to be recognized and accepted by others as good.

Giddens' performative solution to the problem of mutually intolerant traditions is 'Active Trust', leading to a 'positive spiral' of trust-building that creates a functional substitute for 'traditional' community and which builds obligation at the level of personal relations based on 'the communication of difference, geared to an appreciation of integrity'.[44] The process involved is presented as tradition-free: 'integrity' is something that does not require, or seems not to require, adherence to particular traditions. It transcends difference and can be recognized in spite of difference. But it can be understood in terms of the fulfilment of reciprocities such that 'the other is someone on whom one can rely, that reliance becoming a mutual obligation'. This is obligation without tradition, which 'will stabilize relationships in so far as the condition of mutual integrity is met'.[45] It is also, ironically, an echo of Spencer's own vision of society free from religion and based on trust between free contract makers.

Giddens, however, cites a different source: John Dewey's notion of 'liberalism'. Dewey claims that a democratic order requires a 'socially generous' attitude, and the 'capacity to share in a give and take experience'.[46] Dewey supposed, and Giddens perhaps assumes, that this would lead to new forms of collective action. In the 1930s this was going to be 'planning'. For Giddens, however, politics itself requires something different: 'Civil Association', which respects the autonomy of others and amounts to people living in an 'intelligent relationship' with one another governed by rules. This is straightforwardly a liberal concept: it comes directly from Michael Oakeshott[47] as is clear from Giddens' reference to its opposite, an enterprise association. But Giddens, like Bellah, tries to soften this kind of liberalism with something more solidaristic. So Giddens recommends what he calls dialogical democracy, which would not depend merely on active trust of the sort relevant for personal relations – Spencer's solution of contract-making individuals coming to trust one another – but on a 'cosmopolitan engagement with groups, ideas, and contexts other than one's own even where these engagements have nothing directly to do with the domain of the state'.[48]

This kind of dialogic relationship is possible precisely because of the feature that Giddens believes distinguishes post-traditionalism from mere modernity: reflexivity. And this notion allows him to avoid some obvious problems with his account of tradition. The first problem is that it seems to presume the existence of groups, ideas and contexts that are closely related and continuous over time – which is to say something very close to what was always meant by 'tradition'. Giddens concedes that 'combined with the inertia of habit, this means that, even in the most modernized of modern societies, tradition continues to play a role', though he goes on to insist that 'this role is generally much less significant than is supposed by authors who focus attention upon the integration of tradition and modernity in the contemporary world.[49]

'Much less significant' is a quantitative distinction. But Giddens goes beyond this. He argues that not only is tradition less significant, but also that the 'tradition' that remains is fundamentally different from the tradition of the past. This is, apparently, the difference that warrants the 'post' in 'post-traditional': the discontinuity marked by the notion of post-tradition is not simply a matter of the end of traditions, but is among other things a discontinuity within the category of tradition itself. This denial of the continued significance of tradition, however, is somewhat hollow. There would be no point to dialogue, engagement, and the creation of novel forms of personal relationship based on reciprocity with the 'other' unless there was an 'other' who was, at the same time, governed in some significant way by a different tradition.

This internal discontinuity is the result of the discontinuity which he identifies as is 'reflexivity.' Reflexivity is the distinctive characteristic of modern life. 'The reflexivity of modern social life consists in the fact that social practices are constantly examined and reformed in the light of incoming information about those very practices, thus constitutively altering their character.'[50] This means that the apparent continued role of tradition, which he acknowledges, is an illusion. If tradition is justified reflexively it is no longer tradition: 'For justified tradition is tradition in sham clothing and receives its identity only from the reflexivity of the modern.'[51]

This way of making the distinction between mere modernity, in which social practices are questioned, and post-traditionalism, in which the self is created reflexively, creates a muddle. Traditions persist in fact, and need respect at least to enable dialogue between the adherents of different traditions. The existence of 'difference' which is a result of these persistent traditions and their communalization is at least part of what forces individuals into reflexivity and choice. A part, perhaps a large part, of the 'incoming information' about our social practices comes from the encounter with other traditions: this was already a feature of 'modernity'. The fact that one must choose itself marks a fundamental break with tradition. One cannot, for example, wear the head scarf as a continuation of traditional practice. Traditional practice was not a choice. To wear it today is to choose based on reflection on the practice of veiling: choosing to affirm one's identity in this way is a paradigmatic act of a post-traditional, reflexive, act of self-creation. This kind of radical individualism is thus no longer merely an option: we are condemned to it. But weren't we condemned to it already by 'modernity'? Isn't the justification of practices, which is supposed to fundamentally change the nature of the traditions that we continue to accept, precisely the constitutive 'altering' that produces, by definition, the reflexive self?

Post-traditionalism defined

It may be observed that this argumentative strategy makes the category of post-traditionalism immune to refutation by factual observations about the persistence and ubiquity of tradition: the general fact of reflexivity has turned all traditions into post-traditions by definition. But this shifts the explanatory burden, the problem of what is novel about post-traditionalism, to reflexivity. Where does it come from? And this points to a general problem with these distinctions: if it is its own discontinuity, it needs its own explanation; if it is the outcome of something that is already present, it is not a genuine discontinuity. So the argumentative strategy behind the claim of the discontinuous character of post-traditionalism has to exclude arguments that point to continuities. And it has another burden: the discontinuity cannot be the same as the discontinuity that produced 'modernity'. If it is, 'the post-traditional', as a category, collapses into the familiar category of 'the modern'.

Bellah's original point about the character of post-traditional of religion was this: there were once religious frameworks monopolized by religious groups, orthodoxies, but these have now become open to question. He formulates this in terms of the self, and ends with an appeal to something akin to reflexivity:

Not only has any obligation of doctrinal orthodoxy been abandoned by the leading edge of modern culture, but every fixed position has become open to question in the process of making sense out of man and his situation. This involves a profounder commitment to the process I have been calling religious symbolization than ever before. The historic religions discovered the self; the early modern religion found a doctrinal basis on which to accept the self in all its empirical ambiguity; modern religion is beginning to understand the laws of the self's own existence and so to help man take responsibility for his own fate.[52]

Taking responsibility for one's own fate rather than ascribing it to God and meekly accepting the demands of tradition is the product, for Bellah, of *religious* development, beginning with the 'discovery' of the self by the historic religions: so for him this is the past element that leads to reflexivity. But reflexivity is not enough as a basis for social life. Indeed, one might say it is merely corrosive of social life, because there must be some non-reflexive, taken for granted, basis for social relations.

With this we come to a conflict between reflexivity and solidarity. The 'type of community where shared ends and needs make possible the growth of a common life and a common commitment, which can be expressed in a common language',[53] which we have seen is MacIntyre's preferred but unobtainable version of the solidaristic values option, is precisely the type of community that liberalism, which accommodates different ends and needs without a 'common life and a common commitment', cannot create. From the point of view of this kind of community, liberalism is simply an arrangement, a compromise in a society without common commitments. MacIntyre makes this point relentlessly, when he argues that the existence of moral pluralism, in contemporary society, and in English society in the nineteenth century, meant that there was no such common base.

MacIntyre makes another point, which bears directly on the problem of the need for a non-reflexive basis for social life. He said that the very lack of a common project meant that society elevated and depended on what he called 'the secondary virtues of co-operation, of compromise, of a pragmatic approach, of fairness'.[54] The idea of civil association to which Giddens appeals has precisely this character: it is not and cannot be, given the lack of consensus on the religious foundations of the legal and political order, grounded in anything but a kind of compromise. It is essentially about the rules of the game – purposes and goals are individual, and pursued within the framework of the rules, and it is to the rules that citizens must subscribe. It contrasts vividly to the kind of association with shared collective goals: Oakeshott's 'enterprise association'.[55]

Was Spencer right to think that there can be a tradition-free society based on trust between autonomous individuals? Is it a kind of default, as MacIntyre pictures it, based on secondary, and presumably non-traditional virtues, which we fall back on when traditions fail to reproduce themselves?

Is Giddens right to think that there can be a trust-building dialogic relation between the adherents to different contemporary (and reflexive) traditions? Or is the idea of such a dialogue, with its particular notions of generosity, amelioration, participation and so forth, itself an ideology or framework that needs propagation and acceptance? Put even more simply, is cosmopolitan liberalism itself a tradition? There is another question lurking behind this: are there in fact societies that approximate this ideal? What do they look like? Are they post-traditional in the sense of 'tradition-free'? Or does this kind of cooperation itself depend on traditions, on a moral framework or set of values of some sort? And could it be that this is the kind of society we already inhabit, based on a long-standing liberal cosmopolitan tradition of accommodating other cultures?

The idea of rupture

Post-traditionalism as a concept depends on the idea of rupture. But our sense of rupture as well as our sense of continuity is subject to an important illusion. The illusion can be illustrated by Robert Putnam's *Bowling Alone*,[56] which purported to show the decline in associational activities in the United States. Necessarily, this was concerned with associational activities popular in the past, and their decline, such as the bowling leagues referred to in the title. What it could not address, or did not address, was the development of novel forms of association, or forms of association that have not been recognized as such. It is evident that internet-based forms of association have increased, radically, and that phenomena such as women's book clubs have become more important. If we do not take our eyes from the historical rear-view mirror, we are doomed to always seeing traditions recede.

An example of this is the concept of honour. On the one hand it is a relic of the past: honour is relative to rank, and belongs to a society of ranks of the kind that Europe abolished and America never had. It was governed by such sanctions as duelling, which has declined of late. When we encounter the forms of honour in other cultures they are alien and non-modern, such as honour killings. In the nineteenth century honour had a large role in German law,[57] and although the term is alien to Anglo-American law, there is a law of defamation that does something similar. So – did honour simply go away? Or did some of the external forms disappear? Did it persist as one of the elements that enabled capitalism to survive? Or did it survive, even strengthen, as a part of the actual tradition but under different names and guises?

A recent event can put this into focus. A small Toronto Airport posted an advertisement that read 'You're Precious Cargo, not Cattle'.[58] An animal rights activist protested, calling it insulting to cows. The ad was removed. The implication was clear: cows have honour claims, can be dishonoured, and others will defend their honour. We can see this in historical context. Honour became democratized. There was, as a result of changed attitudes toward animals, such as the idea of animal rights, an extension of the democratization of honour to cows. And one can find many other examples of novel applications of honour-like notions, social movements demanding honour, under other names, as well as theoretical claims that validate honour considerations, also under other names, such as in the writings of Axel Honneth on 'recognition'.[59] But might one instead claim, as Peter Berger did, that there was a new concept, dignity, whose 'discovery took place amid the debunked conceptions of honour',[60] and therefore a break in tradition.[61] These are characteristic problems, with no solutions.

Post-traditionalism as a concept depends on the possibly illusory sense that something fundamental has changed. The idea of tradition implies something mental, and the transitions in question, from traditional to modern and then to post-traditional, are mental transitions. But there is typically an ambiguity about cause which undermines the idea of transition: it is not clear whether the external circumstances changed and permitted people to act in accordance with their pre-existing desires, as Bellah suggests was the case with traditional societies, or the desires themselves changed, as new possibilities of objects of desire emerged. And there is another possibility: that the 'tradition' in question was never as rigid as the theory of 'tradition' represented it, and simply changed in the normal way that traditions change, through adaptation and extension to new circumstances. Giddens' idea of reflexivity is a case in point. Did people suddenly become aware in the 1960s that they had practices that they could reflect on, and were therefore forced to either choose to abandon them or to embrace them, in both cases being forced to reflect and choose? Or is this a completely normal and continuous part of social life, and always has been?

In the face of all this indeterminacy, the concept of post-traditionalism must be said to be appealing for other reasons than its cognitive power. The appeal, perhaps, is to be found in its performative implications. We can distinguish two, one discussed by these thinkers, the other found, so to speak, in the streets. The first is exemplified by Giddens' conclusion, to call for dialogue and respect. This is less 'post' than it appears. Dialogue is the fetish of the tradition of liberalism.[62] And the idea that we progress through dialogue fits with a suppressed and unacknowledged grand narrative to the effect that the various traditions of the world are mixtures of moral truth and error, and that somehow the interaction of these traditions will bring about a purified, universal, 'rational good', in the phrase of Hobhouse – the last Spencerian, in many ways. Dialogue then becomes the performative act commanded by the goal of progress, with cosmopolitanism is its apex.[63] It echoes Spencer himself, who envisioned a future in which religious authoritarianism would lose its grip, and people would come to relate to one another as agents able to freely contract with one another and therefore to develop the trusting relations appropriate to the relation of contract. The performative side of post-traditionalism offers this, but also less, because it contemplates – or embraces – the possibility that there can be no progress beyond minimal multi-cultural trust. If this is the case, tradition has disappeared by definition, not in its role in people's lives.

Notes

1 Robert Bellah, *Beyond Belief: Essays on Religion in a Post-Traditionalist World* (Berkeley, CA: University of California Press ([1970] 1991).

2 Herbert Spencer, *The Principles of Ethics*, vol. 1 (New York: D. Appleton and Company, 1895), pp. 477–554.

3 Herbert Spencer, *The Man versus the State: Containing 'The New Toryism', 'The Coming Slavery', 'The Sins of Legislators' and 'The Great Political Superstition'* (London: Williams and Norgate, 1885), pp. 800–1.

4 Stephen Turner, 'Religion and British Sociology: The Power and Necessity of the Spiritual; Sociology in Britain', in John Holmwood and J. Scott (eds), *The Palgrave Handbook of Sociology in Britain* (London: Palgrave, 2014), pp. 97–122.

5 Arthur J. Balfour, *The Religion of Humanity: An Address Delivered at the Church Congress, Manchester, October 1888* (Edinburgh: David Douglas, 1888).

6 Theodore M. Porter, *Karl Pearson: The Scientific Life in a Statistical Age* (Princeton, NJ: Princeton University Press, 2004), p. 90.

7 Karl Pearson, *The Ethic of Freethought* (London: T. Fisher Unwin, 1888), p. 20.

8 E. A. Burroughs, Bishop of Ripon, 'Is Scientific Advance Impeding Human Welfare?', *Literary Digest*, 95 (1927), 32.

9 Bertrand Russell, *Marriage and Morals* (New York: W. W. Norton and Co., [1929] 1957).

10 Christopher Dawson, *Christianity and Sex* (London: Faber & Faber, 1930), esp. pp. 13–16.

11 Benjamin Barr Lindsey and Evans Wainwright, *The Companionate Marriage* (New York: Boni & Liveright, 1927).

12 Charles Ellwood, *The Reconstruction of Religion: A Sociological View* (New York: Macmillan, 1922).

13 Reinhold Niebuhr, *Moral Man and Immoral Society* (New York: Charles Scribner's Sons, 1932).

14 R. H. Tawney, *The Acquisitive Society* (New York: Harcourt, Brace and Howe, 1920); *Religion and the Rise of Capitalism* (New York: Harcourt, Brace & Company, 1926); *Equality* (London: George Allen & Unwin, 1931).

15 John Dewey, 'Challenge to Liberal Thought', *Fortune*, 30 (1944), 155–7, 180–90. Robert Maynard Hutchins, 'Toward a Durable Society', *Fortune*, 27 (1945), 159–60, 194–207.

16 Keith Clements (ed.), *The Moot Papers: Faith, Freedom and Society 1938–1944* (London: Bloomsbury, 2009).

17 T. S. Eliot, *Christianity and Culture* (New York: Harcourt Brace, [1939] 1976).

18 Alan Jacobs, *The Year of Our Lord 1943: Christian Humanism in an Age of Crisis* (Oxford: Oxford University Press, 2018).

19 J. P. Mayer, 'Reflections on Equality', in Leszek Kolakowski and Stuart Hampshire (eds), *The Socialist Idea: A Reappraisal* (New York: Basic Book, 1974), pp. 59–73.

20 Karl Mannheim, *Man and Society in an Age of Reconstruction*, trans. Edward Shils (New York: Harcourt, Brace and Company, [1929] 1940); 'The Crisis in Value' in *Diagnosis of Our Time: Wartime Essays of a Sociologist* (Abingdon, Oxfordshire: Psychology Press [1943] 1997), pp. 12–30; *Freedom, Power, and Democratic Planning* (Oxford: Oxford University Press, 1950); S. Turner and R. Factor, *Max Weber and the Dispute Over Reason and Value: A Study in Philosophy, Ethics, and Politics* (London: Routledge & Kegan Paul, Ltd., 1984), pp. 154–6.

21 Plamena Panayotova (ed.), *The History of Sociology in Britain: New Research and Revaluation* (London: Palgrave Macmillan, 2019).

22 Richard Hofstader, *The American Political Tradition and the Men Who Made It* (New York: A. A. Knopf, 1948).

23 Robert N. Bellah, 'McCarthyism at Harvard', *New York Review of Books* (10 February 2005), www.nybooks.com/articles/2005/02/10/mccarthyism-at-harvard/ (accessed 2 January 2020).

24 Paul Blackledge and Neil Davidson (eds), *Alasdair MacIntyre's Engagement with Marxism: Selected Writings 1953–1974* (Chicago, IL: Haymarket Books, 2005), p. 52.

25 Giovanna Borradori, *The American Philosopher: Conversations with Quine, Davidson, Putnam, Nozick, Danto, Rorty, Cavell, MacIntyre, Kuhn* (Chicago, IL: University of Chicago Press, 1994), pp. 254ff.

26 Robert N. Bellah, 'Introduction', in Bellah and Tipton (eds), *The Robert Bellah Reader* (Durham, NC: Duke University Press, 2006), p. 2.

27 Ulrich Beck, Anthony Giddens and Scott Lash, *Reflexive Modernization: Politics, Tradition and Aesthetics in the Modern Social Order* (Palo Alto, CA: Stanford University Press, 1994).

28 Anthony Giddens, *The Consequences of Modernity* (Stanford, CA: Stanford University Press, 1990), p. 1.

29 Ibid., p. 3.

30 Ibid., p. 6.

31 Anthony Giddens, *Modernity and Self-Identity: Self and Society in the Late Modern Age* (Stanford, CA: Stanford University Press, 1991), p. 107.
32 Bellah, *Beyond Belief*, p. 42.
33 Ibid., pp. 158–9.
34 Ibid.
35 Robert Bellah et al., *Habits of the Heart: Individualism and Commitment in American Life* (Berkeley, CA: University of California Press, 1985).
36 Herbert Spencer, *The Data of Ethics* (New York: A. L. Burt Company, 1879), p. 127.
37 Ibid., pp. 135–6.
38 Alasdair MacIntyre, *Secularization and Moral Change* (New York: Oxford University Press, 1967), p. 51.
39 Ibid., p. 14.
40 Ibid., p. 57.
41 Interestingly, Bellah and MacIntyre later connected. Their relation is discussed in Garrett Potts, 'From Meaningful Work to Good Work: Re-examining the Moral Foundation of the Calling Orientation' (PhD dissertation, Department of Philosophy, University of South Florida, 2019).
42 Anthony Giddens, 'Post-Traditional Civil Society and the Radical Center', *New Perspectives Quarterly*, 15:2 (1998), 16.
43 Ibid.
44 Ibid.
45 Ibid.
46 Ibid., 17.
47 Michael Oakeshott, *On Human Conduct* (Oxford: Clarendon Press, [1975] 1991), p. 112.
48 Giddens, 'Post-Traditional Civil Society', 17.
49 Giddens, *Consequences of Modernity*, p. 38. The reference might be to, among others, Edward Shils, for whom this was a theme. See esp. Lenore T. Ealy, 'The Recovery of Tradition', in Christopher Adair and Stephen Turner (eds), *The Calling of Social Thought: Rediscovering the Work of Edward Shils* (Manchester: Manchester University Press, 2019), pp. 61–78.
50 Giddens, *Consequences of Modernity*, p. 38.
51 Ibid.
52 Bellah, *Beyond Belief*, p. 42.
53 MacIntyre, *Secularization and Moral Change*, p. 57.
54 Ibid., p. 49.
55 Oakeshott, *On Human Conduct*.
56 Robert Putnam, *Bowling Alone: The Collapse and Revival of American Community* (New York: Simon and Schuster, 2000).
57 Ann Goldberg, *Honor, Politics, and the Law in Imperial Germany, 1871–1914* (Cambridge: Cambridge University Press, 2010).
58 Canadian Press, 'Island airport grounds ad 'insulting' to cows', *Toronto Sun*, 30 June 2017, www.torontosun.com/2017/06/30/island-airport-grounds-ad-insulting-to-cows (accessed 21 August 2019).

59 Axel Honneth, 'Grounding Recognition: A Rejoinder to Critical Questions', *Inquiry*, 45:4 (2002), 499–519.

60 Peter Berger, 'On the Obsolescence of the Concept of Honor', in Stanley Hauerwas and Alasdair MacIntyre (eds), *Revisions: Changing Perspectives in Moral Philosophy* (Notre Dame, IN: Notre Dame University Press, 1983), p. 176.

61 Needless to say, a concept like dignity is not 'discovered': *dignitas* was an important Roman concept with legal implications which came to be precisely calibrated to an elaborate system of ranks in Roman society. See Max Radin, 'Roman Concepts of Quality', *Political Science Quarterly*, 38 (1923), 262–89. It is just another term in the honour family of concepts; see Remy Debes (ed.), *Dignity: A History* (New York: Oxford University Press, 2017). What was novel, for these writers, was its egalitarian extension. Berger's argument that the discovery of dignity arose because honour was debunked is simply circular: honour, as he understands the concept, can't be found in societies without ranked social roles because for him honour *means* honour for ranked social roles.

62 Tartly dismissed recently by Raymond Guess, 'A Republic of Discussion: Habermas at Ninety', *The Point* (18 June 2019), https://thepointmag.com/2019/politics/republic-of-discussion-habermas-at-ninety (accessed 11 September 2020).

63 I leave aside the point made by Martha Nussbaum that cosmopolitanism is itself a tradition, reaching back to the ancient world, which is itself in trouble. Martha Nussbaum, *The Cosmopolitan Tradition: A Noble but Flawed Ideal* (Cambridge, MA: Harvard University Press, 2019).

Part III

Contemporary post-constructions
(2000s–present)

10

Busting the 'post'? Postfeminist genealogies in millennial culture

Stéphanie Genz

Introduction

Postfeminism is a concept loaded with contradictions. Loathed by some and celebrated by others, it has appeared in the late twentieth century in a number of cultural, academic and political contexts, from popular journalism and media, to feminist analyses, postmodern theories and neoliberal rhetoric. Critics have appropriated the term for a variety of definitions, ranging from conservative backlash, Girl Power, third wave feminism and postmodern/poststructuralist feminism. In popular culture, it is used as a descriptive marker for a number of (particularly) female characters that have emerged from the 1990s onwards, with Helen Fielding's chick-lit heroine Bridget Jones and the Spice Girls often held up as the poster girls of postfeminism. In academic writings, it sits alongside other 'post' discourses – including postmodernism and postcolonialism – and here, it refers to a shift in the understanding and construction of identity and gender categories (like 'Woman', 'Man' and 'Feminist'). Likewise, in political philosophy and social theory, postfeminism has been read as indicative of a 'post-traditional' era characterized by dramatic changes in basic social relationships, role stereotyping and conceptions of agency. More recently, postfeminism has been anchored within neoliberal society and consumer culture that cultivates individualistic, competitive and entrepreneurial behaviour in its construction of a self-regulating and enterprising subject whose consumption patterns come to be seen as a source of power and choice. Linked to this, postfeminism has also been discussed in relation to contemporary brand culture that shapes not only consumer habits but wider political, cultural and civic practices. Here, the term acquires 'affective relational qualities',[1] emblematic of contemporary *experience economies* where consumers no longer merely consume goods and services but are looking for memorable events that engage them in a personal way.

While commentators have found fault with postfeminism's interpretative potential and flexibility – Coppock and Gamble, for example, deplore that 'postfeminism remains a product of assumption' and 'exactly what it constitutes ... is a matter for frequently impassioned debate'[2] – they also acknowledge its significance and impact. The term continues to be divisive, causing some critics to abandon it because, as Susan Douglas notes, 'it has gotten gummed up by too many conflicting definitions'.[3] At the same time, the cultural presence, resonance and longevity of postfeminism have become hard to ignore, specifically as it continues to evolve with changes in political, cultural and economic environments. As Rosalind Gill concedes, the term's 'continued relevance' and pertinence cannot be denied and '[t]here is, as yet, no parallel for postfeminism'.[4]

To start, I want to trace postfeminism's *genealogy* and consider its position within feminist histories in order to discuss the semantic confusion surrounding a 'post-ing' of feminism. Here the modes of distance and proximity combine in complex ways as the disagreements over and multiplicity of postfeminism's meaning(s) are to a large extent due to the indefiniteness and precariousness of the 'post' prefix itself. Then I will consider *postfeminist transfers* by investigating different incarnations of postfeminism and contemplating the possibility of a twenty-first-century post-boom postfeminist stance – what I designate *bust postfeminism* – that emerges in response to an indeterminate post-2008 recessionary environment. The current historical juncture requires that we question and re-examine how, or even whether, postfeminism is still relevant and in touch with a precarious post-millennium context. In other words, has postfeminism and its associated themes and conceptual vocabulary exhausted their critical usefulness, or does its inherent generativity and adaptability ensure its continuing importance and applicability? How might we categorize this 'new', post-boom postfeminism that responds to this complicated moment in time?

The genealogical approach that I adopt seeks to demarcate a postfeminist landscape that takes into account successive modifications in meaning, allowing for different postfeminist strands to co-exist, overlap, build upon, revise and replace others. Here, postfeminism emerges as a complex and dynamic analytical category – a 'frontier discourse'[5] – made up of an array of relationships and conceptual webs within/between social, cultural, academic and political arenas. The relevance and usefulness of postfeminism rest precisely in its ability as a *critical concept* to complicate longstanding binary distinctions and expose the paradoxes of a late-twentieth- and early-twenty-first-century setting in which old certainties of selfhood/citizenship and erstwhile notions of progress, hope and freedom – what Henry Giroux calls 'the promises of modernity'[6] – have been reconfigured and increasingly appear to be under threat.

Positioning postfeminist genealogies

In order to unravel the definitional possibilities of postfeminism, the continuities and discontinuities with its root concept need to be examined. Confusion rules as postfeminism is variously identified or associated with an anti-feminist backlash, pro-feminist third wave, Girl Power dismissive of feminist politics, trendy me-first power feminism, self-branded celebrity feminism, corporate/neoliberal feminism and academic postmodern feminism. There appears to be a simultaneous denial, use and misuse of feminism, a concomitant and ongoing process of embedding and disembedding that negotiates areas of tension that, I maintain, can be used productively within critical practice and theory. Even though postfeminism concretized as a cultural phenomenon and critical concept in the late twentieth century, the term emerged as early as 1919 after the vote for women had been won by the suffrage movement.[7] This initial mention of postfeminism relied on the supposed success and achievements of the 'first wave' of the feminist movement and enacted a demarcating line between past and present, casting the 'post' in evolutionary or historical terms as a progression of feminist ideas. Yet, it is fair to say that this early-twentieth-century manifestation of postfeminism did not materialize or develop in any specific and tangible ways – cut short by important historical developments such as the outbreaks of both First and Second World Wars – and it was not until the early 1980s that the next significant postfeminist phase occurred. This time, it was the popular press that brought back postfeminism into the cultural limelight where it was discussed mostly as exemplary of a reaction against second wave feminism and its collective, activist politics. Postfeminism – meaning in this case post-second wave – came to signal a generational shift in feminist thinking and in understanding social relations between men and women, beyond traditional feminist politics and its supposed threat to heterosexual relationships.

Approached in this way, postfeminism could be interpreted as a cyclical process of feminist rejuvenation – emerging after momentous and organized stages (or 'waves') of feminist activism and politics – and could be discussed as 'postrevolutionary'[8] in its shift away from collectivist mobilization that characterized both first and second waves of feminism. As Julie Ewington suggests, 'it is not feminism that we are "post" but one historical phase of feminist politics'.[9] Postfeminism encourages feminism to develop an understanding of its own historicity, 'an account of its own temporality that does not simply mimic the modernist grand narrative of progress'. It attributes a historical specificity to second wave feminism, for, as Charlotte Brunsdon asks, 'why should 1970s feminism have a copyright on feminism?'[10] In this chronological sense, the term 'postfeminism' is employed to describe a critical position in relation to the feminism of women's liberation, signifying both the achievements of and challenges for modern feminist politics. Postfeminism's interrogative stance could thus be read as a healthy rewriting of feminism, a sign that the women's movement is continuously in process, transforming and changing itself. This is what Ann Brooks implies in her articulation of postfeminism as 'feminism's "coming of age", its maturity into a confident body of theory and politics, representing pluralism and difference'.[11]

Unsurprisingly perhaps, such evaluations of postfeminism as the new 'improved' feminism free from the dictates of the second wave motherhood were short-lived, as critics started to undo the 'illusions of postfeminism'.[12] As Lynne Alice notes, the 'inflammatory myth of new beginnings and revisionings' disguises the fact that postfeminism can 'operate like a chimera, or perhaps even a conceit', misrepresenting and undermining feminist politics and reducing all feminisms – and their long and diverse histories – to a caricaturized version of 1970s feminism.[13] Here, we need to take into account that the fault lines established between different feminist periods never follow a straightforward chronology but are always created and made to frame the past retroactively, often in line with specific, at times political, agendas. It follows that in some critical investigations, the 'post-ing' of feminism is denounced as an invasion of the feminist body and a vicious attempt to debilitate and sabotage the women's movement.

In my work, I have sought to adopt a more nuanced understanding of postfeminism's appropriation of feminism, beyond a simple rewriting or negation.[14] In its various manifestations, postfeminism exhibits a number of relations to feminism ranging from complacency to hostility, approbation to repudiation. In its most denunciatory expressions, postfeminism clearly performs a historical 'othering' of feminism that shapes it as an archaic monolith unproductive for the experiences of contemporary women and men. Other postfeminist strands reinforce their connections with earlier forms of feminism and open up, as Braithwaite puts it, 'the possibilities of finding and understanding feminisms in places and in ways very different from ... that earlier period'.[15] In this sense, feminist and postfeminist stances are allied and entwined, creating a dynamic context made up of various standpoints and theories. However, these interconnections have often been overlooked and passed over in many critical studies in an attempt to establish two different and easily categorized positions. Much pro- and contra- postfeminist rhetoric relies on a reductive binary structure in order to conjure up a pole of negativity against which postfeminism can be defined and lay bare the faults of feminist orthodoxy, or, alternatively, reminisce nostalgically about a mythical feminist past characterized by a homogeneous and unified women's movement. This *either/or* formulation implies that only one term can subsist by obliterating the other: postfeminism can only exist to the exclusion of feminism, and feminism can only exist to the exclusion of postfeminism.

Instead I want to rearticulate these questions of ownership and definition that have dominated – and at times hampered – examinations of postfeminism and adopt a genealogical approach that highlights postfeminism's multiplicity, its modes of distancing and proximity, embeddedness and disembeddedness in relation to its feminist roots as well as its interconnectedness and overlaps with other post- concepts. In so doing, I also seek to unlock postfeminism's potential for transversing across (disciplinary, geographical, historical) boundaries and situate it within a broader conceptual network in order to deepen its meanings and investigate the range of ideas and themes that sustain it. Postfeminism is not a 'new feminism' in the sense that it represents something radically revolutionary and groundbreaking – it is both retro- and neo- in its outlook and hence irrevocably post-. It is neither a simple rebirth of feminism nor a straightforward abortion (excuse the imagery) but a complex resignification that harbours within itself the threat of backlash as well as the possibility for innovation. In this sense, postfeminism cannot be understood as an alternative to feminism and its social and political agenda. It does not exist in a bounded and organized form as a political and social movement and its origins are more impure, emerging in and from a wide conceptual and contextual web (academia, media and consumer/brand culture; neoliberal politics) that has been influenced by feminist concerns and women's enfranchisement.

Moreover, postfeminism is also located outside of feminist historical periodization and epochal thinking – commonly epitomized by the 'wave' metaphor. This chronology or 'oceanography of feminist movement'[16] comprises the surge of feminist activism in the nineteenth and early twentieth centuries – regularly referred to as the 'first wave' of feminism that culminated around the campaign for women's suffrage in the 1920s – and the 'second wave' resurgence of feminist organizing in the 1960s. The latest invocation – third wave feminism – in particular defines itself as a budding political movement coming to the fore in the 1990s, with strong affiliations to second wave feminist theory and activism. The very invocation of 'third wave feminism' and the mobilization of the adjective 'third' indicate a desire to establish a link with previous feminist waves and ensure a continuation of feminist principles and ideas.[17]

Here, the contrast with postfeminism is clear as many third wavers understand their position as an act of strategic defiance and a response to the cultural dominance of postfeminism. From its initiation, the third wave has resolutely defined itself against postfeminism: in fact, third wave pioneers Rebecca Walker and Shannon Liss were keen to establish an ideological and political split between the two, pronouncing '[w]e are not postfeminist feminists. We are the third wave!'[18] There are of course important differences between postfeminism and the third wave, significantly at the level of foundation and political alignment. Sarah Banet-Weiser for example maintains that postfeminism is 'a different political dynamic than third wave feminism',[19] with the latter defining itself more overtly as a kind of feminist politics that extends the historical trajectory of previous feminist waves to assess contemporary consumer culture. Postfeminism, by contrast, does not exist as a budding political movement and its origins are more diverse and tangled, emerging from within mainstream culture, rather than underground subculture. Moreover, unlike the third wave, postfeminism is not motivated by a desire for continuity and a need to prove its feminist credentials – what Diane Elam terms the 'Dutiful Daughter Complex'.[20] Nonetheless, this rhetoric of antagonism is sometimes misleading as it does not account for the overlap between the third wave and postfeminism, nor does it allow for a politicized reading of the latter. For example, the third wave and postfeminism occupy a common ground between consumption and critique, engaging with feminine/sexual and individual forms of agency. Both third wave feminism and postfeminism draw on popular culture to interrogate and explore twenty-first-century configurations of female empowerment and re-examine the meanings of feminism in the present context as a politics of contradiction and ambivalence. As will be discussed below, the entanglements of feminism and postfeminism are multiple and varied and – as a debating couple – they should not be viewed reductively in opposition, nor in terms of a linear progression.

Post-ing feminism

While the prefix 'post' has long been the subject of academic and theoretical analyses (in particular in its expression as postmodernism, poststructuralism and postcolonialism), it has achieved particular notoriety ever since it attached itself to the social and political phenomenon that is feminism. Proponents and detractors of postfeminism have deliberated over the uses of the prefix and vied for their respective take on how a 'post-ing' of feminism can be effected and understood. What these debates centre on is exactly what this prefixation accomplishes (if anything), what happens to feminist perspectives and goals in the process and what the strange hybrid of 'post-feminism' entails. In my work, I choose to omit the hyphen in my spelling of postfeminism in order to avoid any predetermined readings of the term that imply a semantic rift between feminism and postfeminism. Also, by foregoing the hyphen, I seek to endow postfeminism with a certain cultural independence and critical history that acknowledges its existence as a conceptual entity in its own right. While postfeminism – in its current late-twentieth- and twenty-first-century manifestation – might still be considered an emergent critical concept, it has had over thirty years to solidify into an analytical category and develop a critical history that spans the backlash years of the 1980s, the 'Third Way' 1990s and the uncertain, post-9/11 and recessionary years of the new millennium.

Regardless of our spelling, it is not so much the hyphen but the prefix itself that has been the focus of critical investigations. As Misha Kavka observes, the question that has haunted – or enlivened, depending on your point of view – the discussions can be summarized as 'how can we make sense of the "post" in "postfeminism"'.[21] Even though the structure of postfeminism appears to invoke a narrative of progression insisting on a time 'after' feminism, the directionality and meaning of the 'post' prefix are far from settled. 'Post' can be employed to point to a complete rupture, for as Amelia Jones declares, 'what is post but the signification of a kind of termination – a temporal designation of whatever it prefaces as ended, done with, obsolete'.[22] In this prescriptive sense, postfeminism signals the 'pastness' of feminism – or, at any rate the end of a particular stage in feminist histories – and a generational shift in understanding the relationships between men and women. Here, postfeminism is often evoked by a generation of younger feminists as indicative of the fact that 'we are no longer in a second wave of feminism'.[23] This awareness of feminist change has resulted in a number of bitter ownership battles and wrangling, often cast in familial terms as mother–daughter conflicts.[24]

In response – and very much on the anti-postfeminist side of the divide – the feminist 'foremothers' have attacked their 'daughters' for their historical amnesia and misappropriations of the feminist/familial legacy. According to Lynne Segal, this new breed of feminists 'were able to launch themselves and court media via scathing attacks on other feminists' – even worse, this kind of feminism has been 'appropriated by a managerial elite' that works in the service of neoliberal values and is 'eager to roll back welfare for workfare'.[25] Segal describes how by the 1990s the radical spirit of feminist politics had waned and there was 'a kind of cultural forgetting of the intellectual legacies of feminism'.[26] These anti-postfeminist critics define postfeminism as a sexist, politically conservative and media-inspired ploy that guts the underlying principles of the feminist movement and transforms its collective activist agenda into an individualistic matter of self-interest. This largely pessimistic interpretation was prominent in early media articulations of postfeminism that link it to anti-feminist and media-driven attempts to turn the clock back to pre-feminist times, fuelled by the conservative governments that defined 1980s Reaganite America and

Thatcherite Britain. From this point of view, postfeminism has been read as a 'backlash'[27] and hence primarily a polemical tool with limited critical and analytical value. However, such readings have been superseded increasingly from the 1990s onwards in favour of more complex accounts that argue for a more nuanced understanding of postfeminism that acknowledges the term's diverse entanglements with feminism and other cultural and political theories.

Diametrically opposed to the view of 'post' as 'anti' or 'after' is the idea that the prefix denotes a genealogy that entails revision or strong family resemblance. This approach is favoured by advocates of another 'post' derivative – postmodernism – and here, the prefix is understood as part of a process of ongoing transformation. As Best and Kellner write in their analysis of postmodern theory, the 'post' signifies 'a dependence on, a continuity with, that which follows'.[28] In this sense, the 'post-ing' of feminism does not necessarily imply its rejection and eradication but it means that feminism remains in the postfeminist frame. A third, and perhaps more problematical, interpretation locates the 'post' in a precarious middle ground typified by a contradictory dependence on and independence from the term that follows it.[29] As Sarah Gamble puts it, 'the prefix "post" does not necessarily always direct us back the way we've come'.[30] Instead, its trajectory is bewilderingly uncertain, making it unfeasible and possibly redundant to offer a single definition of any 'post' concept.

Adding to this interpretive struggle is the fact that the root of postfeminism, feminism itself, has never had a universally accepted agenda and meaning against which one could measure the benefits and/or failings of its post- offshoot. At best, feminism can be said to have a number of working definitions that are always relative to particular contexts, specific issues and personal practices. It exists on both local and abstract levels, dealing with specific issues and consisting of diverse individuals while promoting a universal politics of equality for women. Feminists are simultaneously united by their investment in a general concept of justice and fractured by the multiple goals and personal practices that delineate the particular conception of justice to which they aspire. Thus, the assumption that there is – or was – a monolith easily (and continuously) identifiable as 'feminism' belies its competing understandings, its different social and political programmes sharply separated by issues of race, sexuality, class and other systems of social differentiation. It follows that one cannot simply 'hark back' to a past when feminism supposedly had a stable signification and unity. For many feminist media critics in particular, it is postfeminism's relationship with feminism – as a critical and political paradigm – that is paramount and they focus on how, to varying degrees, postfeminist culture incorporates, commodifies, depoliticizes and parodies feminist ideas and terminology, resulting in the worst case in an 'undoing' and 'othering' of feminism. Angela McRobbie (2009) for example has described this discursive process as a 'double move-ment' that takes feminism 'into account' only to repudiate it.[31]

For me, it is important not to fall into a critical trap that takes for granted the meanings of 'post' and 'feminism' and instead allow for con-tradictory and evolving notions of (post)feminism that may co-exist at the same moment. Moreover, we need consider the possibility that – rephrasing McRobbie's formulation – twenty-first-century postfeminism now takes itself 'into account', demonstrating the ability to self-critique, rearticulate and interrogate its own significations, uses and constituencies for a millen-nial generation. In fact, current incarnations of postfeminism adopt a stance of (self-) criticality that calls up various postfeminist tenets in order to scru-tinize them. We see this, for example, in popular culture texts like HBO's *Girls* that explicitly and self-consciously address postfeminist issues – for instance in relation to representations of the female body – while anticipat-ing and inscribing criticism within the narrative itself.[32]

Thus, throughout its critical history, postfeminism has acquired mul-tiple, contested interpretations – from backlash and Girl Power to (neo)liberal feminism and 'affective' self-brand – and it is inflected differ-ently in different historical, cultural, political and social contexts. From this perspective, the attempt to fix *the* meaning of postfeminism looks futile and even misguided as each articulation is by itself a definitional act that (re)constructs the meaning of (post)feminism and its own relation to it. There is no *original* or *authentic* postfeminism that holds the key to its definition. Nor is there a secure and unified origin from which this genuine postfeminism could be fashioned. Instead, I understand postfeminism as a dynamic critical concept capable of adapting to changing historical condi-tions and bringing to the fore a range of contradictions that speak to and inform generations of women and men. Rather than being tied to a spe-cific epistemological field, postfeminism's frame of reference opens out to include not just – as the term suggests – a conceptual and semantic bond with feminism but also relations with other social, cultural, theoretical and political areas – such as consumer brand culture, popular media and neoliberal rhetoric – that might be in conflict with feminism. Hence post-feminism is not the (illegitimate) offspring of – or even a substitute for – feminism but its origins are much more varied and incongruous, addressing the paradoxes of a late-twentieth- and early-twenty-first-century setting in which feminist concerns have entered the mainstream and are articulated in politically contradictory ways.

Due to its inherently 'impure' status and interconnected conceptual web, postfeminism has often been criticized for its disloyalty and bastardiza-tion, for 'feeding upon its hosts'.[33] It has been denounced – particularly by feminist critics – as a contaminating presence, a parasite charged with infiltration and appropriation. A particular point of contention has been postfeminism's commercial appeal and its consumerist implications that are viewed by many as a 'selling out' of feminist principles and their co-option as a marketing device. Here we can identify distinctive postfeminist strands that connect feminist notions of gendered empowerment and choice with cultural practices of commodification and individualism. This thread also brings postfeminism into close political alliance with neoliberal ideas that promote competitive individualism and entrepreneurship in consumer-citizens. These accusations resurface for instance in examinations of popular postfeminist strands – like Girl Power, chick lit and (online) self-branding – that combine an emphasis on feminine 'fun' and female friendship with a celebration of (mostly pastel-coloured) commodities and the creation of a market demographic of (self-branded) 'Girlies', 'chicks' or 'babes'. The end result of this mainstreaming and commoditization – it is feared – is a 'free market feminism' that works 'through capitalism' and is 'based on competitive choices in spite of social conditions being stacked against women as a whole'.[34]

While I do not deny the validity of such critiques, I want to counter the assumption of causality that underlies many of these predominantly early investigations and forces postfeminism into a fixed and delimited structure of analysis and definition. The understanding of postfeminism as an unfaithful reproduction of feminism – or worse, 'a ritualistic denunciation' that renders feminism 'out of date'[35] – is problematic for a number of reasons: it presupposes a distinction between an 'authentic' and unadulterated feminism on the one hand, and a suspect, usually commercialized postfeminism on the other; it assumes that feminist engagements with postfeminism are uniform and it does not take into consideration the range and scope of issues involved in feminist identifications; it adopts a one-dimensional reading of the 'post' – and by implication the 'post-ing' of feminism – as 'anti' feminism; it glosses over some of the overlaps and contradictions that mark postfeminist contexts, thereby foreclosing the interpretative possibilities of postfeminism; it does not allow for an expansive and adaptable postfeminist ethos and new directions across a range of sites, for example in terms of transnational and intersectional perspectives.

At this point we should note the range of postfeminist *transfers* that have caused the concept to travel across disciplinary, geographical and historical boundaries. Indeed, in the few decades encircling the millennium, there has been a veritable explosion of postfeminism across a range of fields: while popular culture remains a key resource for scholars, postfeminism's analytical and conceptual scope has expanded significantly with an upsurge in publications about masculinity, ageing, body politics, race and class.

Postfeminism is now discussed as a global and transnational phenomenon, travelling across borders to become meaningful and localized in various, non-Western settings. As Dosekun has observed, 'post-feminism is readily transnationalized, that is rendered transnational culture, because it is a fundamentally mediated and commodified discourse and set of material practices'.[36] Moreover, the term has gained prominence outside representational and media culture and is now discussed in relation to education, health, digital culture and work, to name but a few current sites of investigation. Rather than its tiredness or redundancy, what this signals is postfeminism's intrinsic productivity, its ability as a conceptual tool to make meaningful the paradoxes that characterize our ways of inhabiting and making sense of millennial existence and culture.

As I discuss in the next section, postfeminism's adaptability and self-reflexivity are evidenced most recently in its shift from a *boom* model that emphasizes 'choice' and the 'freedom' to consume and self-fashion, to a recessionary *bust* postfeminist stance that retains a commitment to consumption but in a pragmatic, pared-down and downsized format that takes issue with the extravagant and 'irresponsible' spending of the Noughties' 'bubble culture'.

Beyond the 'post'? Millennial bust postfeminism

While postfeminism has been the object of widespread critique since its inception, recent investigations have queried not only its social limitations and political allegiances but its intrinsic validity and *raison d'être*. In Charlotte Brunsdon's eyes, postfeminism has become a 'baggy' concept,[37] while for Imelda Whelehan, postfeminism is 'frustrating to analyse because its message requires little unpacking' – ultimately, it is an 'empty signifier' that is 'overburdened' with meaning.[38] In some ways, given its links with the entrepreneurial boom culture of conspicuous consumption and individual gratification that dominated Western economies in the late twentieth and early twenty-first centuries, critical calls that proclaim the redundancy and outdatedness of postfeminism appear logical and even reasonable. It is not surprising then that there have been calls for a revised or updated postfeminism, a millennial rearticulation that reflects a recessionary context infused with anxiety. For example, Nash and Grant propose the term 'post? Feminism' to create a platform for 'new debate' and symbolize that 'feminist engagement with post-feminism is multiple and shifting'.[39] In a similar vein, Rosalind Gill has investigated the relevance of the concept, asking, 'Are we now post-postfeminism?'[40] For her, this question is motivated by what she perceives as the 'new visibility of feminism', a resurgence of interest in feminist issues and debates in corporate/neoliberal arenas, celebrity culture as well as (online) forms of activism. Focusing more directly on the recession as a frame of reference, Diane Negra and Yvonne Tasker also query the pertinence and suitability of postfeminism to connect with the profound political, social and cultural shifts inaugurated by the 2008 economic crisis: 'Postfeminism has shown itself to be significantly related (if not reducible) to the "bubble culture" of the twenty-first century's first decade' that celebrated the 'postfeminist female consumer' as 'an icon of excess as much as admiration'.[41]

In addition, in the course of its proliferation and expansion – evidenced for instance by the ever growing and diverse corpus of postfeminist scholarship – we can detect a certain *embedding* of the term as postfeminism is consolidated into a kind of contemporary master discourse, a postfeminist *grand narrative*. Here, contemporary critics have evaluated and accepted postfeminism as a foregone conclusion, a predictable framework to demarcate their distinct analyses. For example, Angela McRobbie refers to the 'post-feminist stranglehold' that potentially is in the process of being exploded by the 'blossoming of new feminisms across so many different locations'.[42] In a slightly different manner, Gill argues for the continued importance of the critical idiom of postfeminism as 'regrettably, we are a long way from being post-postfeminism'.[43] Here the argument for 'keeping, rather than jettisoning, the notion of postfeminism' is based on the assumption of a 'postfeminist sensibility in which "all the battles" are supposed to have been won, and accusations of sexism come always already disenfranchised: been there, done that, it's all sorted!'[44]

For me, there is no need to coin 'post-' neologisms to reflect the current moment of investigation – indeed, the genealogical approach I have adopted forecloses the notion of a 'closed' postfeminism – postfeminism as fait accompli. Rather, at this historical juncture, it is time to ask (again), what has changed? How has postfeminism evolved and what does post-boom postfeminism – or, *bust postfeminism* if you like – imply? Indeed, we seem to be living in a perpetual state of crisis and anxiety and those points of reference and identification that provided a sense of security and directed our ways of being and seeing – in social, cultural, political and economic terms – continue to be evaporated and replaced by a sense of menace and foreboding. Gone are the days of social optimism, mobility and safety (or, the perception thereof) as we learn how to adapt and cope with the stress and trauma of a seemingly interminable economic crisis and political upheaval, the ensuing atmosphere of austerity and anger at corporate greed, the rollback of opportunities and transfer of risk to culture at large, and a global terrorism that feeds a generalized climate of fear. The current political and cultural moment is also complexly gendered, fears abounding that we are witnessing 'the end of men' and a concomitant 'rise of women',[45] a trend not borne out by economic reality and rising numbers of unemployed women. On the whole, these diverse social, economic and political factors – and their resultant mediatization and effects on cultural forms and representations – necessitate that we investigate how current political changes and the end of a *boom-and-bust* economic model have affected the larger cultural climate and tenets of postfeminism. Certainly, if late-twentieth- and early-twenty-first-century postfeminism was characterized by optimism, entitlement and the opportunity of prosperity, then indisputably such articulations have become more unsustainable and uncertain in a post-2008 recessionary environment that complicates, and possibly nullifies, boom-market mindsets and Noughties confidence in (consumer) 'choice' and 'freedom'.

While the intricacies of a *bust* postfeminist stance are beyond the parameters of this chapter, I want to highlight a number of key characteristics that have emerged in a millennial context. The interplay of economic uncertainty and gender intensifies a number of (post)feminist dilemmas and points of contentions and casts doubt on the discourses of self-regulating entrepreneurship and choice that were the hallmark of celebratory postfeminism of the 1990s and early 2000s and that are embodied in the image of the 'empowered, assertive, pleasure-seeking, "have-it-all" woman of sexual and financial agency'.[46] For example, Lazar's suggestion that 'the postfeminist subject ... is entitled to be pampered and pleasured'[47] needs to be problematized in a recessionary environment that no longer guarantees (economic) success and reward to even the most hard-working individuals. This has a more general effect on postfeminist culture and its depiction of fictional characters: where for example in the case of late-twentieth- and early-twenty-first-century heroines, 'failing' might have been conceived as a 'virtue'[48] – epitomized for example by the professional ineptness and persistent blundering of Helen Fielding's Bridget Jones – such underachievement and incompetence are no longer held up as endearing signs of female identification and imperfection but now turn out to be equivalent to economic suicide as countless, qualified professionals compete in an ever more aggressive and merciless job market. In this sense, the prospect of prosperity and entrepreneurship that may have been viewed with confidence in the pre-recession decades appears less as an individual entitlement than a corporate obligation in times of austerity that masks the rollback of opportunities under the rhetorical guise of necessity, self-restraint and self-care.

Thus, it is plain to see that the larger culture and ethos of postfeminism need to be recalibrated and reassessed in the aftermath of the 2008 economic crisis. Here, we need to engage with a new postfeminist vocabulary which pre-recession was marked by optimism, aspirationalism, and opportunity to prosper, while post-recession becomes unquestionably more pessimistic and less congratulatory. In this recessionary context, the neoliberal/ postfeminist mantra of choice and self-determination is still present but becomes inflected with the experiences of precarity and risk and the insistence on self-responsibilization. Lauren Berlant's theorization of the 'good life' is useful here as she analyses the shrinking or 'fraying of fantasies' of 'upward mobility, job security, political and social equality, and lively, durable intimacy'.[49] Despite, or maybe because of, these conditions of economic and intimate contingency, people remain bound to their situation of profound threat and uncertainty, holding on and hoping against themselves that their fantasies will come good. Berlant describes this affective state, this feeling of our times, as a 'cruel optimism' whereby we are encouraged to believe in the idea of a better and happier future – the 'good life' – whilst such attachments are, simultaneously, obstructed by the precarities and instabilities of daily life.

In the broadest sense then, we need to allow for a shift in postfeminist tone or register – from excess to frugality, carefree spending to economical thrift, light-hearted pleasure to nervous anguish – that can be witnessed for example in recessionary chick flicks such as *Bridesmaids* (2011) that now feature unemployed women and strain to 'resolve female downward mobility through bridal fantasy'.[50] This is in sharp contrast to boom postfeminist representations that hailed young women in particular as free and confident agents with supposedly infinite choice. Variously known as 'can-do girls', 'top girls' or 'supergirls',[51] they were held up as the ideal postfeminist subject who is 'flexible, individualised, resilient, self-driven, and self-made'.[52] This kind of determined, self-motivating individual can be found across boom postfeminist culture, fostering a principle of competition that is both social – compelling individuals to constantly evaluate and compare their own self-enterprise with others – as well as self-directed. The reward for such relentless self-work was to be found in the material pleasures and choices of consumer culture.

This type of consumer postfeminism – exemplified by the urban glamour and shopping sprees of *Sex and the City* – is at odds with a context of austerity in which enterprising individuals might have earned the 'right' to consume but their consumer 'freedom' is now curtailed by limited funds and the value of their self-commodity is progressively in decline. Moreover, the much-touted recipe for success – self-work – is no longer necessarily delivering the promised rewards in a fiercely competitive recessionary marketplace that renders those incapable of capitalizing on their investment increasingly redundant and disposable. In short, if consumption is the key to 'having it all' and unlocking the individual's 'value', then those who cannot 'spend it all' might have to forego their 'freedom' and undersell their 'assets' in neoliberal capitalist consumer cultures. In this context, postfeminism gets a 'reality-check' as the 'right' to be self-reliant now turns into a 'risk' and the promise of upward mobility is increasingly prohibited by the harsh post-boom climate that surrenders those who lack competitive edge – 'failed' consumers and workers – to a 'politics of disposability'.[53]

Beyond these enduring postfeminist matters, I propose that *bust postfeminism* also gives rise to distinct recessionary patterns and themes of heightened visibility in order to bare the structural inequalities and power dynamics that have become glaringly obvious in the harsh post-Noughties climate. Here, *visibility* emerges as a discernible post-boom postfeminist motif that can be witnessed both in popular culture – where it takes the form of sexual sensationalism and *liberal sexism* that is unapologetic and blunt in its portrayal of gendered abuse, witnessed for example in HBO's *Game of Thrones* (2011–)[54] – as well as in relation to contemporary sexualized forms of feminism and activism, exemplified for instance by the global 'Slutwalk' movement and the Ukrainian activist group FEMEN.[55] A number of critics have commented on the increased visibility of feminism more broadly – as McRobbie writes, 'after a long period of castigation and disavowal … feminism once again has a presence across the quality and popular media, and similarly in political culture and in civil society'.[56] Here it is important to remind ourselves that 'visibility' does not always function in the same way – in fact, there might be different kinds of (un)critical visibilities in diverse cultural and political contexts – and 'seeing' does not necessarily lead to social change. Thus, we need to interrogate the nature of visibility itself and its relation to critique whereby making a (political) issue 'visible' or 'speakable' might not be enough as an act of emancipation and political awareness. This might have particularly problematic implications for a range of liberal activist stances – including feminism and gay rights – that have adopted a 'politics of visibility' to foster reconsiderations of gender, race, embodiment and power.[57]

If visibility is one of the recessionary motifs that define *bust postfeminism*, then *affect* is another key term that has come to the fore. My proposition here is that the blunt and precarious post-boom milieu engenders a more *interiorized* and *affective* postfeminist stance that encourages subjects to look inward and focus in on themselves in order to search for meaning/value in these uncertain times. Indeed, one of the reasons for boom postfeminism's continued appeal particularly in popular culture is its promotion of self-goals like 'confidence', 'independence' and 'empowerment', linked to consumerist and neoliberal imperatives that demand that we work on the self as the means to achieve these aims. As a result of more intense external pressures that weigh down on the individual post-recession, these goals now become more inner-directed and internalized, focusing on deeply rooted psychological desires to develop and enhance our sense of self. Many are barred from the 'rewards' of material consumption at this particular moment of downturn when the postfeminist/neoliberal discourses of self-regulating entrepreneurship become, not so much a prerogative, but an institutionalized burden. Accordingly, they turn to *affective* spaces of selfhood in an effort to validate the self and mine meaning (i.e. value) from their individual experiences and attributes (creativity, originality, resourcefulness, etc.).[58]

In relation to postfeminism, what this implies is that we need to move away from the assumption that postfeminist culture and politics act upon individuals from the outside in order to socialize them, for instance in terms of compulsory heterosexiness, responsibilization and entrepreneurialism. Instead, postfeminism is involved in the complex processes of individuation whereby subjects construct their identity, express their agency and actively self-govern in spite of structural/collective barriers.[59] As I have written elsewhere, we now need to 'expand our understanding of the intimate connections between culture and subjectivity' and supplement 'examinations of *what* postfeminist subjectivity entails' with 'an interrogation of *how* postfeminism engages subjects in the perplexing double binds of discipline and choice'.[60] This shift inward underlines postfeminism's *affective* dimension that works from within to penetrate not only the intimate links between subjects but also the relationship of the individual with him/herself. Postfeminism's 'turn to interiority'[61] thus gives rise to a process of intensified individuation that situates postfeminism at the heart of the individual's psyche – as I describe it, postfeminism now 'taps into emotion and affect as crucial elements in the construction, marketing and consumption of … subjectivity'.[62]

Ultimately, what this brief venture into *bust postfeminism* reveals is the concept's intrinsic generativity, its ability to permutate and respond to changing historical conditions and contexts. While postfeminism as a conceptual category and discursive system might still be under construction, its critical history points towards a fertile and productive 'site of risk'[63] that charts new debates and raises new questions probing the inescapable levels of contradiction and diverse points of identification we are confronted with in late modern societies. Postfeminism continues to pose a challenge for critical thinkers, calling upon us to interrogate and possibly reimagine how we carry out critique and apply analytical frameworks – hence, in my eyes there is no doubt that postfeminism is set to extend and deepen its conceptual web and remain a firm fixture of future critical analysis.

Notes

1 Sarah Banet-Weiser, *Authentic TM: The Politics of Ambivalence in a Brand Culture* (New York: New York University Press, 2012), p. 9.
2 Vicki Coppock, Vicki, Deena Haydon and Ingrid Richter, *The Illusions of 'Post-Feminism': New Women, Old Myths* (London: Taylor & Francis, 1995), p. 4; Sarah Gamble, 'Postfeminism', in *The Routledge Companion to Feminism and Postfeminism* (London: Routledge, 2001), pp. 43–54.
3 Susan Douglas, *The Rise of Enlightened Feminism: How Pop Culture Took Us from Girl Power to Girls Gone Wild* (New York: St. Martin's Griffin, 2010), p. 10.
4 Rosalind Gill, 'Post-Postfeminism?: New Feminist Visibilities in Postfeminist Times', *Feminist Media Studies*, 16:4 (2016), 1–22; Rosalind Gill, *Gender and the Media* (Cambridge: Polity, 2007), p. 250.
5 See Patricia S. Mann, *Micro-Politics: Agency in a Postfeminist Era* (Minneapolis, MN: University of Minnesota Press, 1994), p. 208.
6 Henry A. Giroux, 'Neoliberalism and the Machine of Disposability', *Truthout* (8 April 2014), www.truth-out.org/opinion/item/22958-neoliberalism-and-the-machinery-of-disposability (accessed 11 September 2020).
7 See Nancy F. Cott, *The Grounding of Modern Feminism* (New Haven, CT: Yale University Press, 1987), p. 282.
8 Judith Stacey, 'Sexism by a Subtler Name? Postindustrial Conditions and Postfeminist Consciousness in the Silicon Valley', *Socialist Review*, 96 (1987), 7–28.
9 Julie Ewington, 'Past the Post: Postmodernism and Postfeminism', in C. Moore (ed.), *Dissonance: Feminism and the Arts 1970–90* (St Leonards: Allen & Unwin, 1994), pp. 109–21.
10 Charlotte Brunsdon, *Screen Tastes: Soap Opera to Satellite Dishes* (London: Routledge, 1997), p. 101.
11 Ann Brooks, *Postfeminisms: Feminism, Cultural Theory and Cultural Forms* (London: Routledge, 1997), p. 1.
12 See Coppock et al., *Illusions of 'Post-Feminism'*.
13 Lynne Alice, 'What is Postfeminism? Or, Having it Both Ways', *Proceedings of the Feminism/Postmodernism/Postfeminism Conference, November 17–19, 1995: Working Papers in Women's Studies* (Albany, NZ: Massey University, 1995), pp. 7–35.
14 See Stéphanie Genz and Ben Brabon, *Postfeminism: Cultural Texts and Theories* (Edinburgh: Edinburgh University Press, 2009, 2018).
15 Ann Braithwaite, 'Politics and/of Backlash', *Journal of International Women's Studies*, 5:5 (2004), 18–33.
16 Deborah L. Siegel, 'The Legacy of the Personal: Generating Theory in Feminism's Third Wave', *Hypatia*, 12:3 (1997), 46–75.
17 See Siegel, 'Legacy', 60–1.

18 Quoted in Deborah Siegel, *Sisterhood, Interrupted: From Radical Women to Grrls Gone Wild* (Houndmills: Palgrave Macmillan, 2007), p. 128.

19 Sarah Banet-Weiser, 'What's Your Flava? Race and Postfeminism in Media Culture', in Yvonne Tasker and Diane Negra (eds), *Interrogating Postfeminism: Gender and The Politics of Popular Culture* (Durham, NC: Duke University Press, 2007), pp. 201–26.

20 Diane Elam, 'Sisters are Doing it to Themselves', in Devoney Looser and Ann E. Kaplan (eds), *Generations: Academic Feminists in Dialogue* (Minneapolis, MN: University of Minnesota Press, 1997), pp. 55–68.

21 Misha Kavka, 'Feminism, Ethics, and History, or What is the "Post" in Postfeminism', *Tulsa Studies in Women's Literature*, 21:1 (2002), 29–44, 31.

22 Amelia Jones, 'Post-Feminism – A Remasculinization of Culture', *M/E/A/N/ I/N/G: An Anthology of Artists' Writing, Theory and Criticism*, 7 (1990), 7–23.

23 Stacy Gillis and Rebecca Munford, 'Harvesting our Strengths: Third Wave Feminism and Women's Studies', *Journal of International Women's Studies*, 4:2 (2003), 1–6.

24 See Imelda Whelehan, *The Feminist Bestseller: From* Sex and The Single Girl *to* Sex and the City (Houndmills, Basingstoke: Palgrave Macmillan, 2005), pp. 168, 179–80.

25 Lynne Segal, 'Theoretical Affiliations: Poor Rich White Folk Play the Blues', *New Formations*, 50 (2003): 142–56.

26 Lisa Adkins, 'Passing on Feminism: From Consciousness to Reflexivity?', *European Journal of Women's Studies*, 11:4 (2004), 427–44; Segal, 'Theoretical Affiliations', 152.

27 See Susan Faludi, *Backlash: The Undeclared War Against Women* (London: Vintage, 1992).

28 Steven Best and Douglas Kellner, *Postmodern Theory: Critical Interrogations* (London: Macmillan, 1991), p. 29.

29 See Linda Hutcheon, *A Poetics of Postmodernism: History, Theory, Fiction* (London: Routledge, 1988), p. 17.

30 Gamble, 'Postfeminism', p. 44.

31 Angela McRobbie, *The Aftermath of Feminism: Gender, Culture and Social Change* (London: Sage, 2009).

32 See Stéphanie Genz, '"I have work ... I am busy ... trying to become who I am": Neoliberal *Girls* and Recessionary Postfeminism', in I. Whelehan and M. Nash (eds), *Reading Lena Dunham's* Girls: *Feminism, Postfeminism, Authenticity and Gendered Performance in Contemporary Television* (Basingstoke: Palgrave Macmillan, 2017), pp. 17–30.

33 Simon Dentith, *Parody* (London: Routledge, 2000), p. 188.

34 Whelehan, *Feminist Bestseller*, p. 155.

35 Angela McRobbie, 'Post-Feminism and Popular Culture', *Feminist Media Studies*, 4:3 (2004), 255–64.

36 Simidele Dosekun, 'For Western Girls Only?', *Feminist Media Studies*, 15:6 (2015), 960–75, 961.

37 Charlotte Brunsdon, 'Television Crime Series, Women Police, and Fuddy-Duddy Feminism', *Feminist Media Studies*, 13:3 (2013), 375–94.
38 Imelda Whelehan, 'Remaking Feminism: Or, Why is Postfeminism So Boring?', *Nordic Journal of English Studies*, 9:3 (2010), 155–72.
39 Meredith Nash and Ruby Grant, 'Twenty-Something *Girls* v. Thirty-Something *Sex And The City* Women', *Feminist Media Studies*, 15:6 (2015), 976–91.
40 Gill, 'Post-Postfeminism?', p. 2.
41 Diane Negra and Yvonne Tasker (eds), *Gendering the Recession: Media and Culture in an Age of Austerity* (Durham, NC: Duke University Press, 2014), pp. 4, 6.
42 Angela McRobbie, 'Notes on the Perfect: Competitive Femininity in Neoliberal Times', *Australian Feminist Studies*, 30:83 (2015), 3–20.
43 Gill, 'Post-Postfeminism?', pp. 16, 17.
44 Rosalind Gill, 'Unspeakable Inequalities: Post Feminism, Entrepreneurial Subjectivity, and the Repudiation of Sexism among Cultural Workers', *Social Politics*, 21:4 (2014), 509–28.
45 See Hanna Rosin, 'The End of Men', *The Atlantic* (July/August 2010), www.theatlantic.com/magazine/archive/2010/07/the-end-of-men/308135/ (accessed 11 September 2020).
46 Eva Chen, 'Neoliberalism and Popular Women's Culture: Rethinking Choice, Freedom and Agency', *European Journal of Cultural Studies*, 16:4 (2013), 440–52.
47 Michelle Lazar, 'Entitled to Consume: Postfeminist Femininity and a Culture of Post-Critique', *Discourse & Communication*, 3:4 (2009), 371–400.
48 See McRobbie, *Aftermath*.
49 Lauren Berlant, *Cruel Optimism* (Durham, NC: Duke University Press, 2011).
50 Diane Negra and Yvonne Tasker, 'Neoliberal Frames and Genres of Inequality: Recession-era Chick Flicks and Male-Centred Corporate Melodrama', *European Journal of Cultural Studies*, 16:3 (2013), 344–61.
51 See Anita Harris, *Future Girl: Young Women in the Twenty-First Century* (New York: Routledge, 2004); Angela McRobbie, 'Top Girls? Young Women and the Post-feminist Sexual Contract', *Cultural Studies*, 21:4–5 (2007), 718–37; J. Ringrose and V. Walkerdine, 'What Does It Mean to Be a Girl in the Twenty-First Century? Exploring Some Contemporary Dilemmas of Femininity and Girlhood in the West', in C. Mitchell and J. Reid-Walsh (eds), *Girl Culture: An Encyclopedia* (Westport, CT: Greenwood Press, 2007), pp. 6–16.
52 Harris, *Future Girl*, p. 16.
53 See Henry Giroux, 'Neoliberalism and the Death of the Social State: Remembering Walter Benjamin's Angel of History', *Social Identities*, 17:4 (2011), 587–601.
54 See Stéphanie Genz, '"I'm not going to fight them, I'm going to fuck them": Sexist Liberalism and Gender (A)politics in *Game of Thrones*', in R. Schubart and A. Gjelsvik (eds), *Women of Ice and Fire: Gender, Game of Thrones and Multiple Media Engagements* (New York: Bloomsbury, 2015), pp. 243–66.
55 See Stéphanie Genz, 'Baring the Recession: Sexual Sensationalism and Gender (A)politics in Contemporary Culture', in H. Davies and C. O'Callaghan

(eds), *Gender and Austerity in Popular Culture* (London: I. B. Tauris, 2017), pp. 189–209.

56 McRobbie, 'Notes on the Perfect', p. 4.

57 See Monica J. Casper and Lisa Jean Moore, *Missing Bodies: The Politics of Visibility* (New York: New York University Press, 2009).

58 See Banet-Weiser, *Authentic*.

59 See Zygmunt Bauman, 'Identity in the Globalising World', *Social Anthropology*, 9:2 (2001), 121–9.

60 Stéphanie Genz, 'My Job is Me: Postfeminist Celebrity Culture and the Gendering of Authenticity', *Feminist Media Studies*, 15:4 (2015), 545–61.

61 See Tisha Dejmanee, 'Consumption in the City: The Turn to Interiority in Contemporary Postfeminist Television', *European Journal of Cultural Studies*, 19:2 (2016), 119–33.

62 Genz, 'My Job is Me', 546.

63 Genz and Brabon, *Postfeminism*, p. 179.

11

Posthumanism and the 'posterizing impulse'

Yolande Jansen, Jasmijn Leeuwenkamp and Leire Urricelqui

Introduction

With the increasing awareness of the devastating consequences of what some call 'the Anthropocene' and others a 'crisis of humanism', the 'posthuman' has become a focal term in contemporary debates at the crossroads of science, politics and the humanities. Participants in this debate in the last decades of the twentieth century and the first decade of the twenty-first century, have often claimed that we are living in a historical moment in which the human is losing its centrality by 'its imbrication in technical, medical, informatic, and economic networks'.[1] Over the last decade, the human's imbrication in biological, ecological and geological assemblages has been added to that list.[2] Authors in this field insist that we are living in a critical historical moment 'impossible to ignore', and necessitating new theoretical frameworks.[3] Or as philosopher and gender studies scholar Francesca Ferrando put it in 2013: '[I]n contemporary academic debate, "posthuman" has become a key term to cope with an urgency for the integral redefinition of the notion of the human.'[4] Her colleague Rosi Braidotti argues that we need 'new cartographies' to challenge and go beyond the paradigms of the dominant enlightened humanism that understood the 'human' or 'Man' as the unique and superior form of life.[5] Others, however, consider not so much a *crisis* of humanism, but rather the *enhancement* of the human through progress and technological development as the most crucial aspect of the 'post-moment' we are in.[6] The latter version of posthumanism, also called 'transhumanism', expresses an enthusiasm for science and technology, often in tandem with capitalism, that is on a tense footing with the more critical strand of posthumanism. The 'posthuman' thus inspires quite divergent discourses, in terms of either crisis or progress, that are not easily combinable. Critical posthumanism, transhumanism, extropianism, new materialism, technoscience studies and animal studies are examples of these multiple and contrasting fields and approaches, all of them referring to a notion of the 'posthuman', and their variety brings together some of the big tensions of our time.

Debates on the 'posthuman' have been dealing with these tensions from the moment the notion was coined by literary scholar Ihab Hassan in 1977, at an expanding scale across the humanities and sciences. Hassan, a key figure within postmodernism,[7] talked about posthumanism when reflecting on a perceived convergence between the 'two cultures' that had been separating science and imagination, technology and myth since the nineteenth century, as C. P. Snow had famously argued in 1959.[8] One of these cultures was, in Hassan's terms, the 'abstract, technophile, sky-haunted culture dominated by the male principle', i.e. the culture of science and technology that had announced the actual advent of the *homo deus* that had first only been the product of human fantasy. The other culture was the one of 'moist, earthbound arcadians ruled by the female principle'.[9] As we will see in what follows, within the discourse on posthumanism that has developed since the publication of Hassan's article in 1977, we can trace the two cultures' further intertwinement in the interaction between 'transhumanism' on the one hand, and 'critical' or 'cultural' posthumanism on the other. The ways in which each of these strands within posthumanism interprets the 'post' in posthumanism is pivotal for this interaction.

In an article on the notion of 'postraciality', African American Studies scholar Paul Taylor nicely captures how the post-prefix 'is a philosophical operator that expresses a philosophical impulse', which he calls the 'posterizing impulse'.[10] In connection to what Kwame Anthony Appiah calls 'a space-clearing gesture', Taylor summarizes that 'posterizing' is all at once 'a gesture of repudiation, of indebtedness, of skepticism, and of openness, done with an eye toward the inexorability of change over time'.[11] This impulse is characterized by the use of imagery concerning a 'historic shift, break or rupture ... in order to establish distance from some older way of proceeding'.[12]

What we will try to demonstrate in this chapter, is that the 'posterizing impulse' has been part of the posthumanist discourse from the 1970s onwards, but stemmed from the debate about 'transhumanism' that had already arisen in the optimistic 1950s. The actual notion of 'posthumanism', when it was introduced in the 1970s, formed part of the postmodern, reflexive and ironic discourses of the time, which did not so much claim a historical shift or rupture, and did not imply a 'space-clearing gesture' towards a different future, but rather announced a position towards the present, a cultural critique, an explanation of 'how we became posthuman'.[13] This title of literary studies scholar Katherine Hayles's book summarizes this reflexivity: it had more to do with an attitude towards the present in light of a 'posthuman culture' than with a claim about a posthuman age or era, or about 'the future' at all.

It remains a question, however, how much 'post-' was needed here, or whether, perhaps, the gesture towards a 'post-' was rather a 'problem' than a helpful impulse. The latter view has lately quite felicitously been elaborated on by philosopher and biologist Donna Haraway, who understands 'post-' as 'more of a problem.'[14] Instead of 'posterizing', she rather proposes 'staying with the trouble', a rethinking of the place of humanity not among the gods (for the future), but as part of the *humus* that we (sh)are with multiple other species. This rather connects us to a 'com-post' than to a 'posthuman', to what she calls the 'humusities' rather than the humanities or posthumanities.[15]

We will suggest that a philosophical discourse related to 'posthumanism' has emerged today that acknowledges the search for a new 'post' 'beyond' anthropocentrism and modern humanism, especially in the sense of its approach to nature, but that has picked up the reflexivity towards the notion of the 'post' as well, and is aware of how it can remain trapped in the boldness of the posterizing gesture. It therefore seeks an earthly, 'staying with the trouble' kind of 'post', or rather a 'com-post', while being less academic, ironic, and literary than the early postmodern posthuman in the work of Ihab Hassan. See here our zigzag reconstruction.

Postmodern posthumanism in the work of Ihab Hassan

'Posthumanism' was coined by literary scholar Ihab Hassan in 1977, as a broad speculative concept within postmodernism, which had already been turned, in Hassan's words, into 'a tedious travesty' at the time.[16] Hassan introduced the notion in his parodical article 'Prometheus as Performer: Toward a Posthumanist Culture? A University Masque in Five Scenes'. Very postmodernly, Hassan does not assume the role of 'author' or 'philosopher' in the article but instead uses the form of a medieval disputation with eight different kinds of texts as dramatic characters, among them 'pretext', 'text', 'mythotext', 'metatext', 'postext'.[17] The latter ironically 'vainly attempts to conclude the nonaction', while 'pretext' superciliously announces 'the emergence of a new type of culture', which it calls 'posthumanist'.[18] The 'postmodern performance' reflects how the different attitudes and voices within the debate about the Promethean possibilities of man hang together with different attitudes towards time and historicity. The most 'posterizing', philosophical, 'grand narrative'-like voice, 'text', at first just signals a process leading to a posthumanist culture, a culmination of 'the growing intrusion of the human mind in nature and history', the 'dematerialisation of life and the conceptualisation of existence', in short, the Hegelian-Christian narrative of universal history,[19] according to which the emergence of posthumanism is nothing more than the 'natural effect of Western metaphysics'.[20]

In the dynamics of the discussion with 'mythotext', who is focused on the myth of Prometheus, 'text' later on dramatizes this growing intrusion into the announcement of 'a new phase':

> We need to understand that five hundred years of humanism may be coming to an end, as humanism transforms itself into something that we must help-lessly call posthumanism. The figure of Vitruvian Man, arms and legs defin-ing the measure of things, so marvelously drawn by Leonardo, has broken through its enclosing circle and square, and spread across the cosmos.[21]

According to 'text's dialogue partner 'mythotext', however, the myth of Prometheus stealing fire from the gods, 'mirrors our own present'.[22] Prometheus transformed the human condition by means of his cunningness (corresponding to technological ingeniousness) and through interference with the gods, transcending the boundaries between the human and the divine. Impersonating this double-edged sword of cunningness and hubris, he represents the ambiguity of the transformation of the human condi-tion. As we are reminded by 'mythotext' in a scene ominously called 'the Warnings of the Earth', posthumanism can be seen as the culmination of a cunning attitude that human beings have always had: 'Posthumanism seems to you as a sudden mutation of the times; in fact the conjunctions of imagi-nation and science, myth and technology, have begun by the firelight in the caves of Lascaux',[23] and the optimism connected to the Promethean myth is more 'kitsch than vision', since Prometheus 'is a trickster and thief'.[24] From the mythical perspective, the historical 'post' announced by 'text' is therefore just a matter of myopia missing the continuities of the human condition. 'Prometheus is himself the figure of a flawed consciousness strug-gling to transcend such divisions as the One and the Many, Cosmos and Culture, the Universal and the Concrete'[25] – hence the figure of the hubris of man. The figure of Prometheus thus represents the ambiguity of the human urge for technological and scientific progress: a matter of improvement (hero), but by means of hubristic tricks (thief).

Hassan's article can be seen as capturing all the ambivalences of the posthumanist culture that 'text' is announcing: 'to open oneself with hope to the Promethean endeavor is also to recognize its error and terror, its madness within.'[26] And 'mythotext' adds: 'We know all too well the litany of our failures: pollution, population, power that serves only to suppress – in short, man's deadly exploitation of nature and himself.'[27] The ambiguity of the figure of Prometheus can therefore be seen as paradigmatic for the historical development of posthumanist theory: on the one hand, it entails the attitudes of optimism towards the new possibilities of transcendence of 'the human' that technology enables (seeing the heroic side), while on the other hand, it also entails from the outset attitudes of critical reflection on the particular culture that underlies this need to transform the human condition (seeing the hubristic side).

Posthumanism is then characterized early on by the *performance of Prometheus*: 'Performing' Prometheus in the present is a reflection on a transformation difficult to evaluate and assess both qua 'newness' (postness) and qua progress, rather than a singular historical 'post' where one era would be the successor of the other. Posthumanism thus explicitly formed part of postmodernism from the beginning, and it couldn't escape being introduced as a 'dubious neologism, the latest slogan, another image of man's recurrent self-hate',[28] by which 'Zeus & Co' (Inc.) had to perform (once again) the ambivalence of the human access to fire – to knowledge and imagination, science and myth – without having received the wisdom needed to deal with them politically. Hence, ironically and precisely at the time most 'isms' had been declared ideological and dead, Hassan's article both announced the posthumanist culture projecting 'human consciousness into the cosmos, of "mind" into the furthest matter' while at the same time presenting this as just a matter of perspective, the dramatic view of one voice among others.[29] In sum, the emergence of the notion of posthumanism immediately involved a critical cultural reflection on the exploitative tendency that undergirds progressive humanism, while at the same time refraining from the bold historicizing 'space-clearing' 'post' that seems so central to the philosophical gesture of 'posterizing', a gesture that itself formed part in many ways of modern humanism.

Apart from the distinction between a 'posterizing' and a 'critical' posthumanism, Francesca Ferrando distinguishes posthumanism as an 'academic critical position' from a posthumanism in terms of 'a perception of the human which is transhistorical', and which, she notes, is often called transhumanism.[30] In a similar vein, Ranish and Sorgner write:

> Hassan's announcement of posthumanism has little to do with the posthuman in transhumanism. Similar to Foucault's [...] proclaimed 'end of man', post-humanism does not mean 'the literal end of man but the end of a particular image of us'. [...] In other words, for these theorists, our biological nature may remain unchanged, but the self-concept of the human changes, in particular when we consider the integration of technology in our life.[31]

In sum, the 'post' in posthumanism is itself full of ambiguity, simultaneously engaging a historical, a critical and a transhistorical conception of 'the human'. These three conceptions became further entangled after Hassan's prophetic announcement of posthumanism.

Posthumanism among other 'posts' from the 1970s onwards

As an 'ism' without a prior adjective ('posthuman'), 'posthumanism' came up relatively late in comparison to some earlier adjective 'posts' that had emerged as periodizing markers and sociological-historical adjectives, such as 'post-Christian', 'post-colonial' and 'post-secular'.[32] It came up in tandem with other 'post-isms' such as postmodernism and poststructuralism in the 1970s. These notions were characterized by their origins in academic contexts. However, they soon became public notions that summarized a rejection of the ways in which European modernity had tended to hide its colonial, violent, inhuman dimensions by externalizing them either outside of Europe (colonial violence) or by transformations into fascism, totalitarianism or racism against the 'Other' of the Enlightenment. Thus, these post-isms imply a distance taken from modernity itself and the ideologies and practices that had shaped it, such as colonialism, humanism, liberalism, historicism, Enlightenment, capitalism, communism, and the 'grand narratives' of 'Man' and history.

During the 1980s, at the time of the 'end of isms' culminating in the fall of the Berlin Wall, some post-isms became popular (postmodernism in particular) while others lived a largely academic life, making their way through the humanities and social sciences, such as poststructuralism. Posthumanism, for its part, remained relatively reserved to fields of scholarship studying the intersection of science, technology and the humanities, especially in the 1990s (in the work of Donna Haraway and Katherine Hayles in particular).[33]

All the post-isms tended to be rather critically approached in mainstream public cultures. The more radical views connected to 'post-structuralism', often named 'antihumanist', departing from Michel Foucault's and Jacques Derrida's generation, as well as their legacies of anti-bourgeois and anti-capitalist radicalism, were surpassed in the larger societies by the revival of liberal democracy and liberal humanism in their well-known Anglophone (Isaiah Berlin, John Rawls, Anthony Giddens), French (Raymond Aron) and German (Jürgen Habermas/Axel Honneth, Ulrich Beck) versions, and implied a reflexively oriented modernity rather than anything 'post-', even if Jürgen Habermas took his share of conceptualizing 'posts-', postmodernism and post-secularism in particular.

As we already saw, in contrast with the philosophical gesture of 'posterizing', posthumanism emerged from the outset as a form of cultural critique capturing the ironic and ambiguous condition in which both the humanist ideals of modernity and the critiques of modernity by the 'post-isms' had become problematic. Posthumanism thus signalled a new culture where 'imagination and science are agents of change'.[34] For Hassan, imagination and myth were a vital aspect of this change. Therefore, posthumanism emerged not merely as a rational reflection on historical change, but as a critical cultural reflection on the interconnectedness of science and art. It was not only a matter of technological advance, paradigmatic for progressive modernity according to which the 'human form' is transforming rapidly, but also a matter of a change in 'human desire and all its external representations'.[35]

However, it was also through art and the imagination that critical posthumanism became futuristic itself. As a way of reflecting on the limits or ends of man as a progressive being and the gloomy scenarios of where science could take us, art has historically imagined many 'posthumans' in the guise of figures like Doctor Faustus, Frankenstein and Superman, and in stories such as *Brave New World* and *2001 – A Space Odyssey*.[36] This type of imagination was not confined to art, as theoretical reflections on new forms of the 'human' such as Haraway's *Cyborg Manifesto* and Harari's more recent and popular *Homo Deus* show. According to Ferrando, then, posthumanism came 'along within and after postmodernism' (referring to Hassan), as it developed first as a 'political project' aimed at deconstructing the 'Human' in the 1970s, but subsequently transformed into a critical position within literary studies in the 1990s, ultimately leading to a philosophical position 'enacting a thorough critique of humanism and anthropocentrism'.[37]

Transhumanism and posthumanism

Like with most other post-concepts, it is difficult to delineate an unequivocal historical development of posthumanism, even though the term has a relatively precise origin, as we already noted. Thinking 'beyond' or 'after' humanism can be attributed to many authors, who do not necessarily identify themselves as posthumanist thinkers. Even within the philosophical context, the term 'posthumanism' can be attributed to ideas from radically different strands of thought. Moreover, due to the intertwinement with other concepts, such as 'antihumanism' and 'postmodernism', and the emergence of new, related concepts such as 'transhumanism',[38] there is not one evident genealogical narrative to reconstruct. 'Posthumanism' can, therefore, be very roughly defined as 'an umbrella term for ideas that explain, promote or deal with the crisis of humanism'.[39]

If we understand posthumanism as announcing and theorizing the end of man as the centre of the universe, the origins of this idea can be said to have developed long before the term was used. Several authors go back to

Marx,[40] Nietzsche,[41] Heidegger,[42] or Foucault[43] to signal the beginning of the movement they retrospectively call 'posthumanism'. They argue that these theorists were pivotal for establishing the idea that man is not so much the Cartesian rational and autonomous subject that was envisioned by the humanist ideal of Man, while they were also not doing so from an anti-modern standpoint. According to Rosi Braidotti, a shift in how human nature is conceptualized is at the core of all posthumanist theory:

> Far from being the n[in]th variation in a sequence of prefixes that may appear both endless and somehow arbitrary, the posthuman condition introduces a qualitative shift in our thinking about what exactly is the basic unit of common reference for our species, our polity and our relationship to the other inhabitants of this planet.[44]

In short, according to Braidotti, posthumanism should be seen as a historical moment, or rather shift, in which the traditional ways in which human beings as a biological species and as moral creatures have been conceptualized have increasingly become regarded as untenable. However, the question of which idea(s) gave a significant urgency to this shift is difficult to answer.

The diversity regarding the origins of the concept has everything to do with the sort of 'posthuman' that is envisioned. As mentioned, we can generally distinguish two different but interrelated strands of posthumanism. Even though both share 'the notion of technogenesis',[45] as Francesca Ferrando[46] points out, it is in their differences that, crucially, lies an understanding of these two philosophical approaches. First, the strand usually called 'transhumanism' departs from the idea that technological, genetic and biomedical developments can and should ultimately lead to the emerging of a new type of human – the *posthuman*.[47] David Roden calls this more futuristic line of thought 'speculative posthumanism' as it is 'not a normative claim about how the world ought to be but a metaphysical claim about what it could contain'.[48] The second perspective, developed by Stefan Herbrechter, among others, can be called 'critical posthumanism'. It draws on the idea that the humanist ideal of man as a progressive being must be critically reconsidered and revised. It can, therefore, be seen as a 'philosophical corrective to humanism'.[49] If posthumanism aspires to challenge and overcome humanism, transhumanism considers the intellectual and physical limitations of the human being as something that needs to be overcome by the technological control of biological evolution. In what follows, we will go into the central characteristics of both currents to better understand the aspects in which they differ or, even, are radically opposed.

In 1957 the biologist Julian Huxley coined the term *transhumanism* to refer to the possibility of the human species transcending itself in its totality: 'It [transhumanism] is the idea of humanity attempting to overcome its limitations and to arrive at fuller fruition; it is the realization that both individual and social developments are processes of self-transformation.'[50] Although he did not assign to it the same meaning as his successors, the term ultimately denoted a radical transcending of man's biological limitations.[51]

In the 1980s, transhumanists began to identify themselves with this term and line of thought, forming the modern philosophical notion of transhumanism that prevails today. Over the decade, FM-2030[52] and Natasha Vita-More began teaching classes on transhumanism in Los Angeles, Eric Drexler founded the Foresight Institute, and Max More established the Extropy Institute. In 1990, More wrote the foundations of modern transhumanism in *Principles of Extropy* and *Transhumanism: A Futurist Philosophy*. In 1998, philosophers Nick Bostrom and David Pearce founded the World Transhumanist Association and, together with the authors already mentioned as well as others, approved the Transhumanist Declaration.[53] Based on the ideas conceived by More, transhumanism is here defined as:

(1) The intellectual and cultural movement that affirms the possibility and desirability of fundamentally improving the human condition through applied reason, especially by developing and making widely available technologies to eliminate ageing and to greatly enhance human intellectual, physical, and psychological capacities.
(2) The study of the ramifications, promises, and potential dangers of technologies that will enable us to overcome fundamental human limitations, and the related study of the ethical matters involved in developing and using such technologies.[54]

In this way, transhumanists believe that the existing forms of the human are at an intermediate stage that needs to be challenged to advance towards a human form in which bodies, as well as intelligence, will be enhanced for a higher utility and purpose. Reaching this goal means, for them, entering the stage of 'the posthuman'. According to transhumanists, the enhancement of human nature towards a posthuman nature will be reached through technological development: 'By thoughtfully, carefully, and yet boldly applying technology to ourselves, we can become something no longer accurately described as human – we can become posthuman.'[55] The posthuman is thus the future human that will overcome all those undesirable characteristics of the present human condition, such as ageing and death. Furthermore, 'posthumans would also have much greater cognitive capabilities, and more refined emotions (more joy, less anger, or whatever changes each individual prefers)'.[56] Transhumanism is, in this way, a techno-deterministic and techno-utopian form of posthumanism in which the *telos* of humanity's future will be achieved through technology.[57]

For Bostrom, transhumanism is a combination of Renaissance human-ism (hence Hassan's reference to the Vitruvian man) together with specific ideas from the Enlightenment period, where rational humanism, empirical science and critical reason are understood as the path for learning about the world as well as for providing the grounds of morality. Transhumanism is thus rooted in 'rational humanism'.[58] It is what transhumanists understand as a 'eupraxsophy',[59] which is a 'nonreligious philosophy of life that rejects faith, worship, and the supernatural, instead emphasizing a meaningful and ethical approach to living informed by reason, science, progress, and the value of existence in our current life'.[60] That is the above-referred-to exten-sion of the humanist project based on enlightened principles such as reason, progress or secularism. It is a thinking that wants to bring humanism beyond itself, and that understands limits as something to be transcended, to be challenged.

As Cary Wolfe critically puts it, transhumanism 'should be seen as an *intensification* of humanism'.[61] Thus, instead of presenting a framework to approach the problems that a hierarchical understanding of the human versus all other species presents, as we will see critical posthumanism does, transhumanism, on the contrary, strengthens this hierarchy. The human is understood within a linear timeline in which there is demarcated progress to achieve through technological development to become a superior form: the post-human. The post-human will challenge the limits that the body presents for the mind. The post-human(ity) of transhumanism is thus a goal to be achieved. It is the purpose towards which transhumanism heads and therefore remains an intermediate phase between the human and the post-human.

This type of 'posthumanism' can, therefore, be seen as remaining within the humanistic framework – the idea of man as a being that can be improved through knowledge and science remains central. For this reason, Stefan Herbrechter describes this strand of posthumanism – which he calls 'the current technology-centered discussion about the potential transforma-tion of humans' – as 'merely the latest symptom of a cultural malaise that inhibits humanism itself'.[62]

Contrary to transhumanism, *critical posthumanism* presents a theo-retical framework where two critiques converge: on the one hand, post-humanism criticizes the classical humanism and the idea of man as a unique being, that is, 'the universalist posture of the idea of "Man" as the alleged "measure of all things"'; on the other hand, posthumanism ques-tions 'species hierarchy and the assumption of human exceptionalism'.[63] That is, posthumanism presents a post-anthropocentric critique of the established hierarchy of the species, in which man is placed above the rest as a superior being:

In the West, the human has been historically posed in a hierarchical scale to the non-human realm. Such a symbolic structure, based on a human exceptionalism well depicted from the Great Chain of Being, has not only sustained the primacy of humans over non-human animals, but it has also (in)formed the human realm itself, with sexist, racist, classist, homophobic, and ethnocentric presumptions.[64]

Posthumanism's critique, therefore, opposes transhumanism's goal. It is 'a critique of the Enlightenment subject's claim to mastery, autonomy, and dominance over material and virtual worlds',[65] to put it in terms that clearly echo Horkheimer and Adorno's critique of Enlightenment rationalism in *Dialectic of Enlightenment*.[66]

According to Pramod Nayar, posthumanism proposes a deconstruction of the dualisms that encompass the idea of 'the human' as a neutral and timeless idea, which can be universalized to define the exclusivity and superiority of the human species. Critical posthumanism 'rejects both human exceptionalism ... and human instrumentalism',[67] that is, it rejects the uniqueness of human beings as well as the belief that humans have the control over the natural world. Thus, this critical approach questions the philosophical projects of humanism and transhumanism that situate human reason and rationality in the centre, by proposing a broader and more inclusive understanding of the concept of life. As such, posthumanism aims, first of all, to debunk the belief, central to humanism, that man alone has dignity in contradistinction to animals because he has reason and consciousness.

An important source for the latter idea was Renaissance humanist Giovanni Pico Della Mirandola's *Oration on the Dignity of Man*.[68] In this text – later denoted as 'the manifesto of humanism'[69] – Mirandola aims to specify what it is about human nature that makes 'man' such a miraculous, admirable and eminent creature.[70] In his characterization of the human Mirandola distinguishes 'man' from both animals and the divine, and concludes that the excellence of man is characterized precisely by this intermediate state: unlike animals, man has the capacity to overcome the constraints of nature because of his intellectual capacities, which brings man closer to the divine, but the real wonder is man's potentiality and openness towards different ways of being:

But upon man, at the moment of his creation, God bestowed seeds pregnant with all possibilities, the germs of every form of life. Whichever of these a man shall cultivate, the same will mature and bear fruit in him. If vegetative, he will become a plant; if sensual, he will become brutish; if rational, he will reveal himself a heavenly being; if intellectual, he will be an angel and the son of God.[71]

Mirandola thus thought that the dignity of man consists in his capacity to transcend the natural constraints of nature through his free will and intelligence to develop into a higher form of being (the posthuman perhaps).

Another, interrelated, point of critique that is central to critical posthumanism (and not to transhumanism) is what Herbrechter calls the 'ideology of development'.[72] This denotes the humanist and Enlightenment belief that man is a progressive being, open to all kinds of development in virtue of his rational capacities. This idea is epitomized in Leonardo da Vinci's Vitruvian Man, which became a symbolic figure for Western humanism. This humanist conception of man invokes a higher form of humanness, or *humanitas*, which is embodied in the Vitruvian Man: the *homo universalis*. This 'universal man' (explicitly not female), which is central to the cosmos, is meant to characterize a human being that has developed all his potential talents and intellectual faculties to perfection, and, as such, has distinguished himself from the lower, mere 'natural', beings and positioned himself in a more approximate relation to the divine. This metaphysical conception of man became rationalized during the Enlightenment, in the form of Descartes' *res cogitans* and Kant's transcendental reason, but this did not mean that these conceptions were any less metaphysical.

Due to scientific and technological developments during the seventeenth and eighteenth century, the conceptualization of humanity as a progressive species and 'civilization' became a central idiom, which nonetheless culminated in a 'system' which had dehumanization as its counter-narrative. As Herbrechter explains: 'The inhuman in the human takes two forms: on the one hand, the inhumanity of the "system", which only uses humanism as its ideology, and, on the other hand, the inhuman which inhabits the human as its "secret" core ...'.[73] The first type of inhumanity is related to the anthropocentrism which is presented as universal and must be countered by acknowledging that '[h]umans and their humanity are historical and cultural constructs ... and they therefore have to be placed within larger contexts like ecosystems, technics or evolution'.[74] The second type of inhumanity is related to the way in which humanist essentialism creates inferior forms of being, and posthumanism in this sense, therefore, means 'to acknowledge all those ghosts, all those human others that have been repressed during the process of dehumanization: animals, gods, demons, monsters of all kinds'.[75]

These two tendencies of antihumanism have resulted in both the externalizing of the nonhuman to other species, sexes, races and premodern stages of evolution in order to define the Western humanist (modern) subject as natural dominator over other forms of life (the 'other inhuman'), as well as in the creation of dichotomies between the rational essence of man and its internal otherness (the animality, physicality, instinctiveness, subconsciousness, and mortality inherent to human life). However, as the creation of this 'external other' is generally understood as a way of dealing with the 'internal other', where physicality, irrationality and animality are projected on the external other, the effort to go beyond the humanistic discourse through recognizing antihumanist tendencies within (historical materialism, Freudian unconsciousness, Lacanian structuralism or the Nietzschean will to power), risks losing from sight the constructive relation of this tendency with the external inhuman other. This becomes clear when we consider the way in which 'anti'-humanism played a role in critiques of modernity.

The fact that humanism projected inhumanness onto external others has resulted in critical responses from (formerly) dehumanized others to the mechanisms of subordination that relegated them to this status. Noteworthy examples are Simone de Beauvoir's feminism and the anti-colonial and anti-racist works of, among others, Aimé Césaire, W. E. B. Du Bois, and Frantz Fanon. Many of these responses were not so much a wholesale rejection of Western humanism or a desire to move beyond it, but in many cases the response was to advocate for a new notion of humanity in which other forms of being could be positively affirmed and alternative forms of experience could be metaphysically grounded. Fanon recognized that Western humanism had created an ideology of European whiteness that had dialectically created the Black Other as a necessary negation of the White Subject, but in order to overcome this negative relation he foresaw the emergence of a new type of humanity as the only viable way to assert oneself ontologically and politically in the world. He writes in *The Wretched of the Earth*:

> It [decolonization] brings a natural rhythm into existence, introduced by new men, and with it a new language and a new humanity. Decolonization is the veritable creation of new men. But this creation owes nothing of its legitimacy to any supernatural power; the 'thing' which has been colonized becomes man during the same process by which it frees itself.[76]

For Fanon it is precisely the affirmation of the colonized subject's humanity which becomes the mechanism that sets them free (from being *damnés*). From that perspective, negating the humanist and modernist framework and its Manicheist logic from a 'post-' position would rather be remaining within the framework of humanism. To reject humanism in this context would then risk denying a new form of humanity that emerged precisely out of a critique of the inhuman tendencies within Western humanism. In this vein, Africana philosopher Lewis Gordon stated in the 1990s that only the dominant group has the privilege to move away from humanism since, after all, it has always been their 'humanity', while other communities have to fight for 'the humanistic prize'.[77] In addition, Zakiyyah Iman Jackson has argued that posthumanism leaves aside the critiques on humanity produced by black scholars. Posthumanists began to present criticisms of 'man's' 'epistemological integrity'[78] by questioning different conceptions whose roots lead to Enlightenment thought. However, as Jackson notes, posthumanism has remained 'committed to a specific order of rationality, one rooted in the epistemological locus of the West, and more precisely that of Enlightenment man'.[79]

Paul Taylor has drawn a similar conclusion in his discussion of 'postraciality'. He argues that we should reject strong versions of postraciality, as the 'idea that we have achieved a postracial condition is part of the ideological dimension of a particular racial paradigm' which is characterized by 'its determination to whitewash racial history and the mechanisms of ongoing racial stratification – to obscure, ignore or erase the evidence that race still matters in a variety of definite, concrete, and distressingly familiar ways'.[80] This means that 'the act of repudiation',[81] which is common to all 'posterizing gestures', risks dismissing and obscuring the particular histories, traditions and experiences that developed from racial systems in favour of a non-racial universalism.

In other words, the critiques that developed in reaction to Western humanism have themselves been part of its history and development. Even though these responses wanted to leave behind a certain type of essentialist and exclusionary logic, rejecting all the hierarchizing dichotomies that humanism had generated, they simultaneously risked rejecting, obscuring and disregarding the histories, ideas and imagined futures that evolved from and within these dichotomies. In this sense, 'posthuman' imaginaries still have tended to invoke a universal teleology towards an abstract – genderless, colourless and bodiless – human, creating a blind spot for present forms of racism, sexism and colonial legacies.

Posthumanism in the present

Why is there a new interest in these 'post' phenomena over the last five or ten years, and perhaps why is 'posthumanism' one of the more popular ones? A few sequences of events in the first decades of the 2000s seem to have stimulated the re-emergence of the post-isms. The easy neoliberalism that wanted to be no -ism of the 1990s was first shaken by the events of 9/11 and their aftermath, then further by the financial crisis of 2008, the rising levels of inequality and the sealing off of the 'white world' from the Global South, after that by rising populism, and, since about 2015, by increasing public awareness of the depth of the global environmental crisis and the role of humanity in it, summarized by the term 'Anthropocene', and later the 'Capitalocene'[82].

Posthumanism is perhaps the 'philosophy of the time', as Rosi Braidotti and Francesca Ferrando claim, because it brings together the reflexive attitude of the other 'post-isms' with a relatively large arsenal of alternative ways of thinking and doing, of affirmation instead of being mainly critically oriented, and because it has been directed, from the beginning, towards the sciences as well as the humanities.[83] It thus brings together a few of the older post-World War II grand narratives of deception with modernity and capitalism, referring to Heidegger's critique of technology in the first place, with an awareness of the impact of humanity and modernity/coloniality on the whole world and the Earth itself. Anthropologist Claude Lévi-Strauss had formulated this constellation early on in 1979, after having been asked whether he saw himself as an antihumanist:

> What I have struggled against, and what I feel is very harmful, is the sort of unbridled humanism that has grown out of the Judeo-Christian tradition on the one hand, and on the other hand, closer to home, out of the Renaissance and out of Cartesianism, which makes man a master, an absolute lord of creation.[84]

It is the increasing awareness of the falsity of this lordship, the how and the why of it, as well as the awareness that it has to end, that is a shared sense among the more critical versions of posthumanism, as well in the larger public, which can explain the notion's popularity. However, we are not sure that 'post-' helps to find a helpful temporal orientation here. We, the authors of this article, tend to feel closer to Haraway's wager that commemorating, com-posting, *sympoiesis* in multispecies practices of kinship-making, rather oriented towards the *re-* than to the *post-*, even if reflexive rather than futuristic, would be a stronger, more imaginative way to go.[85]

Notes

1 Cary Wolfe, 'What Is Posthumanism?', in C. Wolfe (ed.), *What is Posthumanism?* (Minneapolis, MN: University of Minnesota Press, 2009), pp. xi–xxxiv, pp. xv–xvi.

2 See, for example, Bruno Latour, *Facing Gaia: Eight Lectures on the new Climatic Regime.* (Cambridge: Polity Press, 2017); Donna Haraway, *Staying with the Trouble: Making Kin in the Chthulucene* (Durham, NC: Duke University Press, 2016); Anna Lowenhaupt Tsing, *The Mushroom at the End of the World: Living in Capitalist Ruins* (Princeton, NJ: Princeton University Press, 2015).

3 Wolfe, *What is Posthumanism*, pp. xv–xvi.

4 Francesca Ferrando, 'Posthumanism, Transhumanism, Antihumanism, Metahumanism, and New Materialisms: Differences and Relations', *Existenz:*

An International Journal in Philosophy, Religion, Politics, and the Arts, 8:2 (2013), 26–32, 26.

5 Rosi Braidotti, 'Posthuman Feminist Theory', in Lisa Disch and Mary Hawkesworth (eds), *The Oxford Handbook of Feminist Theory* (Oxford: Oxford University Press, 2018), pp. 673–98, p. 689; 'Posthuman Critical Theory', in D. Banerji and M. R. Paranjape (ed.), *Critical Posthumanism and Planetary Futures* (New Delhi: Springer India, 2016), pp. 13–32, p. 17; 'Posthuman Critical Theory', *Journal of Posthuman Studies*, 1:1 (2017), 9–25, 11. Braidotti here defines cartography as: 'a theoretically based and politically informed map of the present or 'actual moment' in terms of scholarly and discursive production.' Its task is 'to provide insights into multiple dimensions: to be critical about the actual conditions, but also creative in terms of new figurations or navigational tools that aim at *actualizing* the virtual' (ibid., 11).

6 Francesca Ferrando and Rosi Braidotti, *Philosophical Posthumanism* (London: Bloomsbury, 2019), p. 2; Ferrando, 'Posthumanism, Transhumanism', pp. 26–7, n. 1; Stefan Herbrechter, *Posthumanism: A Critical Analysis* (London: Bloomsbury, 2013), p. 34; Neil Badmington, *Posthumanism* (New York: Palgrave, 2000), p. 2; N. Katherine Hayles, *How We Became Posthuman: Virtual Bodies in Cybernetics, Literature and Informatics* (Chicago, IL: University of Chicago Press, 1999), p. 247.

7 For a discussion of Hassan's work in relation to postmodernism, see Hans Bertens' chapter in this volume.

8 C. P. Snow, *The Two Cultures* (Cambridge: Cambridge University Press, [1959] 2001).

9 Ihab Hassan, 'Prometheus as Performer: Toward a Posthumanist Culture?', *The Georgia Review*, 31:4 (1977), 830–50, 839.

10 Paul C. Taylor, 'Taking Postracialism Seriously', *Du Bois Review*, 11:1 (2014), 9–25, 16.

11 Ibid.

12 Ibid.

13 Hayles, *How We Became Posthuman*.

14 Haraway, *Staying with the Trouble*, p. 212, n. 2.

15 Ibid., pp. 11, 32.

16 Hassan, 'Prometheus as Performer', 832.

17 Ibid., 831.

18 Ibid.

19 Ibid., 835.

20 Herbrechter, *Posthumanism*, p. 34.

21 Hassan, 'Prometheus as Performer', 843.

22 Ibid., 832.

23 Ibid., 835–6.

24 Ibid., 847. See also Trijsje Franssen, 'Prometheus: Performer or Transformer?', in Robert Ranish and Stefan Lorenz Sorgner (eds), *Post- and Transhumanism: An Introduction* (Frankfurt am Main: Peter Lang, 2014), pp. 73–82, p. 74.

25 Hassan, 'Prometheus as Performer', 838.

26 Ibid., 847.

27 Ibid., 848.

28 Ibid., 843.

29 Ibid.

30 Francesca Ferrando, 'The Body', in Ranish and Sorgner (eds), *Post- and Transhumanism*, pp. 213–26, p. 219.

31 Robert Ranish and Stefan Lorenz Sorgner citing Foucault (*The Order of Things: An Archaeology of the Human Sciences*, 1966) and Hassan (*Prometheus as Performer*, 1977), 'Introducing Post- and Transhumanism', in Ranish and Sorgner (eds), *Post- and Transhumanism*, pp. 7–27, p. 15.

32 Stefan Herbrechter notes that the concept 'posthumanism' was already used by Thomas Blount in 1656, and 'post-Human' by H. P. Blavatsky in 1888 (Herbrechter, *Posthumanism*, pp. 33–4). It could be interesting to trace these old versions of the notion, but they do not form part of the scholarly culture of post-war 'posts' on which we are focusing here.

33 Donna Jeanne Haraway, 'A Cyborg Manifesto: Science, Technology and Socialist-Feminism in the Late Twentieth Century', in Haraway, *Manifestly Haraway* (Minneapolis, MN: University of Minnesota Press, 2016), pp. 3–90; Hayles, *How We Became Posthuman*.

34 Hassan, 'Prometheus as Performer', 838.

35 Ibid., 843.

36 For an overview of these 'posthumans', see 'Chronology I: The Posthuman', in Bruce Clarke and Manuela Rossini (eds), *The Cambridge Companion to Literature and the Posthuman* (Cambridge: Cambridge University Press, 2016), pp. xxv–xxix.

37 Ferrando, 'The Body', 219.

38 For all the subcategories that can be said to fall under 'posthumanism', see Ferrando and Braidotti, *Philosophical Posthumanism*, p. 1.

39 Ranish and Sorgner, 'Introducing Post- and Transhumanism', p. 14.

40 Badmington, *Posthumanism*, p. 5.

41 Herbrechter, *Posthumanism*, p. 31.

42 Ferrando and Braidotti, *Philosophical Posthumanism*, p. 2.

43 Cary Wolfe, 'What Is Posthumanism?', p. xii.

44 Rosi Braidotti, *The Posthuman* (Oxford: Polity Press, 2013), p. 2.

45 The notion of 'technogenesis' was coined by Bernard Stiegler to refer to the co-evolution of the human animal together with the technicity of tools, a concept that Katherine Hayles adopts as well.

46 Ferrando, 'Posthumanism, Transhumanism', 28.

47 Ranish and Sorgner, 'Introducing Post- and Transhumanism', p. 8.

48 David Roden, *Posthuman Life: Philosophy at the Edge of the Human* (London: Routledge, 2015), p. 9.

49 Herbrechter, *Posthumanism*, p. 3.

50 Julian Huxley, 'Knowledge, Morality, and Destiny: The William Alanson White Memorial Lectures, Third Series', *Psychiatry*, 14:2 (1951), 127–51, 139.

51 Ranish and Sorgner, 'Introducing Post- and Transhumanism', p. 10.

52 FM-2030 was the adopted name by transhumanist and futurist philosopher Fereidoun M. Esfandiary.

53 For information about the association and the declaration: https://humanity plus.org/philosophy/transhumanist-faq/ (accessed 6 February 2020).

54 Ibid.

55 Max More, 'The Philosophy of Transhumanism', in Max More and Natasha Vita-More (eds), *The Transhumanist Reader: Classical and Contemporary Essays on the Science, Technology, and Philosophy of the Human Future* (Oxford: Wiley-Blackwell, 2013), pp. 3–17, p. 4.

56 Ibid.

57 Cf. Pramod K. Nayar, *Posthumanism* (Cambridge: Polity Press, 2014), pp. 7–8.

58 Bostrom, Nick, 'A History of Transhumanist Thought', *Journal of Evolution and Technology*, 14:1 (2005), 1–25, 2.

59 The term was coined by Paul Kurtz, known as the father of secular humanism. See More, 'Philosophy of Transhumanism', 4.

60 Ibid.

61 Wolfe, 'What Is Posthumanism?', p. xv.

62 Herbrechter, *Posthumanism,* p. 3.

63 Braidotti, 'Posthuman Feminist Theory', p. 674. See also Braidotti, 'Posthuman Critical Theory'.

64 Ferrando, 'Posthumanism, Transhumanism', 28. As David Livingstone Smith explains, the Great Chain of Being or *scala naturae* is the conception 'of the universe as a vast hierarchy with God, the supremely perfect being, sitting astride its apex, with inanimate matter lying at its base and everything else situated at one or another of the many levels arrayed in between. Although the details of the scheme vary from one culture to another and from one epoch to the next, all versions of it are broadly similar. Plants are near the bottom, not much higher than the soil from which they grow. Simple animals like worms and snails are more perfect than plants, so they occupy a slightly more elevated rung. Mammals are higher still, and we humans have a privileged rank just below the angels, and two steps beneath the Creator.' It is the representation of the Cosmos 'as static and unchangeable, complete and continuous. There was no room for novelty.' David Livingstone Smith, *Less than Human: Why We Demean, Enslave, and Exterminate Others* (New York: St. Martin's Press, 2011), pp. 39, 41.

65 Zakiyyah Iman Jackson, 'Animal: New Directions in the Theorization of Race and Posthumanism', *Feminist Studies*, 39:3 (2013), 669–85, 672.

66 Theodor W. Adorno and Max Horkheimer, *Dialectic of Enlightenment: Philosophical Fragments*, ed. Gunzelin Schmid Noerr, trans. Edmund Jephcott (Stanford, CA: Stanford University Press, 2002).

67 Nayar, *Posthumanism*, p. 8.

68 Giovanni Pico della Mirandola, *Oration on the Dignity of Man* (1496), trans. A. Robert Caponigri (Chicago, IL: Henry Regnery, 1951), p. 7.

69 A. Robert Caponigri, 'Introduction', ibid., p. xiii.

70 Mirandola, *Oration on the Dignity of Man*, p. 3.

71 Ibid., pp. 8–9.

72 Herbrechter, *Posthumanism*, p. 8.

73 Ibid.

74 Ibid., p. 9.

75 Ibid.

76 Frantz Fanon, *The Wretched of the Earth*, trans. Constance Farrington (New York: Grove Press, 1963), pp. 36–7.

77 Lewis Gordon, 'African-American Philosophy: Theory, Politics, and Pedagogy', in Steven Tozer (ed.), *Philosophy of Education* (Urbana, IL: Philosophy of Education Society, 1999), pp. 39–46, 39, as quoted in Jackson, 'Animal', 672.

78 Jackson, 'Animal', 670.

79 Ibid., 672. Jackson refers to the essays by Sylvia Wynter about coloniality and the emergence of the ideas of Natural Man and Natural Reason, in particular to Wynter's article 'The Ceremony Must be Found: After Humanism', *boundary 2*, 12:3/13:1 (1984), 19–70.

80 Taylor, 'Taking Postracialism Seriously', 13.

81 Ibid., 17.

82 Jason Moore (ed.), *Anthropocene or Capitalocene* (Oakland, CA: PM Press, 2016).

83 Ferrando and Braidotti, *Philosophical Posthumanism*, p. 1.

84 Claude-Lévi-Strauss, 'Entretien avec Jean-Marie Benoist', *Le Monde* (26 January 1979), 21–2 (our translation). Original: 'Ce contre quoi je me suis insurgé, et dont je ressens profondément la nocivité, c'est cette espèce d'humanisme dévergondé issu, d'une part, de la tradition judéo-chrétienne, et, d'autre part, plus près de nous, de la Renaissance et du cartésianisme, qui fait de l'homme un maître, un seigneur absolu de la création.'

85 Haraway, *Staying with the Trouble*. Lévi-Strauss captured this direction in the interview from 1979: 'The respect of man by man cannot be based on certain particular dignities which mankind would attribute to itself, for then a fraction of mankind may always decide that it embodies these dignities more eminently than others. Rather, a kind of principal humility should be established at the outset; man, beginning by respecting all forms of life outside his own, would be protected from the risk of not respecting all forms of life within humanity itself' ('Entretien', 21–2). Original: 'Le respect de l'homme par l'homme ne peut pas trouver son fondement dans certaines dignités particulières que l'humanité s'attribuerait en propre, car, alors, une fraction de l'humanité pourra toujours décider qu'elle incarne ces dignités de manière plus éminente que d'autres. Il faudrait plutôt poser au départ une sorte d'humilité principielle; l'homme, commençant par respecter toutes les formes de vie en dehors de la sienne, se mettrait à l'abri du risque de ne pas respecter toutes les formes de vie au sein de l'humanité même.'

Epilogue: Lessons for future posts

Adriaan van Veldhuizen

Introduction

This volume is not merely a collection of essays on post-concepts. It is an attempt to understand – from a comparative, historical point of view – what post-concepts are, where they came from and what they do. This attempt stems from the observation that during the last century post-concepts have become common throughout the social sciences and the humanities. As the last two chapters, especially, demonstrate, there are no signs of this tendency abating. Many more post-concepts certainly lie ahead of us; we are not post-post. Therefore, by examining the peculiarities of several historical post-concepts, this volume aims to offer insights for students of more recent post-concepts as well.

This extended epilogue brings the threads of this volume together by summarizing some of the most important insights that emerge from the eleven preceding chapters.[1] It frames these key insights with help of the methodological framework laid down in the introduction. It also argues that the principles used in this volume not only help us understand historical post-concepts, but also prove valuable in assessing contemporary post-concepts, and perhaps even future ones. Therefore, the second part of this epilogue focuses on a post-concept that is central to contemporary public life and debate, but has not yet been discussed in much detail in this volume: post-truth.

Studying post-concepts: A historical phenomenon

Before turning to the five methodological principles detailed in the introduction – *transfer*, *interconnectedness*, *performativity*, *positioning*, and *conceptual webs* – I should highlight that this volume is an exercise in intellectual history, not philosophical analysis. The chapters in this book do not assume that post-terms are either conceptually stable or in need of further definitional clarity. Instead, the chapters trace these terms through time, attentive to their changing and sometimes even contradictory meanings. Compared to other publications on the use of post-concepts, this historicizing approach is a distinctive feature of the chapters collected in this volume.[2] So, it might be useful to first present some results of this historicizing view.

Roger Backhouse observes that inventing post-concepts is a tradition typical for the social sciences and the humanities. In the natural sciences and economics, the use of such concepts is less common. And when post-concepts do occur in these disciplines, they are used differently than in the human sciences. Deployed as descriptive labels, they are generally applied in historiographical contexts, as ways of periodizing the histories of those disciplines themselves. However, as Backhouse's analysis of one of these rare economic post-concepts – post-Keynesian – nicely shows, there are exceptions to this rule. Although post-Keynesian was initially charged with 'a purely temporal meaning', it subtly evolved into a term with more complex and layered connotations.

Intellectual history therefore appears to be an excellent heuristic tool to get a grip on the multiplicity of meanings and the misunderstandings that spring from it. It not only allows historians to trace gradual changes in meaning, but also, as illustrated by Howard Brick's discussion of post-capitalism, enables them to show how a concept can die out and pop up again years later. How exactly conceptual histories are written is perhaps of secondary importance. In fact, this volume illustrates that conceptual histories can take different forms. While some chapters adopt a traditional chronological framework, Stéphanie Genz presents her history of post-feminism as a genealogy. Yolande Jansen, Jasmijn Leeuwenkamp and Leire Urricelqui do the same in their chapter on posthumanism. Other chapters even bring in quantitative elements, or show how post-concepts developed in two or more contexts at the same time. Which of these approaches is most helpful for the task at hand obviously differs from concept to concept. Importantly, however, all of these methods make abundantly clear that the meaning of the post-prefix is never fixed over time. Post-concepts should therefore be considered as dynamic phenomena, as even the seemingly static or descriptive ones can experience significant changes of meaning through the years.

Apart from diachronic differences in meaning, there are often synchronic differences as well. In such cases, a multiplicity of meanings can be discerned at one and the same moment in time. K. Healan Gaston shows such differences in the interpretation of the concept post-secular by discussing two of its founding fathers: a Catholic and a Protestant. The confusion produced by such a proliferation of meanings, is perhaps shown most strikingly by

Genz, whose chapter on postfeminism distinguishes two mutually exclusive ideas associated with one and the same concept. But synchronic uses of a post-concept are not always incompatible: the debate on posthumanism, 'transhumanism' and 'critical posthumanism' emerged at the same time and in dialogue with each other.

Most of these synchronic differences seem to spring from the elusive character of the post-prefix. In her famous 1992 piece 'Notes on the "Post-Colonial"', Ella Shohat distinguished between post-concepts that denote a movement beyond a certain way of thinking and post-concepts that refer to a passage into a new period.[3] A comparable attempt to bring clarity in the meaning of the 'post' can be found in the question posed by Kwame Anthony Appiah in 'Is the Post- in Postmodernism the Post- in Postcolonial?'. Over the years, Appiah's focus on the dual capacity of post-concepts has inspired many similar questions, which were reflected in titles of articles and books: 'Is the Post- in Postcolonial the Post- in Post-Soviet?', 'Is the "Post" in "Post-Totalitarian" the "Post" in "Postcolonial"?', 'Is the "Post" in "Postsecular" the "Post" in "Postcolonial"?'.[4] Collectively answering these questions 'no', these authors have offered a deluge of meanings of posts. Perhaps everyone writing about these concepts, whether in comparison or in themselves, should consider Genz's dictum: 'For me, it is important not to fall into a critical trap that takes for granted the meanings of "post" and "feminism" and instead allow for contradictory and evolving notions of (post)feminism that may co-exist at the same moment.'[5]

Transfer *of post-concepts*

This brings me to our first methodological principle presented in the introduction: the *transfer* of post-concepts. Post-concepts are constantly transferred across disciplinary, linguistic and geographical boundaries, often acquiring new meanings in each new setting. Postmodernism offers an excellent example of this conceptual wanderlust: not only Hans Bertens, who devotes a full chapter to postmodernism, but virtually all other authors in this volume touch upon the concept. Postmodernism was not travelling alone: we see that post-structuralism went transatlantic from France to the US, while post-ideology oscillated between France, Germany and the US. The latter concept even found its genesis in an international organization – the Congress for Cultural Freedom – that introduced the concept not only in different countries, but also in a plethora of academic, political and cultural circles. Postfeminism is observed moving from national contexts to a transnational context, and post-Christian transferred from critics of religion to Christian authors. Posthumanism moved from cultural critique to philosophical and futuristic discourses. Sooner or later, most post-concepts start to move, so that research on post-concepts inevitably tends to become interdisciplinary.

Interconnectedness *of post-concepts*

As mentioned, many authors have asked whether the 'post' in 'post-X' is the same as the 'post' in 'post-Y'. This kind of question is relevant, as the chance of stumbling upon one post-concept while studying another are high. It seems that post-concepts have a magnetic appeal to each other. Many authors in this volume find examples of this interconnectedness of post-concepts. Stéphanie Genz shows that the debate on the concept of postfeminism is closely related to discussions of postcolonialism. For his part, Andrew Sartori argues that those who study postcolonialism cannot do so without also looking at post-structuralism. Edward Baring, writing on post-structuralism, connects his object of study to postmodernism. Indeed, postmodernism seems to be connected to virtually every other post-concept. Because of the mutual attraction of post-concepts, the chapters in this volume touch upon many more post-concepts than the table of contents seems to suggest. Post-Marxist, post-bourgeois, post-political, post-industrial and post-imperial all appear in various chapters, thereby illustrating that post-terms themselves form a kind of conceptual web – on which I will elaborate below.

There is at least one striking reason for post-concepts to be so closely connected: the fact that some of them were proposed or popularized by the same authors. Already in the early 1950s, Charles Olson, in his analysis of 'the post-modern, post-humanist, post-historic era', showed how easily post-concepts can relate to each other.[6] Likewise, in 1957, Irving Howe described Wallace Stevens as 'a forerunner of post-crisis, post-ideological man',[7] while a reviewer of Howe's *Politics and the Novel* coined the term 'post-political man'.[8] In the years that followed, Howe discussed 'post-Resistance France' and wrote about '"postmodern" fiction'.[9] Howe seems to have introduced several post-concepts and directly or indirectly connected them in his writings. This observation ties in with examples from the chapters of this volume, wherein authors such as Will Herberg, Hans Hoekendijk, Fredric Jameson, Robert Bellah, Ihab Hassan and Daniel Bell each employed multiple post-concepts. The post-prefix was a linguistic tool some authors used more often than others, in part as a matter of literary style and aesthetics.

Performativity *of post-concepts*

A discussion on literary aesthetics, however, might distract us from the fact that the post-prefix is more than a stylistic phenomenon. It is also much more than a synonym for 'after', referring simply to historical sequences.[10] The 'post' has consequences in the real world; it *does* something. This brings me to the third methodological principle: *performativity*.

A clear-cut example of this performative use can be found in Suki Ali's book *Mixed-Race, Post-Race*. She mentions that her use of the term post-race 'emphasises deconstructive approaches to identities, and draws on theories of performativity, passing and new ethnicities'.[11] By choosing this terminology Ali 'challenges the tenacity of "singularity" within the hegemonic "race" rhetoric, binaried ways of thinking and limits to language which deny possibilities for mixed identifications'.[12] The performative power of the term post-race, one could say, facilitates a new reality.

In Chapter 3 of this volume, I argue that the authors discussing the post-ideological era used performative or creative language too. They cooperated in shaping new intellectual landscapes. Post-concepts do not only reflect a juxtaposition of consecutive historical epochs, but also tend to *create* those epochs. Especially when used as tools for periodization, many post-concepts share qualities with other 'colligatory concepts', such as 'Middle Ages' and 'Renaissance'.[13] In the use of such concepts, one particular characteristic of an era is taken to stand for that era as a whole. In a metaphorical manner, one is invited to see everything that happened in the sixteenth century in the light of the rebirth that allegedly took place during the 'renaissance'. This kind of colligatory language is not confined to historians constructing eras; because of their ability to shape perceptions, post-terms are used as political or even polemical tools as well. The 'post' is easily applicable to politics, in so far as it can be used by contemporaries to express and create a desired situation: 'We are working together for a post-racial era', or, on the contrary, 'I don't want to live in a post-literary society!'.

The 'post' *as* positioning *concept*

Because of their political and normative impact, the performative aspect of post-concepts is closely related to the fourth methodological principle of this volume: their ability to serve as positioning concepts.[14] As K. Healan Gaston points out, according to some authors, modern society not only 'was becoming' post-secular, but also 'should become' post-secular.[15] The importance of this 'should' is discussed in various forms in this volume. Andrew Sartori describes postcolonial as a 'political periodizer' and Roger Backhouse writes that 'the term post-Keynesian had political implications'.[16] Stéphanie Genz underscores that feminism itself is a 'social and political phenomenon'; she therefore draws attention to the political aspects of postfeminism.[17] In Chapter 3, I write that although post-ideology pretended to describe the depoliticization of society, it became a political ideology in itself.[18]

When people use post-concepts to distance themselves from other intellectual positions, the 'post' can, as a subcategory in positioning, also gain a polemical or pejorative meaning. Herman Paul observes that '[i]n the 1950s and early 1960s, "post-Christian age" would come to serve primarily as a *Kampfbegriff* between two specific groups of Christian intellectuals'.[19] Because of this polemical undertone, people are often hesitant to call themselves 'post-X'. Edward Baring also notices this: 'Intellectuals are often reluctant to let their ideas be reduced to slogans, or be seen as just one of a group. And certainly, if we take post-structuralism to be a school with a rigid set of doctrines that have to be accepted without question, it is clear that there is no such thing.'[20] Ultimately, in a considerable amount of cases, post-concepts are labels given by one group or person to another. And this other is often not a friend. This leads to another reason for emphasizing that post-concepts should never be taken for granted as situational descriptions, but rather should be carefully considered as performative positioning tools with a political or even polemical stance vis-à-vis other concepts or positions.

The conceptual webs *of post-concepts*

This brings me to the fifth and final methodological principle. Obviously post-concepts are portmanteaux and this volume focuses on the first half of each of them: post. But this is not the only part that matters. As each post-concept positions itself vis-à-vis a root concept, understanding the prefix requires understanding the root concept, too.[21] Linguistically, this situation hints at a somewhat paradoxical relation between the 'post' and its root concept: although the present is dissociated from the past, it is still defined by the past. Although this negative self-definition of post-concepts seems to underscore the primacy of the root concept, the situation is actually more complex. The understanding of the post-concept depends not only on knowledge of the root concept but also on comprehension of wider conceptual webs and networks within which they function.

For this reason, this volume has attempted to approach post-concepts as comprehensively as possible. Writing about post-structuralism, for example, Edward Baring not only demonstrates the importance of the root concept but also shows how both structuralism and post-structuralism were embedded within wider discourses. Baring is not alone in this attention to discursive context: all authors in this volume emphasize that it is only through these surrounding conceptual networks that we can grasp the position of a post-concept. Because of the kaleidoscopic nature of tradition, for instance, Stephen Turner places the adjective post-traditional in a dialogue with neighbouring concepts such as modernism and liberalism. In a different vein, Herman Paul observes that theorists of the post-Christian might have adopted different stances on the post-Christian age but nonetheless relied, in varying degrees, on the same historicist legacy.

In conclusion, we could argue that, taken together, the various post-concepts form a Wittgensteinian family. All members share a part of their name and certain capacities, but rarely all of them. Interestingly, one particular member of the post-family has good relations with a remarkable number of its relatives: post-war. Although some post-concepts made their first appearances in the interwar-period or even earlier, most of them flourished in the post-war period and many had a close relation to the Cold War. Altogether, this age of posts suggests that post-concepts, as a family, are themselves a cultural sign of the post-war years.

The 'age of posts' has been observed before, albeit in a rather negative manner. In 1992 philosopher Ulrich Beck called the prefix post 'the key word of our time', stressing that '[i]t hints at a "beyond" it cannot name, and in the substantive elements that it names and negates it remains tied to the familiar'.[22] In the same year, and even less complimentary, he described the prefix as a sign of 'helplessness' in social theory, comparing it to 'a blind man's cane'.[23] Beck's normative approach of the post-family as a negative marker of its own time is significant, but at the same time conceals other capacities of the prefix. All things considered, many of the concepts discussed in this volume anticipated the possibility of a new era, a fresh start, offering glimpses of a post-capitalist, post-ideological or post-political society. Other concepts indeed expressed a more reluctant attitude, fearing a post-Christian age or, later, lamenting a postfeminist future. But even these posts were not mere expressions of intellectual impotence; they referred to transitions that could be stopped or accelerated. So, following Beck, I would argue that post-concepts should indeed be studied together and contextually. As a family, this collection expresses more than the sum of its parts. However, contrary to Beck, the whole family should not be collectively dismissed as an unimaginative cluster of signs of helplessness. Post-concepts are just as often markers for the use of (political) agency, and accompany successful attempts to reshape society.

Eating a post-truth pudding

To what extent do the insights summarized so far apply to contemporary post-concepts? In the remainder of this epilogue, I would like to argue that the methodological principles put forward in this volume not only help us understand historical post-concepts but also help us to make sense of new ones. We can illustrate this capacity by applying our methodological framework to 'post-truth', the *Oxford English Dictionary*'s Word of the Year 2016.

The term post-truth can be traced back to 1992 and the days of the 'culture war'. Back then, it was considered a neologism for 'lying'. In an article in *The Nation*, Steve Tesich stated that since the Vietnam War, American political discourse had become clouded by a growing number of lies. After discussing the lies in Richard Nixon's presidency and Ronald Reagan's lack of truthfulness during the Iran/Contra scandal, Tesich concluded that the American people voluntarily had chosen to live a post-truth life.[24] After this article, however, the concept disappeared from the radar. Twelve years later, in 2004, the American journalist Ralph Keyes returned to the concept. In his *The Post-Truth Era: Dishonesty and Deception in Contemporary Life*, Keyes pointed at the nonchalance with which people – politicians in particular – tend to tell lies.[25] Although the book stirred some attention, the concept 'post-truth' did not stick.

When it re-emerged in the 2010s, it did so with different connotations. In 2012, journalists Ari Rabin-Havt and David Brock published *The Fox Effect*, a book on American news channel Fox News. It discussed 'the era of post-truth politics', in which '[t]he facts no longer matter, only what is politically expedient, sensationalistic, and designed to confirm the pre-existing opinions of a large audience'.[26] In the authors' interpretation, post-truth came close to what Harry Frankfurt in 1986 had called 'bullshitting'.[27] It was no longer synonymous with lying, but instead expressed an indifference towards truth as such.

As this short survey suggests, even though the concept post-truth only has a short history, we already see diachronic differences of meaning. What about meanings that can be distinguished synchronically? One does not have to search very long to find an overabundance of interpretations on social media such as Facebook, Twitter and Instagram. In academic publications the situation is not much clearer. Although the concept has appeared in many articles over the last few years, authors work with different definitions of the concept. Moreover, those who reflect on their use of post-truth do not always succeed in bringing much clarity. In an article on 'The post of post-truth in post-media', for instance, Polish author Adrian Mróz discerned three interpretations of the concept:

(1) The use of appeals to emotions and beliefs as constitutive varieties of circumstances that overshadow traditional notions of 'objective facts'.

(2) The affective bodily circumstances, social reality, and idea network under which a sentence is subjectively felt as true or rejected as false.

(3) A statement of circumstances (1)–(2), at times identifies with the meaning of the statement.[28]

In his article 'Truth, Lies and Tweets: A Consensus Theory of Post-Truth', philosopher Vittorio Bufacchi stated that the 'prefix in Post-Truth has a meaning more like "belonging to a time in which the specified concept has become unimportant or irrelevant"', adding that '[s]imilarly, the prefix "post" in Post-Truth is not a chronological reference to something that occurs "after" truth, instead it is a statement about the fact that truth is no longer essential, that truth has become obsolete and that truth has been superseded by a new reality'.[29] Bufacchi noted that his definition is broader than, though not contradictory to, the more famous one in the *Oxford English Dictionary* (OED): 'Post-Truth [is] "an adjective defined as relating to or denoting circumstances in which objective facts are less influential in shaping public opinion than appeals to emotion and personal belief".'[30]

Meanwhile, the interpretations by Mróz, Bufacchi and the OED all differ from the concept of 'bullshit' as introduced by Frankfurt and adopted by several authors who wrote about post-truth. In books and articles by the latter we find elaborations on the differences between 'pre-post-truth bullshit' and 'post-truth bullshit' and the difference between 'lying, misleading, bullshit, and the propagation of ignorance'.[31] After studying these synchronic and diachronic differences in meaning, we should conclude that within just a few years, many books have been published on this one particular post-concept, without reaching any consensus about its meaning.

Applying the first methodological principle guiding us in this volume – the concept of *transfer* – we notice that post-truth's itinerary included many different discourses over the last few years. It is striking to see how a concept that first appeared in journalism became a regular presence in academia, politics and policy.[32] Post-truth's transfer from journalism to other domains is clearly visible in books such as *Post-Truth: The New War on Truth and How to Fight Back* by Matthew d'Ancona. This author started from what he saw in the newspapers and then moved to an analysis of society, concluding with a reflection on the epistemological position needed to fight the loss of truth he experienced on his way.[33]

This route is just one example of how post-truth could penetrate almost any discipline, country or discourse. Scrolling through academic books and journals, we find a study on post-truth and pedagogy, as well as an *International Affairs* issue on 'International Relations in the Age of "Post-Truth" Politics'. Historian David Černín blogged on 'History in the Age of Post-Truth', whilst Robert Johnson did the same for post-truth and theology. Murray Forsyth gave a cautionary account on the influences of post-truth on medicine, and Angela Condello and Tiziana Andina published *Post-Truth, Philosophy and Law*.[34] Looking across geographical boundaries, a similar view emerges: post-truth was named 'Word of the Year' in the UK, the US and in a slightly different form (*postfaktisch*) in Germany, while Brazil was, according to communications scholar Ana Cristina Suzina, 'hijacked by post-truth'.[35]

Let us now turn to the second methodological principle of this volume: the interconnectedness of post-concepts. Perhaps because post-truth is widely discussed by post-loving philosophers and social theorists, it easily finds connections to other post-concepts. Over the last four years, it was combined with an incredible amount of other post-concepts – post-justice, post-fact, post-factual, post-shame, post-sexual and post-trust are only a few of them.[36] Amid the frequent occurrence of these relatively new post-concepts, moreover, there is one post that is brought up in almost every publication on post-truth: postmodernism. Already in *The Post-Truth Era*, Ralph Keyes wrote that 'to devout postmodernists, there is no such thing as literal truth, only what society labels as truth'.[37]

In general terms, we could argue that the discourse of postmodernism implied an encouragement to rethink the monolithic truth-claims constructed by previous generations of philosophers. Some voices perceived postmodernism as a self-applied safeguard against totalizing ideologies, whereas others saw postmodernism propagating an all-consuming relativism. The latter interpretation, emphasizing the relativistic tendencies of postmodernism, explains many of the connections to post-truth. Jaclyn Partyka has written that '[i]n many ways, our current climate of fake news and alternative facts is an aftershock of postmodernism'.[38] In an ultimate attempt to discredit postmodernism and to present it as the forerunner of post-truth, Michiko Kakutani notes that '[e]ven Mike Cernovich, the notorious alt-right troll and conspiracy theorist, invoked postmodernism in a 2016 interview with *The New Yorker*. "Look, I read postmodernist theory in college. If everything is a narrative, then we need alternatives to the dominant narrative," he said'.[39] Conversely, the philosopher Carlos G. Prado warned that '[a]ttempts to connect post-truth to postmodernism, even when critical, effectively lend post-truth something of a philosophical history that is, in fact, bogus'.[40]

Many other authors address this connection more tentatively. It is telling that a number of them reflect on this interconnectedness mainly through questions. Beginning his book on post-truth politics, Joshua Forstenzer wrote: 'We may thus ask: Has the intellectual movement that is postmodernism played a role in the rise of post-truth politics?'[41] Truman Chen titled a blog post 'Is Postmodernism to Blame for Post-Truth?'[42] and Lee McIntyre's chapter devoted to this connection was named 'Did Postmodernism Lead to Post-truth?'.[43] Even the title of Tina Besley, Michael A. Peters and Sharon Rider's afterword for their book on post-truth ended with a question mark: 'Afterword: Viral Modernity: From Postmodernism to Post-Truth?'[44] Although the exact answers given by these authors differ, they feel the need to suggest a strong connection between the two concepts.

In the particular case of post-truth, our third methodological principle, which is *performativity*, might be best discussed together with the fourth methodological principle, *positioning*. To start with the latter: for obvious reasons, people seldom identify themselves as 'post-truth'. Instead, it is most often a label given pejoratively to others. The first publications on post-truth used the term as a derogatory remark. Here, we should realize that this kind of remark is never strictly descriptive; it defines another's position as well. So, although it might sound overly academic to call these insults 'performative positioning tools', that is precisely what they are.

However, post-truth has a special quality here, since it not only discredits specific individuals but also seeks to characterize our current age. As both Herman Paul and I note in our chapters, the use of a post-prefix – in the sense of implying the closure of an age, era or epoch – may draw on historicist epochal thinking. Post-prefixes both create and characterize the eras in question. In the case of post-truth, this epoch-shaping capacity casts a negative light on our current age. Every book or article performatively presenting our era as the 'age of post-truth' contributes to this image of our own age as lacking truthfulness. For this reason, Stuart Sim notes in his *Post-Truth, Scepticism & Power* that '[p]ost-truth has to be recognized as an ideological movement … one that is out to dominate the public realm by undermining the accepted character of political discourse'.[45] Throughout his book, Sim shows that post-truth discourse is related not only to epistemology, postmodernism and politics, but also to a broad network of conspiracy theories.

This brings me to the last methodological principle: the *conceptual webs* in which post-truth operates. If there is one conclusion to be drawn from the case of post-truth, it is that the term's meanings not only changed over the years but also depended strongly on their contexts. What started as a journalist's remark eventually turned into a theme for serious reflection by critical theorists and philosophers such as Carlos Prado and Steve Fuller. The latter even used the 'post-truth standpoint' as a heuristic tool in philosophical debates.[46] With this movement from journalism to academics and politics, the conceptual webs surrounding post-truth changed as well. Whereas 'post-truth' initially referred to specific individuals – American presidents in particular – it later came to denote conspiracy theorists, groups in society and the current age at large. And while it was first applied to everyday politics, it increasingly became a term of art in debates on modern political culture on the one hand, and epistemology on the other.

As mentioned, postmodernism figures most prominently in the conceptual network surrounding post-truth. This leads to connections with other conceptual webs. While discussing postmodernism, for instance, one easily dives into debates on modernism, relativism, historicism and pragmatism. Indeed, we find post-truth here too. With this in mind, we must conclude that, just as with the other post-concepts in this volume, post-truth offers points of entry into several central debates in the age of the post. However, there may be small but meaningful differences between post-truth and the older post-concepts. Perhaps post-truth primarily expresses how the post-war longings and warnings for change, as expressed in many earlier post-concepts, resulted in a sense of disillusionment. In other words, this 'post' is just as much about losing the past as it is about winning the future.

Notes

1 I would like to thank K. Healan Gaston, Herman Paul and Selin Kuşçu for their comments on earlier versions of this epilogue.
2 One could think of linguistic or philosophical publications, but also of a volume like: Krystyna Kujawińska Courtney, Izabella Penier and Sumit Chakrabarti (eds), *The Post-Marked World: Theory and Practice in the 21st Century* (Newcastle upon Tyne: Cambridge Scholars Publishing, 2013).
3 Ella Shohat, 'Notes on the "Post-Colonial"', *Social Text*, 31/32 (1992), 99–113, 101. Khaled Furani for instance, described the 'post' in post-secular as a 'transcending endeavor' and a 'paradigmatic notion'. Jeffrey Nealon even discussed the first 'post' in post-postmodernism as 'a marker of postmodernism's having mutated … the way that a tropical storm passes a certain threshold and becomes a hurricane'. Khaled Furani, 'Is There a Postsecular?', *Journal of the American Academy of Religion*, 83:1 (2015), 1–26, 8; Jeffrey T. Nealon, *Post-Postmodernism: Or, The Cultural Logic of Just-In-Time Capitalism* (Stanford, CA: Stanford University Press, 2012), pp. ix–x.
4 Kwame Anthony Appiah, 'Is the Post- in Postmodernism the Post- in Postcolonial?', *Critical Inquiry*, 17:2 (1991), 336–57; David Chioni Moore, 'Is the Post- in Postcolonial the Post- in Post-Soviet? Toward a Global Postcolonial Critique', *PMLA*, 116:1 (2001), 111–28; Micheal Kilburn, 'Is the "post" in "post-totalitarian" the "post" in "postcolonial"?', in Eóin Flannery and Angus Mitchell (eds), *Enemies of Empire: New perspectives on imperialism, literature and historiography* (Dublin: Four Courts Press, 2007), 211–24; Graham Huggan, 'Is the "Post" in "Postsecular" the "Post" in "Postcolonial"?', *Modern Fiction Studies*, 56:4 (2010), 751–68; Robin James, 'Is the post- in post-identity

the post- in post-genre?', *Popular Music*, 36:1 (2017), 21–32; Shu-mei Shih, 'Is the Post in Postsocialism the Post in Posthumanism?', *Social Text*, 30:1 (2012), 27–50.

5 See Stéphanie Genz's chapter in this volume.

6 Charles Olson, 'The Present is Prologue', in Donald Allen and Benjamin Friedlander (eds), *Collected Prose: Charles Olson* (Berkeley, CA: University of California Press, 1997), p. 207, as cited in Mark Greif, *The Age of the Crisis of Man: Thought and Fiction in America, 1933–1973* (Princeton, NJ: Princeton University Press, 2013), p. 399.

7 Irving Howe, *A World More Attractive: A View of Modern Literature and Politics* (New York: Horizon Press, 1963), p. 162.

8 Benjamin De Mott, 'Two Liberals, One Aesthete', *The Hudson Review*, 10:3 (1957), 465–71, 471.

9 Irving Howe, 'Between Fact and Fable', *The New Republic* (31 March 1958), 17.

10 Elsewhere in this volume, Howard Brick even states that postcapitalist in many cases is not a temporal signifier at all.

11 Because Ali refers to Butler, for whom performativity is not a voluntaristic act, performativity works in different directions here. Both 'race' and 'post-race' are performatively produced. Sometimes this seems to be a self-conscious practice while at other moments it appears to be an organic process. Suki Ali, *Mixed-Race, Post-Race: Gender, New Ethnicities and Cultural Practices* (New York: Routledge, [2003] 2020), p. 9.

12 Ibid., p. 18.

13 On colligatory concepts, see William Henry Walsh, 'Colligatory Concepts in History', in Patrick Gardiner (ed.), *The Philosophy of History* (Oxford: Oxford University Press, 1974) and Christopher Behan McCullagh, 'Colligation and Classification in History', *History and Theory*, 17:3 (1978), 267–84.

14 Penelope Corfield emphasises how post-concepts 'exemplify a general sense of change, albeit by specifying what has gone rather than what has come. They further endorse, without proving, a vague belief that history proceeds by switching from one discrete stage to another, each with its own special characteristics.' Penelope J. Corfield, 'POST-Medievalism/Modernity/Postmodernism?', *Rethinking History*, 14:3 (2010), 379–404, 383.

15 See K. Healan Gaston's chapter in this volume.

16 See Andrew Sartori's and Roger E. Backhouse's chapters in this volume.

17 See Stéphanie Genz's chapter in this volume.

18 See my own chapter in this volume.

19 See Herman Paul's chapter in this volume.

20 See Edward Baring's chapter in this volume.

21 On some rare occasions, post-concepts became a root concept themselves. For example, K. Healan Gaston mentions post-post-Christian, and Stéphanie Genz discusses post-postfeminism. Other post-concepts discussed in this volume became root concepts as well, see, for instance, Larry A. Hickman, *Pragmatism as Post-Postmodernism: Lessons from John Dewey*. (Ashland, OH:

Fordham University, 2007); Jennifer M. Lehmann, *Deconstructing Durkheim: A Post-Post-Structuralist Critique* (London and New York: Routledge, 1993); Paul Jay, 'The Post-Post Colonial Condition: Globalization and Historical Allegory in Mohsin Hamid's "Moth Smoke"', *ariel*, 36:1–2 (2005), 51–71.

22 Ulrich Beck, *Risk Society: Towards a New Modernity* (London: SAGE, 1992), p. 9.

23 Ulrich Beck, 'Modern Society as a Risk Society', in Nico Stehr and Richard V. Ericson (eds), *The Culture and Power of Knowledge* (Berlin: De Gruyter, 1992), pp. 199–214, p. 199.

24 Steve Tesich, 'A Government of Lies', *The Nation*, 254:1 (1992), 12–14.

25 Fascinatingly Keyes already mentions businessman Donald Trump as an example of post-truth for claiming successes he never had. Ralph Keyes, *The Post-Truth Era: Dishonesty and Deception in Contemporary Life* (New York: St. Martins, 2004), pp. 14–15.

26 David Brock and Ari Rabin-Havt, *The Fox Effect: How Roger Ailes Turned a Network into a Propaganda Machine* (New York: Anchor, 2012), p. 283.

27 Harry G. Frankfurt, 'On Bullshit', *Raritan Quarterly Review*, 6:2 (1986), 81–100.

28 Adrian Mróz, 'The Post of Post-Truth in Post-Media: About Socio-Situational Dynamic Information, *Kultura i Historia*, 32:2 (2017), 23–37, 24.

29 Vittorio Bufacchi, 'Truth, Lies and Tweets: A Consensus Theory of Post-Truth', *Philosophy & Social Criticism*, 47:3 (2021), 347–61, 348.

30 Ibid., 348.

31 Authors explicitly elaborating on the connection between post-truth and bullshit: James Ball, *Post-Truth: How Bullshit Conquered the World* (London: Biteback Publishing, 2017); Evan Davis, *Post-Truth: Why We Have Reached Peak Bullshit and What We Can Do About It* (London: Little, Brown, 2017). And for examples of views that put the two concepts on a distance to each other, see Bruce McComiskey, *Post-Truth Rhetoric and Composition* (Logan, UT: Utah State University Press, 2017), p. 12; David Block, *Post-Truth and Political Discourse* (Cham: Palgrave Pivot, 2019), p. 119.

32 A good example of an early article using post-truth in its latest form is written by Jeet Heer. The political element is very clear, since post-truth is a concept especially designed for the description of Trumpian politics: Jeet Heer, 'Donald Trump Is Not a Liar. He's Something Worse: A Bullshit Artist', *New Republic* (1 December 2015), https://newrepublic.com/article/124803/donald-trump-not-liar (accessed 21 February 2020).

33 Matthew d'Ancona, *Post Truth: The New War on Truth and How to Fight Back* (London: Ebury Press, 2017).

34 Michael A. Peters et al. (eds), *Post-Truth, Fake News: Viral Modernity & Higher Education* (Singapore: Springer, 2018); *International Affairs*, 94:2 (2018); David Černín, 'The Role of History in the Age of Post-Truth' (24 April 2019), www.oulu.fi/blogs/historyattheageofposttruth (accessed 30 January 2020); Robert Johnson, 'Truth and the Theological Learning Community in a "Post-Truth" Culture' (2017), www.cbts.edu/truth-theological-learning-community-post-truth-culture

(accessed 30 January 2020); Murray G. Forsyth, 'Post-Truth Era is Destroying Society and Medicine', *British Medical Journal*, 367 (2019); Angela Condello and Tiziana Andina (eds), *Post-Truth, Philosophy and Law* (London: Routledge, 2019).

35 Ana Cristina Suzina, 'Brazil, Hijacked by Post-Truth', *OpenDemocracy.net* (22 October 2018), www.opendemocracy.net/en/democraciaabierta/brazil-hijacked-by-post-truth/ (accessed 30 January 2020).

36 A short survey on Google using the term 'post-truth and post' led to these results, spanning thousands of pages already.

37 Keyes, *Post-Truth Era*, p. 139.

38 Jaclyn Partyka, 'Fictional Affect and Metaliterate Learning through Genre', in Thomas P. Mackey and Trudi E. Jacobson (eds), *Metaliterate Learning for the Post-Truth World* (New York: American Library Association, 2019), p. 182.

39 Michiko Kakutani, *The Death of Truth: Notes on Falsehood in the Age of Trump* (New York: Tim Duggan Books, 2018), p. 52.

40 Carlos G. Prado, *America's Post-Truth Phenomenon: When Feelings and Opinions Trump Facts and Evidence* (London: Praeger, 2018), p. 5.

41 Joshua Forstenzer, *Something Has Cracked: Post-Truth Politics and Richard Rorty's Postmodernist Bourgeois Liberalism* (Cambridge, MA: Ash Center for Democratic Governance and Innovation Harvard Kennedy School, 2018), p. 4.

42 Truman Chen, 'Is Postmodernism to Blame for Post-Truth?', *Philosophy Talk* (17 February 2017), www.philosophytalk.org/blog/postmodernism-blame-post-truth (accessed 1 February 2020).

43 Lee McIntyre, *Post-Truth* (Cambridge, MA: MIT Press, 2018), p. 123.

44 Peters et al., *Post-Truth, Fake News*, p. 217.

45 Stuart Sim, *Post-Truth, Scepticism & Power* (Cham: Palgrave McMillan, 2019), p. 3.

46 Steve Fuller, 'The Post-Truth About Philosophy and Rhetoric', *Philosophy & Rhetoric*, 50:4 (2017), 473–82; Steve Fuller, 'The Dialectic of Politics and Science from a Post-Truth Standpoint', *Epistemology & Philosophy of Science*, 5:2 (2018), 59–74; Steve Fuller, *Post-Truth: Knowledge as a Power Game* (London: Anthem Press, 2017).

Index

EU authorised representative for GPSR:
Easy Access System Europe, Mustamäe tee 50,
10621 Tallinn, Estonia
gpsr.requests@easproject.com

www.ingramcontent.com/pod-product-compliance
Lightning Source LLC
Chambersburg PA
CBHW070410100426
42812CB00005B/1699